AF737420

The Politics of Desire

The Politics of Desire

Foucault, Deleuze, and Psychoanalysis

Edited by
Agustín Colombo, Edward McGushin,
and Geoff Pfeifer

ROWMAN & LITTLEFIELD
Lanham • Boulder • New York • London

Published by Rowman & Littlefield
An imprint of The Rowman & Littlefield Publishing Group, Inc.
4501 Forbes Boulevard, Suite 200, Lanham, Maryland 20706
www.rowman.com

86-90 Paul Street, London EC2A 4NE

Copyright © 2022 by The Rowman & Littlefield Publishing Group, Inc.

All rights reserved. No part of this book may be reproduced in any form or by any electronic or mechanical means, including information storage and retrieval systems, without written permission from the publisher, except by a reviewer who may quote passages in a review.

British Library Cataloguing in Publication Information Available

Library of Congress Cataloging-in-Publication Data

Names: Colombo, Agustín, editor. | McGushin, Edward, editor. | Pfeifer, Geoff, editor.
Title: The politics of desire : Foucault, Deleuze, and psychoanalysis / edited by Agustín Colombo, Edward McGushin, and Geoff Pfeifer.
Description: Lanham : Rowman & Littlefield Publishers, 2022. | Includes bibliographical references and index. | Summary: "This book will gather contributions from international scholars with the aim of exploring the political reflection of Deleuze-Guattari's and Foucault's critical encounter with psychoanalytic thought: their possible connections, their divergences and the fields of reflection that this encounter opens, the problems and debates that lead Foucault and Deleuze to engage with psychoanalysis"—Provided by publisher.650
Identifiers: LCCN 2021062436 (print) | LCCN 2021062437 (ebook) | ISBN 9781538144244 (cloth) | ISBN 9781538144251 (ebook)
Subjects: LCSH: Desire. | Deleuze, Gilles, 1925–1995. | Foucault, Michel, 1926–1984. | Psychoanalysis—Philosophy.
Classification: LCC BF575.D4 P56 2022 (print) | LCC BF575.D4 (ebook) | DDC 150.19/5—dc23/eng/20220217
LC record available at https://lccn.loc.gov/2021062436
LC ebook record available at https://lccn.loc.gov/2021062437

Contents

1 Introduction 1
Agustín Colombo, Geoff Pfeifer, and Edward McGushin

SECTION 1: OEDIPUS, UNCONSCIOUS, AND SEX **3**

2 Rethinking Oedipus: Foucault and Deleuze on Knowledge, Forgetting, and Fractured Selves 5
Corey McCall

3 Knowledge, the Unconscious, and Desire 23
Serene Richards

4 Psychoanalysis in Question: Foucault, Castel, Deleuze-Guattari 41
Philippe Sabot

5 The Christian Invention of the Sexual: In Pursuit of Psychoanalysis 57
Frédéric Gros

6 Phantasms and Their Vicissitudes 69
Laura Hengehold

7 Sex(uality) as State of Exception 89
Cindy Zeiher

8 Twisted (A Tribute): Foucault, Deleuze, and the Rhizomatic Book 101
Lynne Huffer

SECTION 2: OBEDIENCE, REVOLUTION, AND RESISTANCE 121

9 You Can't Always Want What You Get: The Psychoanalytic Ambivalence of Michel Foucault 123
Julian Bourg

10 On Foucault and Deleuze's Disagreement about Desire and Pleasure: Desire as an Object of Veridiction 145
Agustín Colombo

11 Desire's Tyranny: Deleuze and Guattari on Desire, Capitalism, and Authoritarianism in the Contemporary Moment 161
Geoff Pfeifer

12 Foucault's Troublesome Hypothesis: Notes on a New History 179
John Rajchman

Index 189

About the Author 195

Chapter 1

Introduction

Agustín Colombo, Geoff Pfeifer, and Edward McGushin

Freud's conceptual apparatus—that is, the unconscious, the conflictual nature of the psyche, the Oedipal complex, repression, castration, neurosis and hysteria, the sublimation of instinctual desire, and its redirection toward socially acceptable ends—radically transformed not only psychology and clinical practice but also social and political philosophy and theory. For some, the rise of a social and political theory grounded on Freud's concepts offered a new perspective to think the relations between the individual, the social, and the political—one that some have seen as distinct from, in competition with, and a place from which to critique other existing social theories and theoretical positions on the political such as Marxism, liberalism, and conservatism. For others, Freud's theoretical innovations offered the opportunity to extend and further build out the conceptual apparatus that had grown up around some of those older traditions, revitalizing them and making them anew.

Michel Foucault, Gilles Deleuze, and Félix Guattari were at the forefront of a generation of thinkers who grew up in the midst of this philosophical and theoretical transformation and debate. In different ways, these thinkers came to be skeptical of much of both Freud's presuppositions and theoretical apparatus and the ways they were being deployed in the domain of political and social theory. Such skepticism is, however, also tempered by an acceptance and onboarding of some of Freud's key concepts as key notions in Deleuze and Guattari's and Foucault's own work.

This collection of chapters aims to explore the political dimension of both Deleuze-Guattari's and Foucault's critical works in relation to psychoanalysis. In doing so, the main goal of the book is not to engage in a critique of the discipline of psychoanalysis as such but to investigate how Foucault and Deleuze's critique of psychoanalysis gives rise to a political reflection that draws on some of psychoanalysis key notions. Among these, the concept of desire is central not only because of the key role that it plays in both Foucault's and Deleuze and Guattari's critique of and political engagement with psychoanalysis but also because desire allows to grasp the different ways in which Foucault and Deleuze politically engage with psychoanalysis: for Deleuze, desire is the central dimension through which revolution becomes possible, whereas for Foucault desire is a key element at work in the modern mechanisms of subjection.

This book gathers contributions from international scholars with the aim of exploring both the interplay and contrast of Deleuze and Guattari's and Foucault's political critique of psychoanalysis through desire: their possible connections, the divergences and the fields of reflection that this encounter opens, and the problems and debates that led Foucault and Deleuze to engage with psychoanalysis. In doing so, the different chapters of the book tackle a variety of topics such as the contrast between Foucault's and Deleuze's political understanding of desire and pleasure; the genealogy of desire as a way to investigate the historical shaping of psychoanalysis; the relationship between psychoanalysis and the normalizing mechanisms of power (e.g., biopolitics, discipline); the ways in which psychoanalysis interplays with neoliberalism; the status and the role of desire in revolt, resistance, and transformation; Foucault's and Deleuze's different approaches to the unconscious; the political aspect of desire in the reflection on identity; and the way in which Foucault's and Deleuze's critique of psychoanalysis challenges Freud's and Lacan's perspectives on desire. The diversity of the authors' perspectives as well as the recent publication of crucial material, like *Confessions of the Flesh*, Foucault's fourth volume of *The History of Sexuality*, propose a new and original reflection on a key topic of two of the main figures of the contemporary thought.

Taking desire as the main concept on which Foucault's and Deleuze's political approaches to psychoanalysis pivot, connect, and disconnect in some of the ways outlined earlier, the book is organized in two sections. The first section gathers chapters that investigate how Foucault's and Deleuze's critique of psychoanalysis gives rise to a political reflection which draws on main psychoanalytical topics such as the Oedipus complex, the unconscious, and sex. The articles of the second section address the way in which Foucault's and Deleuze's critique of psychoanalysis allows us to think anew crucial political concepts such as obedience, revolution, and resistance.

Through reflection on desire, Foucault and Deleuze provided us new conceptual tools to understand how politics and power run through our daily lives. In the 50th anniversary of Deleuze and Guattari's *Anti-Oedipus*, one of the major references that inspires the many chapters in this book, we aim to pay homage to these two important figures of contemporary thought by enriching and opening new lines of thought and problematization of the political reflection on desire that Foucault and Deleuze developed.

Section 1

OEDIPUS, UNCONSCIOUS, AND SEX

Chapter 2

Rethinking *Oedipus*

Foucault and Deleuze on Knowledge, Forgetting, and Fractured Selves

Corey McCall

Oedipus Rex has become a figure of forgetfulness for us. Even with Freud's eponymous complex, we can see that Oedipus is such a figure: the male ego works by forgetting the desire for the mother and the competitive rage at the father. But even outside this once-dominant Freudian framework, Oedipus remains a figure of forgetting. Consider, for example, James Baldwin's reference to Oedipus in his early essay "Many Thousands Gone," from his first collection *Notes of a Native Son* (1948): "Oedipus did not remember the thongs that bound his feet; nevertheless the marks they left testified to that doom toward which his feet were leading him."[1] Baldwin invokes Oedipus here to show that even if we deny how racism structured American experience in the past, it still haunts us. Indeed, denying the past makes it even more difficult to work through. "In our image of the Negro breathes the past we deny, not dead but living yet and powerful, the beast in our jungle of statistics."[2] Although he did not often comment on the American scene and the concept of "race" became an explicit concern of his only late in his career, Foucault would likely agree with Baldwin that Oedipus is a figure of forgetfulness. Despite the marks on his flesh that signify his doom, he does not remember. According to Foucault, the dominance of the Freudian myth makes it impossible to see that Oedipus is a figure of knowledge and power. Both Foucault and Deleuze will deny that this forgetting simply takes the form of what Foucault will term "the repressive hypothesis" in the first volume of *The History of Sexuality*. Foucault and Deleuze do not wish to forget Oedipus entirely, though they provide alternatives to the dominant Freudian account of Oedipus's significance, but their aims are not simply critical.

Michel Foucault and Gilles Deleuze seek to think Sophocles's *Oedipus* in ways contrary to this dominant Freudian reading. This is most evident in Deleuze and Guattari's *Anti-Oedipus* and their critique of Freud's Oedipal complex and its psychoanalytic conception of desire and selfhood. Of course, Foucault also wants to rethink sexuality and psychiatric power independently of what had become by the 1960s in France a stifling Freudian orthodoxy. As part of this project of thinking Oedipus otherwise than Freud, both thinkers provide distinctive readings of Sophocles's plays. This chapter focuses on these readings in order to begin to determine how and why Sophocles's Oedipus Cycle matters to them—for the development of their distinctive philosophical voices and the points where their projects meet through their various attempts to read *Oedipus* otherwise than Freud. In other words, both philosophers are at least implicitly attempting to wrest *Oedipus* from the Freudian Oedipal complex through their respective readings of Sophocles, but they are doing more than this, for their readings of Sophocles shed light on themes in their work that will come into focus subsequently. Echoing the title of a 1967 essay by Jean-Pierre Vernant, my interest lies in the portrait of Oedipus "without the complex" found in the work of Foucault and Deleuze.

Rather than focusing on these later critiques of Freud found in texts such as the first volume of *The History of Sexuality* or in *Anti-Oedipus*, this chapter stages the encounter between Foucault and Deleuze earlier, beginning with Foucault's reading of *Oedipus Rex*, which is now included as a supplement to his inaugural Collège de France lecture course, the 1970–1971 *Lectures on the Will to Know*. "Oedipal Knowledge" is a lecture that Foucault first gave in Buffalo, New York, in March 1972 and later that year at Cornell University.[3] Foucault's examination of the question of knowledge in Sophocles's *Oedipus Rex* anticipates many of the themes that will animate Foucault's later work, in particular his work on the care of the self in the final two volumes of *The History of Sexuality* and his final lecture courses. What specifically interests Foucault in the play is the question of self-knowledge—that is, the self-reflexivity of Oedipus's knowledge for which he is both the subject and the object as well as the different types of knowledge present in the play, from perceptual knowledge to that of leaders and slaves, testimony, and enigmatic knowledge ("knowledge that deliberately withdraws into enigma and incompleteness").[4] On Foucault's reading, the tragedy largely consists of transitions between these various types of knowledge and their effects on Oedipus's earlier and later selves.

In his 1966 appreciation of Marcel Duhamel's crime novel imprint "La Série Noire," Deleuze traces a similar sort of movement from certain knowledge to incomplete knowledge (enigma or error). Deleuze claims that the crime novel can be read as a revision of Greek tragedy, a claim he elucidates in terms of Sophocles's *Oedipus*. Whereas older detective novels featured a genius who philosophically solves the crime through either a (French) deductive or an (English) inductive veridical method (Deleuze's examples here are Gaboriau's Tabaret and Lecoq or Doyle's Holmes), the hard-boiled noir fiction found in Duhamel's series no longer presents the detective as a genius uniquely equipped to discover the truth; instead, they operate according to the principle of error. The detective is no longer an authority who possesses the Cartesian or empirical methodology that yields the truth but rather an error-prone buffoon who happens to catch the crook, if not by sheer luck then through brute force. In other words, the detective novel traces a transition from philosophy back to tragedy.[5]

Deleuze returns to Sophocles a couple years later in *Difference and Repetition*. This time, he glosses Hölderlin's German translation of *Oedipus* in order to show how the poet rediscovers the fractured self (a divided self that Foucault claims is already present in Sophocles's version of the play).[6]

> The Kantian initiative can be taken up, and the form of time can support both the death of God and the fractured I, but in the course of a quite different understanding of the passive self. In this sense, it is correct to claim that neither Fichte nor Hegel is the descendant of Kant—rather, it is Hölderlin, who discovers the emptiness of pure time and, in this emptiness, simultaneously the continued diversion of the divine, the prolonged fracture of the I and the constitutive passion of the self.[7]

The source for this always already fractured, dispossessed self is Hölderlin's translation of *Oedipus*. Hölderlin ultimately declines Kant's proposed solution to this rendering of the self; for him time's passage undermines the self in much the same way that Oedipus is always already doomed.

In these relatively early years of their respective careers, Foucault and Deleuze are both interested in Oedipus's philosophical provocation, that is, in how Sophocles's tragic cycle demands a philosophical response. These philosophical provocations provide the basis for this chapter. In order to stage the comparison of Foucault and Deleuze, I begin with Walter Benjamin's review of André Gide's *Oedipe*, which he sees representative of a trend that seeks to modernize ancient drama.

OEDIPUS'S MODERN DISGUISES: BENJAMIN AND FOUCAULT, KNOWLEDGE AND POWER

In his brief 1932 review entitled "Oedipus, or Rational Myth," Walter Benjamin analyzes various instances of the modern revival of the Oedipus myth, focusing in particular on the work of André Gide. The occasion for

Benjamin's essay was the publication of Gide's version of Oedipus the previous year.[8] I begin with this text because it nicely summarizes what I take to be the philosophical stakes of the figure of Oedipus in the work of Deleuze and Foucault in the late 1960s and early 1970s. The basic question for Benjamin here is "Why modernize Sophocles's *Oedipus*?" and he cites several influential recent attempts, by artists such as Stravinsky and Picasso, to "divest Greek characters of their traditional clothing, or rather to disguise them by clothing them in modern dress," a trend, Benjamin informs us, that had been dubbed "Neoclassicism."[9] Although this modernizing tendency had once been seen as controversial, it has since become almost commonplace, though Benjamin notes that the problem with the English play *Hamlet in Tails* may have simply been that "the play is too modern to be modern."[10] Benjamin analyzes this neoclassical tendency and provides three reasons for it. First, ancient figures such as Oedipus are simultaneously familiar and "remote from contemporary concerns." Furthermore, Benjamin notes that these modernizing attempts are all constructivist experiments, in which the playwrights oppose their modern reinterpretations to the "natural and organic" interpretation of the Greek theater.[11] Finally, these reinterpretations seek to test whether Greek art is indeed eternal, which means simply that it remains subject to endless reinterpretation:

> And, in the third place, there is also a covert or open intention involved: namely, the desire to make a genuine test—one grounded in the philosophy of history—of the eternal character of Greek art, which is to say, its constantly self-renewing relevance.

Furthermore, Benjamin asserts that this desire for "constantly self-renewing relevance" provides us the key to Gide's reinterpretation.[12] The problem is that Gide's modern reinterpretation comes at the expense of historical specificity as well as the horror the audience feels when confronted with Oedipus's fate. Gide's modern Oedipus is no one in particular.

In other words, Gide here comes close to Freud, whose everyman Oedipus represents men's deepest and most repressed desires. Both Gide and Freud modernize Oedipus by refashioning him in our modern guise, a bourgeois Oedipus fit for mass consumption. Despite their manifold differences—for example, Gide wants to use Oedipus as a vehicle to display the rational kernel of Greek myths while Freud uses Oedipus as a symbol of the repressed irrational desire of the psyche held together only by the rational ego—their figures of Oedipus are won at the cost of denying the historical specificity of the play itself. This also provides the basis for Jean-Pierre Vernant's critique of Freud's repurposing of the Oedipus myth, that is, that it comes at the cost of forgetting the historical specificity of Sophocles's plays themselves:

> For Freud, the impact of tragedy is connected with the particular nature of the material that Sophocles uses in *Oedipus Rex*, that is to say, in the last analysis, the dreams of making love with one's mother and murdering one's father. These, he writes, are the key to tragedy. [. . .] In support of his thesis, Freud writes that when attempts have been made, in dramas similar to *Oedipus Rex*, to reproduce a tragic effect using material other than Oedipal dreams the result has been total failure. And he cites as examples a number of bad modern dramas. At this point one is speechless with amazement. How can Freud forget that there are plenty of other Greek tragedies besides *Oedipus Rex* and that, of those of Aeschylus, Sophocles, and Euripides that have come down to us, there is virtually not a single one that has anything to do with Oedipal dreams? Does this mean that they are bad plays, producing no dramatic effect?[13]

As with Gide's rationalist reinterpretation, Freud's more notorious use of the Oedipus myth was premised upon a forgetting of the various historical contexts and the artistic forms that produced Sophoclean tragedy. And this is perhaps also why Benjamin refers to this as a problem for the philosophy of history, prompting us to ask how we ought to repurpose the past. In other words, how do we render the past relevant without forgetting its various contexts of meaning?

A similar sort of modernizing tendency can certainly be found in Deleuze's reference to Oedipus as a precursor to the modern crime novel, so the question here should be whether Deleuze provides us with yet another version of a decontextualized modern Oedipus.[14] Foucault, on the other hand, sees Oedipus as an exemplary figure of the will to know, and is careful to read him within the Greek context, though this is a context that can never be completely reconstructed into a harmonious whole. If, as he writes in the Course Summary, the task of the lecture course has been to "put together, fragment by fragment, a 'morphology of the will to know,'" then the figure of Oedipus must be part of this fragmentary composition. A fragmentary composition is, presumably, one that fails to provide the whole story but consists merely as a series of clues or hints that someone will have to subsequently piece together under the melancholy condition that this reconstruction will remain forever incomplete with any desire for completeness left unfulfilled.[15] In other words, Deleuze's explicit link between Oedipus and the detective novel remains implicitly a task for us, Foucault's detectives of the present. So, while Foucault's modernization of Oedipus is less evident than Deleuze's, it remains our task to decipher the clues of *Oedipus*.

A significant aspect of Oedipus's continued relevance lies in the feature that Foucault's lecture first emphasizes, what we might call Oedipus's self-reflexivity: Oedipus's knowledge does not primarily concern the various features of the world around him, but rather it concerns himself. Of course, this makes Oedipus both the subject and object of the play. As Foucault puts it,

> The one who seeks is the object of the search; the one who is ignorant is the one it is a question of knowing about; he who unleashed the dogs is himself the prey; the trail on which he set them takes them back to the point where he is waiting for them.[16]

But this reflexive knowledge, in which one is both subject and object, doctor and patient, evinces a struggle that Foucault characterizes as "the battle to know," a battle which will take center stage in Foucault's subsequent works on the care of the self. As I mentioned previously, Foucault discerns five kinds of knowledge operating within the play (knowledge in terms of medium, origin, bearers, the relationship to time, and the "the source of obscurity that veils them").[17] He then proceeds to show, through a formal analysis of the play, how it unfolds as a series of doublings, between, for example, the divine and human, Oedipus's Corinthian and the Theban halves, Oedipus the king and Oedipus the king's murderer, Oedipus the one who exiles and Oedipus the one who is exiled.[18] Foucault dubs this process of doubling the "mechanism of the *sumbolon*," which he characterizes as "a composite figure of excessive, monstrous halves that no man's eyes can any longer bear to see"—Oedipus's monstrosity.[19]

One finds two types of knowledge in the play: divine knowledge, as represented by the oracle and the blind seer Teiresias, and the human knowledge of testimony and confession. Foucault claims that Oedipus himself represents a third type of knowledge, that of the tyrant—the sovereign who substitutes truth with power and a desire to rule and take his slain father's place. Things aren't quite so simple, though, for Oedipus is not completely bereft of knowledge: his legitimacy derives from the knowledge displayed in solving the Sphinx's riddle. As Foucault puts it, though he easily solves this riddle, he remains a riddle to himself until the end of the play, when his monstrosity is finally revealed. Foucault reads the play as one concerning a conflict between two kinds of knowledge: the divine knowledge of signs and seers and the human knowledge of tyrants, exemplified by *techne* and *tuche* (roughly, art and luck). Oedipus turns his back on the gods and seals his fate not out of ignorance but precisely because he eschews divine knowledge in favor of the human.

> Oedipus the tyrant, both sovereign and judge, wants to discover the truth by himself, by finding those who saw and heard. To the old oracular procedures to which the piety and terror of the people have pushed him, to the procedure

> of the purgatory oath, to which, without his assent, Creon opens himself up, Oedipus constantly prefers his own questions: Who did it, who can testify about it? If Oedipus turns his back on the oracular procedure, it is through an impulse of pride, of excess, which the Chorus denounces as soon as the guilt of the king begins to dawn.[20]

Oedipus the tyrant, figure of monstrous excess, will be forced to submit to the power of Creon due to his crimes. And the laws, which the tyrant sought to establish through decree, will once more become the "sublime laws," product of divine decree. The play, then, portrays the struggle between two types of knowledge, and, therefore, two rival versions of power relations.

> What disappears with the fall of Oedipus is that old oriental form of the expert king (*roi savant*), of the king who controls, governs, pilots, and sets the city right with his knowledge, fending off disasters or plagues; more directly it is the updated version that Greek "tyranny" tried to give this old form when it wished to put the cities right by using, diverting, and often twisting the gods' oracles; maybe it is the even more contemporary image that some in Sophocles's own time sought to project, those who "shot their arrows further than the others" and got themselves recognized as "first citizens." (LWK, 256)

(That last sentence contains an unmistakable reference to Pericles.) Foucault concludes his essay by considering that the figure of Oedipus might still remind us today of another regime of knowledge: one that doesn't depend upon concepts of order and measure, concepts we inherited from the Aristotelian account of knowledge. For Foucault, tragic wisdom consists in the reminder that truth might still take the form of transgression and excess. Reading *Oedipus* today, Foucault claims, reminds us of the various connections and affiliations between power and knowledge, connections and affiliations that we often forget when we accept the conception of knowledge as pure, disinterested, and scientific.[21]

Miriam Leonard focuses on the reinterpretations of Oedipus offered by Vernant and Foucault and points out that they are both attempting to replace Freud's psychoanalytic Oedipus with a political one by critiquing the assumption that Oedipus reveals a timeless truth about human nature focused on the will. This will manifests what Foucault calls "a very serious defect," namely "that of assuming that the human subject, the subject of knowledge, and forms of knowledge are somehow given beforehand and definitively and that economic, social, and political conditions of existence are merely laid or imprinted on this definitely given subject."[22] By 1974, Foucault will draw upon his "Oedipal Knowledge" lecture to think about Oedipus as a figure of power and knowledge. Unlike Vernant, who considers the tragedy of Oedipus in terms of the contradictions between the demands of democracy and the temptations of tyranny, Foucault sees only Oedipus the tyrant in "Truth and Juridical Forms." In this way, as Leonard notes, Foucault's return to the figure of Oedipus a few years after "Oedipal Knowledge" anticipates his later work on disciplinary power in *Discipline and Punish* while it also acknowledges its debt to Deleuze and Guattari's *Anti-Oedipus*. Indeed, Foucault states that his project has already been accomplished with more depth by Deleuze and Guattari as he reiterates that none of them are doing structuralism.

> I'll digress long enough to point out that everything that I'm trying to say, everything that Deleuze and Guattari have shown with much more depth in *Anti-Oedipus*, is part of a group of studies that, contrary to what newspapers say, are not concerned with what is traditionally called "structure." Neither Deleuze, nor Jean-François Lyotard, nor Guattari, nor I ever do structural analyses; we are absolutely not "structuralists."[23]

Instead, what he is trying to do is bring to light power relations that have remained hidden due to a focus on economic structures. By 1973, Oedipus has become the representative figure of the connection between power and knowledge that still operates within contemporary society. Indeed, he proposes to analyze this Oedipus complex instead of the Freudian one.[24] According to Foucault's power-knowledge complex, Oedipus is not a figure of forgetfulness that provides the timeless model for the repression of desire. Instead of the etymology to which Freud and subsequently writers such as James Baldwin refer that derives the meaning of Oedipus's name from the fact of his swollen foot, Foucault draws upon a neglected etymology that links Oedipus's name with sight and knowledge.

> But let's not forget that this wordplay is multifarious, or that the Greeks themselves had already noted that in *Oidipous* we have the word *oida* which means both "to have seen" and "to know." I would like to show that Oedipus in this mechanism of the *sumbolon*—of communicating halves, of the interplay of responses between the shepherds and the gods—is not one who didn't know but, rather, the one who knew too much. He is the one who joined his knowledge and his power in a certain reprehensible way, and whom the *Oedipus* story was meant to expel finally from history.[25]

Although Foucault denies that Oedipus himself represents forgetfulness, Foucault needs to recall Oedipus's forgotten significance as the man who was both too knowledgeable and too powerful.

In 1932, Walter Benjamin asked how and why contemporary artists and authors continued to disguise Oedipus in modern garb and thereby decontextualized him. By contrast, Foucault wants contemporary readers to recall the forgotten lesson concerning the various entanglements between power and knowledge exhibited by that monstrous tyrant, Oedipus. In this respect, Deleuze's interests are closer to Benjamin's, for Deleuze does not return to the *Oedipus* cycle to recover its significance for modern readers. Like Benjamin, Deleuze's interests lie both in the modern inheritors of Oedipus and in the modern disguises that Oedipus wears. In the following section, I will consider one modern disguise and one modern interpreter, beginning with Deleuze's treatment of the modern detective before turning to his analysis of Hölderlin's *Oedipus*.

OEDIPUS THE DETECTIVE: DELEUZE—KANT—HÖLDERLIN

At the outset of *Difference and Repetition* (1968), Deleuze claims that we should conceive of philosophy as part detective novel and part science fiction.

> By detective novel we mean that concepts, with their zones of presence, should intervene to resolve local situations. They themselves change along with the problems. They have spheres of influence where, as we shall see, they operate in relation to "dramas" and by means of a certain "cruelty." They must have a coherence among themselves, but this coherence must not come from themselves. They must receive their coherence from elsewhere.[26]

He attributes this insight regarding the dependence of concepts to Empiricism. That is, because concepts lack independence, they are constantly being created anew. Empiricism creates concepts, rather than conceiving of them as pure and eternal (as with Plato) or as a fixed and necessary form for experience (as with Kant).

Deleuze had already developed the connection between philosophy and the detective novel in a short essay published in 1966. As I noted in the introduction, this chapter is an appreciation of Marcel Duhamel's series devoted to detective fiction. The trajectory of the detective novel that Deleuze traces in this piece mirrors the development of philosophy found in *Difference and Repetition* and other works: from a closed system that was thought to be orderly and secure to an empiricist one that permits novelty at the expense of secure, a priori foundations for thought.

> In the old conception of the detective novel, we would be shown a genius detective devoting the whole power of his mind to the search and discovery of the truth. The idea of truth in the classic detective novel was the effort and

operations of the mind. So it is that the police investigation modeled itself on the philosophical inquiry, and conversely, gave to philosophy an unusual object to elucidate: crime[27]

Detective fiction follows modern philosophy by distinguishing those detectives who follow Descartes and proceed deductively and those who follow Hobbes and proceed inductively. The French and English types of detectives closely resemble their philosophical forbears in their respective methodologies.

Furthermore, detective fiction follows in the wake of both philosophy and tragedy. Crime fiction posits two parallel series, that of the detective and the criminal. "By a metaphysical law of reflection, the cop is no more extraordinary than the criminal—he, too, professes allegiance to justice and truth and the powers of deduction and induction."[28] The criminal series and the detective series can both trace their lineage back to one individual: they coincide in Oedipus.

Still, we shouldn't be too surprised that the crime novel so faithfully reproduces Greek tragedy, since Oedipus is always called on to indicate any such coincidence. While it is the only Greek tragedy that already had this detective structure, we should marvel that Sophocles' Oedipus is a detective, and not that the detective novel has remained Oedipal.[29]

Although detective fiction may trace its origins to both philosophy and tragedy, Duhamel's series comes to represent a shift in the nature and the role of the detective. The detective no longer pretends to search for the truth, but instead becomes a figure who compensates for error, once the murder suspect is arrested for a petty crime and the truth is only accidentally revealed, for example. The truth is revealed only subsequently and incidentally: it is a matter of chance. Justice is ultimately done, but the detective is not its agent. The power of falsehood becomes the driving force of the genre.[30] The crisp distinction between good cop and bad criminal begins to break down, and parallel series begin to merge, thereby positing a return to Oedipus, who is tragically both a tyrannical ruler and a defiled criminal.

Deleuze has updated Benjamin's list of Oedipus's modern disguises to include the detective and criminal, disguises that in fact were there all along. Deleuze reminds us that one more modern re-interpreter of the Oedipus myth should take his place with the likes of Picasso, Stravinsky, and Gide, for Hölderlin too belongs among this company. What, according to Deleuze, are the philosophical stakes of Hölderlin's reinterpretation of Oedipus?

In order to answer this question we must return to *Difference and Repetition*, this time to Deleuze's account of Hölderlin's creative transformation of Kant through Oedipus. The second chapter of Deleuze's daunting book focuses on time, specifically on the phenomenology of time-consciousness: how time is experienced, and how our conscious, reflective experience of time depends upon prior passive syntheses that inform pre-reflective organic ground of time. Deleuze attributes this discovery to Kant, for it was Kant who detected what Descartes had previously missed, namely that the experience of one's self is temporally mediated. On Descartes's account, the guarantor of time is his occasionalist Deity who remakes the universe at each instant. But this occasionalism presents the universe as an indefinite series of slices that seem to flow only because God wills it again and again, from the beginning until the end of time. And it is God who unifies individual conscious experience through the guarantee that the universe will be made anew.

Deleuze rightly notes that Kant's prohibition against the speculative deployment of God to underwrite the certitude of conscious experience renders the serenely unified conception of time and the self that we find in Descartes's thought as well as in much of the Western philosophical tradition utterly problematic. The self becomes fragmented because Kant takes time seriously. This means that he neither spatializes time (as Aristotle had when he understood time as the measure of motion) nor does he ground it in an entity or entities outside time (as we find, for example, in Descartes's God or Plato's Forms). Nevertheless, Kant fails to articulate the radical implications of the self's fragmentation through time, a task that will fall to intellectual successors such as Hölderlin, Nietzsche, and Deleuze himself. Instead, he shrinks from the abysmal thought of this fragmented self and retreats into the practical: while the theoretical grounding for claims cannot be won by resorting to metaphysical concepts of God, freedom, and immortality, these thoughts can and must be deployed when we act. While there can be no legitimate cognition that involves the concept "God," we think and act based upon it.[31] The practical serves to secure the self in the face of the fragmentation wrought by time. Deleuze claims that Hölderlin's *Oedipus* makes explicit the implications of Kant's attempt to consider time on its own terms. But how?

Aaron Schuster reminds us that Deleuze dubs Hölderlin the true heir of Kant's conception of the fragmentary self rent to pieces by time.

> Hölderlin is the thinker who takes up and radicalizes the Kantian paradox of inner sense, precisely through his intense engagement with Greek tragedy. [. . .] Hölderlin worked on highly original translations of *Oedipus Rex* and *Antigone* for sometime in the late 1790s to 1803; they were published in 1804, the last works of his lucid period before his final breakdown and refuge in his friend Zimmer's tower; the pall of schizophrenia somehow hangs over these texts.[32]

Schuster claims that Hölderlin's highly original interpretation of these Theban plays centers around the role of religion—Oedipus's tragic fate is sealed when he decides to root out the evil curse that has befallen Thebes, a decision the consequences of which will reverberate through the generations.[33] Oedipus just is this break marked by this decision—the difference that fractures Oedipus and makes it impossible to identify him with who he was before this tragic action. "For a brief moment we enter into that schizophrenia in principle which characterizes the highest power of thought, and open being directly on to difference despite all the mediations, all the reconciliations, of the concept."[34]

Recall that Foucault begins by reading the play in formal terms and then uses this formal reading to draw conclusions about the forgotten implication of power and knowledge in the play. Hölderlin, too, begins his "Remarks on Oedipus" by analyzing the formal characteristics of tragic poetry. Whereas Foucault focuses on the *sumbolon* as the formal structuring element of the play, Hölderlin understands the play in terms of a similar formal break, that of the caesura. The caesura breaks Sophocles's plays in two into two asymmetrical parts and thereby structures the tragic break that characterizes the action of the play: tragedies are broken plays about broken people that fail to realize they are broken until it is too late. The basis for Hölderlin's understanding of both the form and content of the play is paradox, and identity can only be grasped through difference.[35] In his fragmentary analysis of the play, Hölderlin begins by claiming that modern poetry should be elevated to the status it had in the ancient world if poets want to live comfortably before claiming that modern poetry cannot possibly measure up to ancient models, for poetic technique is lacking among modern poets.[36] Unlike the seventeenth-century partisan defenders of ancient and modern poetry who engaged in a spirited debate over whether ancient or modern poetry was superior or his German Idealist contemporaries who sought a synthesis between ancient and modern poetry, Hölderlin wants to find a way to keep both in dynamic tension with each other, a dynamic tension that renders both strange and thereby avoids the temptation of synthesis. This is the reason that Deleuze's *Oedipus*, inspired by Hölderlin's schizophrenic one, is not *Oedipus* in another modern disguise.

What modern poets forget is the lawfulness of poetry: the formal measure inherent in tragedy is that of the caesura or the radical break that occurs within the play that renders it tragedy. This radical split breaks the play asunder (recall that Foucault was interested in the doubling or *sumbolon* that occurred within the play). Foucault follows Hölderlin's interpretation by claiming that Oedipus follows the oracular pronouncement to purify the city by political means (what Foucault calls tyrannical means). Subsequently, what Hölderlin terms Oedipus's "wonderfully furious curiosity" transgresses its limits. Oedipus, the secure autonomous tyrant, slowly becomes insecure as his monstrous nature dawns upon him, a realization that Hölderlin describes as being

> tempted again by life, the desperate struggle to find himself, the brutal, almost shameless strife to gain control of himself, the madly wild seeking for consciousness. [. . .] In the end there dominates in [Oedipus's] speeches the insane questioning for a consciousness.[37]

Foucault and Hölderlin differ in the conclusions they draw based on the formal conditions of *Oedipus Rex*: Foucault concludes that this shows the collusion between power and knowledge (a theme which will become increasingly important in the coming years), while Hölderlin's conclusions are motivated, at least in part, by his interest in Oedipus's desire to know in order to show how that desire to know proves his tragic undoing.

Hölderlin begins his analysis by pointing out some general characteristics of poetry (ancient versus modern poetry in particular) before turning to the play itself as an exemplar of the tragic mode. This leads him to consider the play in terms of Oedipus's search for self-consciousness. He concludes by considering Oedipus's search as exemplary once more, this time in terms of the nature of human consciousness. Tragedy, Hölderlin concludes, is a poetic form concerned with the collusion between humans and gods ("how the god and man mate") that is the presentation of "the tremendous."[38] This collusion of humans and gods invariably leads in tragedy to their separation. "At such moments man forgets himself and the god and turns around like a traitor. [. . .] In the utmost form of suffering, namely, there exists nothing but the conditions of time and space."[39] One hears an echo of Kant's transcendental aesthetic here in the reference to the conditions of time and space. It is the suffering of this separation that Kant too quickly heals through the moral self of pure practical reason.[40]

Having strayed from Freud's own tyrannical reduction of Oedipus to a mere complex, we can see that both Foucault and Deleuze recognize the philosophical stakes of the figure of Oedipus and tragedy more generally. Each thinker develops Benjamin's insight regarding the need to modernize Oedipus found among contemporary artists and thinkers. Indeed, they add to the list of genres and figures in which one finds this modernizing impulse: from reminders of the coincidence of power and knowledge to detective fiction and Hölderlin's attempts to squarely face the implications of Kant's philosophy. Nevertheless, this monstrous figure remains an uncanny presence in the work of both thinkers precisely because they do not simply modernize Oedipus: both thinkers read Oedipus on his own terms and thereby remind us of the strangeness of Sophocles's *Oedipus*, the ancient monstrous human who unfortunately remains all too relevant for us today.

NOTES

1. James Baldwin, "Many Thousands Gone," *Collected Essays*. Ed. Toni Morrison (New York: Library of America, 1998), 22. Cf. Eddie S. Glaude, Jr. *Begin Again: James Baldwin's America and Its Urgent Lessons for Our Own* (New York: Crown, 2020), 44–46 for a discussion of Baldwin's theory of tragic memory and this passage in particular.

2. Baldwin, "Many Thousands Gone," 22.

3. Michel Foucault, "Oedipal Knowledge," *Lectures on the Will to Know and "Oedipal Knowledge": Lectures at the Collège de France 1970-1971*. Ed. Daniel Defert. Trans. Graham Burchell (New York: Palgrave Macmillan, 2013), 229. Hereafter cited as LWK.

4. LWK, 230.

5. Gilles Deleuze, "The Philosophy of Crime Novels," *Desert Islands and Other Texts 1953-1974*. Ed. David Lapoujade. Trans. Michael Taormina (Los Angeles: Semiotext(e), 2004), 82.

6. Aaron Schuster claims that one of Deleuze's most sustained engagements with German Idealism comes through his reading of Hölderlin's *Oedipus*. See Aaron Schuster, *The Trouble with Pleasure: Deleuze and Psychoanalysis* (Cambridge, MA: MIT Press, 2016), 63. I elaborate on Schuster's reading later.

7. Gilles Deleuze, *Difference and Repetition*. Trans. Paul Patton (New York: Columbia University Press, 1994), 87. Hereafter cited as DR.

8. André Gide, *Oedipe* (Paris: Pléiade, 1931), though Benjamin cites the Ernst Robert Curtius German translation of Gide's edition, which was published as *Oedipus, oder Der vernunftige Mythos*. Benjamin's text was originally published as a review in *Blätter des hessicshen Landtheaters*.

9. Walter Benjamin, "Oedipus, or Rational Myth," *Walter Benjamin: Selected Writings*, Volume 2, 1927-1934. Ed. Michael W. Jennings, Howard Eiland, and Gary Smith (Cambridge: Harvard University Press, 1999), 577. This conception of modernization will become important for both Benjamin and Foucault in their discussions of Baudelaire and what Foucault calls in "What is Enlightenment?" the "heroization of the present."

10. Benjamin, "Oedipus, or Rational Myth," 577. Constructivism in a theatrical context originates in the work of the Soviet dramatist V. E. Meyerhold, who pioneered a new pedagogy of acting he called "biomechanics" that conceived of the human body as a machine as he proclaims "the body a machine and the worker the machinist." Although Benjamin does not develop the idea here, there are undeniable connections between Meyerhold's constructivism and the revolutionary theater of Bertolt Brecht as well as Benjamin's own work on the modern mechanization of art. For a historical overview that connects Meyerhold with the work of Deleuze and Guattari, see Gerald Raunig, "*Machinae Et Orgia*: Revolutionary Theatre Machines in the Soviet Union

of the Early Twentieth Century," *Third Text*, 23, no. 1 (January 2009): 25–34. For a fuller treatment, see Gerald Raunig, *A Thousand Machines: A Concise Philosophy of the Machine as Social Movement* (Cambridge, MA: MIT Press, 2010).

11. Benjamin, "Oedipus or Rational Myth," 577.

12. Ibid., 578.

13. Jean-Pierre Vernant and Pierre Vidal-Naquet, "Oedipus Without the Complex," *Myth and Tragedy in Ancient Greece*. Trans. Janet Lloyd (New York: Zone Books, 1990), 90–91.

14. In the following section, I will conclude that because Deleuze follows Hölderlin in reinterpreting Oedipus, he ultimately does not simply give us another Oedipus in modern guise.

15. Foucault claims at the outset that this fragmentary morphology has motivated his work and will continue to motivate his future research, and, though it is beyond the scope of this chapter, it would be interesting to trace whether this did in fact motivate his subsequent work. One obvious way in which he did not carry out this research program can be found in the emphasis on practices, and particularly practices of the self, that dominates his later work, but the emphasis on the will to know never completely disappears. There are undeniable similarities between Foucault's notion of the fragment and German Romanticism, similarities which I have begun to explore in my essay "Foucault's Alleged Irrationalism: The Legacy of German Romanticism in the Work of Michel Foucault," *Idealistic Studies*, 37, no. 1 (2007): 1–13.

16. Foucault, "Oedipal Knowledge," LWK 229.

17. LWK, 230.

18. LWK, 235.

19. LWK, 236.

20. LWK, 252.

21. LWK, 256–257.

22. Miriam Leonard, "Tragic Will and the Subject of Politics," *Phoenix*, 59, no. 2 (2005): 133–142. The Foucault quotation is from the first section of "Truth and Juridical Forms," *Essential Works of Foucault 1954-1984, Volume 3: Power*. Ed. Paul Rabinow. Trans. Robert Hurley et al. (New York: The New Press, 1994), 2.

23. Ibid., 17.

24. Ibid.

25. Ibid., 25. Note that Foucault here draws upon his analysis of *Oedipus* in terms of the *sumbolon* first presented in "Oedipal Knowledge."

26. DR, xx.

27. Gilles Deleuze, "The Philosophy of Crime Novels," *Desert Islands and Other Texts 1953-1974* (Los Angeles: Semiotext(e), 2004), 81. Hereafter cited as DI.

28. DI, 82.

29. Ibid.

30. DI, 83.

31. And we can use these ideas regulatively to lend coherence to our cognitions.

32. Schuster, op. cit., 63.

33. Ibid., 64.

34. DR 58, cited by Schuster, 65.

35. See Joshua Billings, *Genealogy of the Tragic: Greek Tragedy and German Philosophy* (Princeton: Princeton University Press, 2014), 189, citing Friedrich Hölderlin, *Essays and Letters*. Trans. Jeremy Adler and Charlie Louth (London: Penguin, 2008), 316: "'The meaning of tragedies,' Hölderlin writes in an undated note, 'is most easily grasped through paradox.' Paradox, the co-presentation of opposites, is the guiding principle of Hölderlin's thought on tragedy. Unity, Hölderlin believes, can only be grasped through difference."

36. Friedrich Hölderlin, *Essays and Letters on Theory*. Trans. and Ed. Thomas Pfau (New York: SUNY Press, 1988), 101.

37. Ibid., 104–105.

38. Ibid., 107.

39. Ibid., 108.

40. Joshua Billings argues that Hölderlin reads *Oedipus at Colonus* as a modern tragedy: "It is modern for its depiction of a form of fate that is less visceral, and more spiritual than that typical of tragedy—death as a kind of anti-climax or absence." "The Ends of Tragedy: *Oedipus at Colonus* and German Idealism," *Arion* 21, no. 1 (Spring/Summer 2013): 118. Cf. Joshua Billings, *Genealogy of the Tragic: Greek Tragedy and German Philosophy* (Princeton: Princeton University Press, 2016).

REFERENCES

Baldwin, James. "Many Thousands Gone," *Collected Essays*. Ed. Toni Morrison. New York: Library of America, 1998.

Billings, Joshua. *Genealogy of the Tragic: Greek Tragedy and German Philosophy*. Princeton: Princeton University Press, 2014.

Benjamin, Walter. "Oedipus, or Rational Myth," *Walter Benjamin: Selected Writings*, Volume 2, 1927-1934. Ed. Michael W. Jennings, Howard Eiland, and Gary Smith. Cambridge: Harvard University Press, 1999.

Deleuze, Gilles. "The Philosophy of Crime Novels," *Desert Islands and Other Texts 1953-1974*. Ed. David Lapoujade. Trans. Michael Taormina. Los Angeles: Semiotext(e), 2004.

Foucault, Michel. "Oedipal Knowledge," *Lectures on the Will to Know and "Oedipal Knowledge": Lectures at the Collège de France 1970-1971*. Ed. Daniel Defert. Trans. Graham Burchell. New York: Palgrave Macmillan, 2013.

———. "Truth and Juridical Forms," *Essential Works of Foucault 1954-1984, Volume 3: Power*. Ed. Paul Rabinow. Trans. Robert Hurley et al. New York: The New Press, 1994.

Gide, André. *Oedipe*. Paris: Pléiade, 1931.

Glaude, Eddie S., Jr. *Begin Again: James Baldwin's America and Its Urgent Lessons for Our Own*. New York: Crown, 2020.

Hölderlin, Friedrich. *Essays and Letters on Theory*. Trans. and Ed. Thomas Pfau. New York: SUNY Press, 1988.

Leonard, Miriam. "Tragic Will and the Subject of Politics," *Phoenix*, 59, no. 2 (2005): 133–142.

Raunig, Gerald. "Machinae Et Orgia: Revolutionary Theatre Machines in the Soviet Union of the Early Twentieth Century, " *Third Text*, 23, no. 1 (January 2009): 25–34.

———. *A Thousand Machines: A Concise Philosophy of the Machine as Social Movement*. Cambridge, MA: MIT Press, 2010.

Schuster, Aaron. *The Trouble with Pleasure: Deleuze and Psychoanalysis*. Cambridge, MA: MIT Press, 2016.

Vernant, Jean-Pierre and Pierre Vidal-Naquet, "Oedipus Without the Complex," *Myth and Tragedy in Ancient Greece*. Trans. Janet Lloyd. New York: Zone Books, 199.

Chapter 3

Knowledge, the Unconscious, and Desire

Serene Richards

INTRODUCTION

The forgotten women of nineteenth-century Paris's Salpêtrière hospice, or museum, as some have described it, were involuntarily interned and diagnosed with "hysteria" through a series of symptoms imagined by members of the psychiatric staff. In this chapter, I investigate the collaboration between psychiatric knowledge and the state, and the subsequent modes of subjectification that this endeavor lends itself to, or what Deleuze and Guattari would call part of the forces of anti-production that quash desire(s). What transforms a line of flight into a line of death? The chapter begins by examining Jean-Martin Charcot's practice of "provoked" observation and reinvention of hysteria to the tune of a positivist science during his time as head of psychiatry at the Salpêtrière in Paris during the nineteenth century. My argument engages Foucault's work on the subject of the unconscious of knowledge, and the relationship between the human sciences and power: the former delineating the conditions of possibility of life and the living. We will see how psychoanalysis emerges as a counter-science in Foucault's work, capable of seeing an incomplete representation of the subject or "science of man." Finally, I turn to Deleuze and Guattari for whom any psychoanalytic endeavor not only recognizes Foucault's description of an incompleteness in representation, completeness being impossible, but neither does it seek to fulfill nor isolate deviant behavior as such. I argue that desire permeates the social, composing the cartographic lines that make up someone's life and being. The great challenge is, and will remain, how to prevent a line of flight—understood not as an escape but as a creation—becoming a line of death.

Psychiatry or the Knowledge of Beautiful Souls

> The hysteric is a divine spirit that is always at the edge, the turning point, of making. [. . .] She is given images that don't belong to her, and she forces herself, as we've all done, to resemble them.[1]

In 1656, Louis XIV converted a gunpowder factory into the Salpêtrière hospice for the internment of the poor women of Paris. The Salpêtrière was a branch of the General Hospital, the latter founded as part of the "Great Confinement" during the seventeenth century. The General Hospital, contrary to its name, did not serve a primarily medicinal purpose, but rather was designed for the ethical transformation of the poor; the aim was to inculcate a new ethic of work in each and all, for "God wants men and women to earn their bread by manual labour [working the body] and by the sweat of their brow."[2] From very early on, the evidence suggests that psychiatry and capitalism exist in close proximity, epitomized in this new system of confinement, designed to combine the demands of budding capitalism, philanthropic concern, and the new science of psychiatric knowledge.

By the turn of the twentieth century, "the Salpêtrière was what it had always been: a kind of feminine inferno, a *citta dolorosa* confining four thousand incurable or mad women. It was a nightmare in the midst of Paris's *Belle Epoque*."[3] In this space, women were to be treated for madness while coexisting together through work, that is, labor. Their work consisted in menial tasks, generally unproductive, or rather, uneconomical, but this was not the point: from idleness to prostitution, deviances of all kinds had to be cured, and a new value of work instilled. The new psychiatric knowledge that permeated the space positioned itself as the modus operandi of treatment and cure and presented itself as a science in the hopes of embodying a sense of neutrality and authority. As Foucault points out, this appeal to scientific neutrality, and the authority that accompanies it, masks, instead, its subordination to "the imperatives of a morality" all the while reiterating its divisions all "under the guise of the medical norm."[4] Indeed, Foucault argues that this knowledge

> became associated with an insistent and indiscreet practice, glibly proclaiming its aversions, quick to run to the rescue of law and public opinion, more servile with respect to the powers of order than amenable to the requirements of truth [. . .] it promised to eliminate defective individuals, degenerate and bastardised populations. In the name of a biological and historical urgency, it justified the racisms of the state, which at the time were on the horizon.[5]

For Foucault, this was a system of correction wedded to the values and morals of the ruling order of things, specialized in identifying, separating, and pathologizing deviancy "under the guise of the medical norm." This state racism, inseparable from scientific and biological knowledge—in the form of eugenics in some instances—is part of the long discourse on biopolitics that Foucault will go on to elaborate in more detail in his 1975–1976 lectures at the Collège de France, *Society Must Be Defended*.[6]

In 1841–1842 the number of women admitted involuntarily to the Salpêtrière recorded as suffering from hysteria was 1 percent, by 1883 this figure grew to just over 20 percent.[7] This sharp rise in the number of women diagnosed with hysteria coincides with the tenure of Jean-Martin Charcot, who, after working at the hospice for a number of years, was made chief of the Clinic in 1862. What is the relationship, if any, between Charcot and the rise in registered so-called hysterical women? The first thing to note is that the notion of hysteria was not a novel idea, rather it can be understood as an atemporal floating signifier whose semantic content has varied over the centuries. The Hippocratic school in the fifth century BC named hysteria after the Greek for "uterus," likely initiating the concept's association with women rather than men. As a result of hysteria's fluctuating meaning over the preceding centuries, this particular affliction, in a sense, defied classification: categorization being a primary concern for physicians. Jean-Martin Charcot, therefore, took up the task of organizing the multifarious spread of symptoms hitherto associated with hysteria and categorized them into a sort of coherence. Adopting a positivist method familiar to the natural sciences, "Charcot's goal was to subsume the seemingly random symptoms under positive laws; and he succeeded, asserting on the grounds of 'attentive and sufficiently repeated observations' that the symptoms unfolded with complete predictability."[8] As Georges Didi-Huberman puts it, it is almost as though Charcot "reinvented hysteria," isolating it as "a pure nosological object."[9] Which is to say that "what Charcot wanted or expected in principle from this method was for it to bear an idea, an accurate concept of 'pathological life,' the life of the nervous system in this case."[10] In re-situating the symptoms as deriving primarily from hereditary factors, Charcot was able to make of hysteria an object of knowledge, classifying certain symptoms in-line with the demands of a positive science. Perhaps most unsettling of all was that Charcot's method not merely involved observation of patients but rather "provoked" observation, in order to simultaneously obtain facts and put them to work.[11]

Yet, who were these women, interned at the *Salpêtrière* for hysteria? A fascinating detail is recorded alongside the names of the women interned and diagnosed with hysteria: a list of their various occupations. It would seem that they all held working-class jobs, working as "women-seamstresses, laundresses, flower-sellers—who lived outside the framework of a bourgeois value system."[12] The occupations of the Salpêtrière women are of little to no relevance to Charcot, who believed hysteria to be an essentially biological illness, and who was seemingly more concerned with constructing a discourse that could be understood as characteristic of women such as those interned, going so far as to delete and manipulate data and information that would have potentially disrupted the smooth running of his imposed hypotheses. As Foucault explains it,

> the more frequent practice of deleting from the succession of dossiers what had been said and demonstrated by the patients regarding sex, but also what had been seen, provoked, solicited by the doctors themselves, things that were almost entirely omitted from the published observations.[13]

Rather than being an incidental detail, the occupations of these women and the daily struggles encountered in a society increasingly concerned with surplus labor, doing work that is tied up with exchange value, enduring growing poverty and social exclusion are of paramount importance for Deleuze and Guattari, for whom there is a social production of the unconscious, including class struggle, as we will encounter later on in this chapter.

A key theme that runs throughout Foucault's work on the relationship between power and the science of man is an analysis of how the various techniques of power function with respect to life, and in a sense, we can discern that the relationship is one of instituting life itself, thereby giving rise to questions of subjectification and deciding on the mode of the possible in terms of living, being, and acting. The connection here is between a knowledge largely derived and produced though the state internment of the deviant, or mad, and a certain governance of life, and is, in this way, decidedly biopolitical. The women of the Salpêtrière were never cured; indeed many of them perished in the hospital. As Hélène Cixous describes,

> The great hysterics have lost speech, they are aphonic, and at times have lost more than speech: they are pushed to the point of choking, nothing gets through. They are decapitated, their tongues are cut off and what talks isn't heard because it's the body that talks, and man doesn't hear the body.[14]

For Charcot and others, it did not matter what was said or left unsaid, for what was heard was what chimed well with a structure that could give rise to a diagnosis: repeatable and observable. The manipulating and discarding of documents including unsettling, perhaps even contradictory, information formed part of this practice of knowledge production, utilized with the aim of an intervention in mind, of managing conduct and behavior. Despite its best efforts, this knowledge remained imperfect. Indeed, caught between acts which on occasion failed to repeat the experiment, and an emerging philanthropic concern for madness, their practice elicited its own unsettling anxiety, with a nagging suspicion that something has gone awry. At the heart of this new scientific consciousness was Charcot and others' fear of the unknown, that madness itself could change form (as it often does), and that knowledge could not always be seen in the actions of the interned women. As Didi-Huberman notes, one did not "submit" to an asylum's organization but rather it was understood that one entered into it: "One enters into it as one enters into the routine of daily life, an infinitesimal and at the same time unlimited routine: the banal tenderness of the State."[15] A certain dissonance then, between the goodwill of the beautiful soul and the destructive potential of their actions, perhaps the sense that the experiment really is just that: an experiment. Charcot's fear was perhaps most palpable when it came to be known that several magicians and magnetizers of the time began advertising their performances with slogans such as "Based on Professor Charcot's experiments at the Salpêtrière."[16] Imitation is flattery or a poignant reminder of that which psychiatric knowledge conceals of itself; of its own unknown and uncertainty. The Salpêtrière can be thought of as representative of an antagonism that characterizes a knowledge that believes in its certainty; all the while accompanying it is the nagging suspicion that there is more to it, or less, a conjuring of *mana*, as Mauss would call it, is often necessary to smooth over the cracks. The Salpêtrière, a hospital, or a museum as some have called it, was also "the capital of smoke screens, the capital of sandmen."[17] Foucault saw this clearly, and it was for this reason that for him it was essential to shed light on the unconscious of knowledge, the unthought that accompanies the exactitude of reason.

Knowledge and the Unconscious

Foucault was not a psychoanalyst but a philosopher chiefly concerned with the formation of the subject, or the human being. From the early 1950s, Foucault was preoccupied with what he saw as the growing "anthropologisation of philosophy." In one of his first lectures at the University of Lille in 1952–1953 entitled "Connaissance de l'homme et réflexion transcendentale" Foucault lays the groundwork for his project on the growing influence of anthropological themes in nineteenth-century philosophy.[18] Indeed, in 1953 Foucault convened his first seminar at the *École normale supérieure* on "Kant's Anthropology and Freud," which, to date, remains unpublished. Foucault's interests in nineteenth-century anthropological questions continued through to his stay in Hamburg in 1960 where he began to translate Kant's *Anthropology from a Pragmatic Point of View* (1798). In 1961, Foucault submitted two theses: one was an early version of his book *Madness and Civilization* that was examined at the Sorbonne and a second entitled "Kant: Anthropology. Introduction, Translation, Notes," supervised by Jean Hyppolite. Foucault's examiners suggested that his introduction to Kant should be developed and published as a separate work. So, when, Foucault's translation of Kant's *Anthropology* was published in 1964, only a few pages out of a total of 128 pages actually appeared in the introduction to Kant's work. The remaining pages were developed and published, just two years later, under the title *The Order of Things*. Clearly, Foucault was heavily preoccupied with investigating how this new field of empirical knowledge, known as the new "science of man," or anthropology, could emerge and play a crucial role in the techniques of government, and, in turn life, determining the conditions of possibility of living, which he would term biopower or biopolitics.

Alenka Zupančič has somewhat misleadingly suggested that Foucault's *The History of Sexuality Volume I* amounts to an "account of psychoanalysis."[19] Yet, if Foucault gave any account of psychoanalysis, he provided it in *The Order of Things*, where Foucault distinguished and appreciated psychoanalysis as a counter-science. While *The History of Sexuality*, published in 1976, 10 years after *The Order of Things*, still picks up where the latter left off, it illustrates much of the conceptual movements by way of an analysis of the objectification of sexuality by the human sciences, which, in turn, serves to illustrate the relationship between power and the governance of life, or what Foucault calls, for the first time, the paradigm of biopolitics or biopower.[20] Foucault is not so much interested in what power *is* as much as *how* power is articulated in the social field: identifying its hold over life and analyzing power's hold over life in turn on processes of subjectification.

In many ways, it remains difficult to pin Foucault's work down into a specific discipline or thematization, and this is perhaps due to the problematizations that Foucault concerned himself with, namely how a new "science of man" could lend itself to the governance of life. In an interview with the journal *La Quinzaine littéraire* in March 1968, Foucault was asked to define his work. He offers the following, modest, response:

> [My work is an attempt to] try to find something that would be like the *unconscious* in the history of science, and in human knowledge. If you like, the working hypothesis is, broadly put, the following one: the history of science, the history of knowledge(s), do not simply obey the general law of the progress of reason, it is not a human consciousness, it is not human reason that is a kind of guardian of the laws of its own history. There exists, beneath what science knows of itself, something that it does not know; and its history, its future, its episodes, its accidents, obey a certain number of laws [*lois*] and determinations. These laws and determinations, these are what I have tried to reveal. I have tried to excavate an autonomous domain that would be that of the *unconscious*

> of knowledge, that would have its own proper rules, just as the human being's *unconscious*, too, has its own rules and determinations.[21]

Foucault points to that hidden kernel of our knowledge that continues to exist in close proximity to us. We tirelessly and ceaselessly redouble our efforts to conceal this "unconscious of human knowledge," professing completeness and mastery, while the human being's unconscious remains a mystery. Throughout history, numerous efforts have been made to *tame* the human being, to expel the irrational, the passions, and the inhuman.[22] Foucault is not necessarily interested in how these limits are decided upon, for instance, over what qualities constitute the irrational. Rather, Foucault's analysis is twofold: on the one hand, Foucault looks at how these authorial truths work in tandem with a technique of government, and, on the other, he sheds a light on what remains after this necessarily impossible task has been decided upon, the so-called taming of man. As the shadow of man's impotence continues to haunt the exactitudes of his reason while points of resistance and lines of flight continue to disrupt the representations.

Foucault highlights these themes in *The Order of Things*; the latter, in large part, constitutes an analysis of the effect of the epistemic shift resulting from the predominance of the human sciences. The key difference from Classical thought, argues Foucault, is that the conditions of possibility of living, of life, now come to be interrogated, and in many respects implied, by way of an articulation of the human being in the form of "man," the subject or the cogito. The key shift, in other words, occurs on the level of clearly defining the limits of the possible and the conditions of possibility of life, which paradoxically comes from life itself, from the new science of man, with man situated as both the subject and object of such knowledge, and made to exist retroactively throughout history according to new epistemic laws. For Foucault,

> When natural history becomes biology, when the analysis of wealth becomes economics, when, above all, reflection upon language becomes philology, and Classical *discourse* (Emphasis in original), in which being and representation found their common locus, is eclipsed, then, in the profound upheaval of such an archaeological mutation, man appears in his ambiguous position as an object of knowledge and as a subject that knows: enslaved sovereign, observed spectator, he appears in the place belonging to the king.[23]

In this context, "Man" finds himself at the center of the world and as the primary *source* of order: that it is only through him that all knowledge can be made possible. Foucault calls man, in this sense, an empirico-transcendental doublet. With modern thought, the emphasis is one of revelation, of revealing the conditions of knowledge in accordance with the empirical contents a predetermined mode of problematization allows for. The analysis then limits itself to one of a positivist nature, where the "truth of the object determines the truth of the discourse that describes its formation."[24] In other words, the discourse itself anticipates an already self-defined truth, so that whatever one seeks is, in a sense, already predetermined. For Foucault, the effect is a discourse situated between positivism and eschatology, where man is produced as a "truth" within it: both reduced and promised at the same time. Hence, a discourse that is both empirical and transcendental that enables an analysis of man as a subject and site of knowledge—as empirically determined and continually referred back to an origin.

Problems arise, however, since being the site of knowledge implies also being the site of misunderstanding and errancy within a potential discourse: the not-known.[25] The unthought, or unconscious of knowledge, as both external and yet necessarily linked to man, is, "in one sense, the shadow cast by man as he emerged in the field of knowledge; in another, the blind stain by which it is possible to know him."[26] Or, in psychoanalytic terms, the subject is always already constituted in relation to a foreclosure; what is foreclosed is precisely that which cannot be symbolized, an impossible, that returns as a symptom, such that "what was foreclosed from the Symbolic returns in the Real—in the form of hallucinatory phenomena"—and "returns in the Real of the symptom."[27] Man, in its construction, carries with it its shadow: that, for the human sciences it is at once a matter of discounting as nonsense, and of unveiling, of knowing, of transcribing. Indeed, during the late nineteenth and early twentieth centuries a new interest arose concerning the notions of glossolalia and aphasia, to the extent that psychiatrists interpolated linguists to aid in formalizing an analysis: asking, for example, whether glossolalia could be considered a language.[28] It is for these reasons that Foucault suggests that psychoanalysis, along with ethnography, emerge as counter-sciences, since they flow in the opposite direction to the human sciences. The human sciences looks backward, tirelessly making and constructing man as he appears, while psychoanalysis and ethnography "ceaselessly 'unmake' that very man who is creating and re-creating his positivity in the human sciences."[29] In both cases, there is no attempt to construct a general concept called man nor is there an attempt to isolate a unique *quality* or *essence* of man. Rather, both ethnography and psychoanalysis have access to a multiplicity of experiences, develop concepts, and express a continual dissatisfaction with what may otherwise appear to be established knowledge. Indeed, as far as psychoanalysis is concerned, it is not a question of approaching the unconscious "with their back to it" and waiting for it to reveal itself. Rather, psychoanalysis "points directly toward it," not in the direction of rendering sayable something which is implicit but rather "toward what is there and yet is hidden."[30] In advancing over the space of what is representable, that which is ipso facto non-representable, psychoanalysis discovers in it that it is possible for there to be "system (therefore signification), rule (therefore conflict), norm (therefore function),"[31] thereby challenging what had long been discounted as mythology. Psychoanalysis shows that in the un-representable space lies the very conditions of possibility of knowledge about the living human being. For Foucault, only when these ephemeral elements that escape all signification emerge can we recognize madness—not as something "of another world" as "straying of reason," but as something

> perilously nearest to us—as if, suddenly, the very hollowness of our existence is outlined in relief; the finitude upon the basis of which we are, and think, and know, is suddenly there before us: an existence at once real and impossible, thought that we cannot think, an object for our knowledge that always eludes it.[32]

Psychoanalysis recognizes itself in this moment: sensing that which is closest to it and at the same time appears impossible. When phantasy and the imagination were subsumed under the ego cogito, and the phantasm long ago expelled from the subject of experience with the advent of modern science, appearing only in the form of mental alienation and illusions, its presence did not disappear but rather transformed as man's shadow. The phantasm, or the unthought, having been foreclosed from the constitution of the subject now returns only as symptom. When psychoanalysis is confronted with the analysand bearing this symptom, this madness that is all too familiar, it realizes it is all too close, recognizing even itself in it. Such that

> psychoanalysis "recognizes itself" when in it is confronted with those very psychoses which nevertheless (or rather, for that very reason) it has scarcely any means of reaching: as if psychosis were displaying in a savage illumination, and offering in a mode not too distant but just too close, that towards which analysis must make its laborious way.[33]

Psychoanalysis is made to confront these psychoses and finds itself in them. It cannot reach this madness but can only be reminded of its own madness in it, seeing in it only a glimpse of that which it could be, and toward which it "must make its laborious way."

For this reason, Alenka Zupančič's suggestion that "what is dramatically missed (and missing) in Foucault's account of psychoanalysis is, quite simply, the concept of the unconscious"[34] is somewhat misguided. Zupančič adds that "the fact that in his account of psychoanalysis he never actually quotes Freud or Lacan also speaks to that effect."[35] As has been elucidated so far, Foucault's project aims elsewhere; it is not a question of providing an account of psychoanalysis nor necessarily to critique psychoanalysis, lest we forget that the first volume of *The History of Sexuality* is subtitled *The Will to Knowledge*. Foucault, in part, aims at discerning what effect the human sciences have on our conceptualization both of ourselves and in turn over the conditions of possibility of living amid the paradigms of discipline and biopolitics. Moreover, Foucault is concerned with the close relationship between the form of knowledge of the human sciences and government, the former lending itself as a technique of power, rendering possible interventions into life the extent to which is not possible without this knowledge, a necessarily imperfect one at that.

Indeed, Zupančič points at that for Lacan: "There is a structural gap that pertains to discursivity as such, and this gap is what gives to the unconscious its structure, and it is involved—by default—in all relations of power."[36] Similarly, for Foucault, as we have seen, this is the unconscious of knowledge—the shadow of consciousness that continues to exist and haunt knowledge and discourse. Zupančič argues that "whatever the object of power, the latter never operates simply in relation to this object, but also in relation to its own structural gap."[37] As we encountered, there is much similar ground here; for Foucault this is precisely the unknown that power seeks to know. Foucault would later go on to examine the use of statistics as a technique of power which is simultaneously that through which the known is articulated and through which the unknown can be measured, guessed, estimated, and ultimately made concrete as image—thought not without faults since there exists both known unknowns and unknown unknowns. Indeed, this is precisely the impossible task: the unknown giving rise to greater unknowns, like an untamable shadow haunting language, knowledge, and man—an irreparable gap.

That is not to say that these planes of thought are equivalent, though the point has been to, in a sense, refine Foucault's problematization in light of numerous misunderstandings. In *What Is Philosophy*, Deleuze and Guattari provide clarification over their long-held stance that philosophy is essentially the creation of concepts. Importantly, the concepts that one creates should always be adequate to a particular problem. In this case, it is clear that Foucault's problem lies elsewhere than that of psychoanalysis, strictly speaking, and, in *The History of Sexuality* that is on the relationship between knowledge and power, as a technique or *how* of power, understood through the concept of biopolitics. This knowledge(s)—that is in itself incomplete though presented as full representations—have served, Foucault believes, as techniques of power intervening in the management of populations and effectuating forms of subjectification. This is not to say that knowledge "comes first," that is, that power merely receives knowledge and applies it in a linear process of production. Rather, as Deleuze explains in his work on

Foucault, "these power-relations, which are simultaneously local, unstable and diffuse, do not emanate from a central point or unique locus of sovereignty."[38] They amount to a technique or strategy of non-stratification; "The practice of power remains irreducible to any practice of knowledge."[39] For this reason, Deleuze reminds us that Foucault would call this a microphysics of power, not to denote something small or minutiae but rather to emphasize the sense of power's mobility, irreducible to one type of knowledge. Indeed, as Deleuze puts it,

> The sciences of man are inseparable from the power relations which make them possible, and provoke forms of knowledge [*savoirs*] which can more or less cross an epistemological threshold or create practical knowledge [*connaissance*]: for example, a "*scientia sexualis*" involves the relation between penitent and confessor, believer and director; while psychology involves disciplinary relations. We are not saying that the sciences of man emanate from prison, but that they presuppose the diagram of forces on which prison itself depends.[40]

It is this functional relation, this interdependence, that functions as a technique of government that interests Foucault. The women interned at the Salpêtrière were the subjects and objects of an imperfect knowledge; as Cixous said, "She is given images that don't belong to her, and she forces herself, as we've all done, to resemble them."[41] It is precisely for this reason that, for Deleuze and Guattari, it is not enough to discover the unconscious and interpret it according to programs or representations, rather the unconscious itself must be produced. For Deleuze, psychoanalysis—tied up with the representation of Oedipus—impedes the formation of utterances. The flows of desire are reduced to representations where "the intensities lose their steam and the connections are broken."[42]

Producing the Unconscious

How would it be if these insane people were right?[43]

The uniting factor in Foucault's and Deleuze and Guattari's writings on psychiatry and psychoanalysis is the unequivocal belief that the latter cannot be thought apart from the political. As Foucault writes,

> It is to the political credit of psychoanalysis [. . .] that it regarded with suspicion (and this from its inception, that is, from the moment it broke away from the neuropsychiatry of degenerescence) the irrevocably proliferating aspects which might be contained in these power mechanisms aimed at controlling

> and administering the everyday life of sexuality. [. . .] It was owing to this that psychoanalysis was [. . .] in theoretical and practical opposition to fascism.[44]

High praise indeed, and, in the preface to *Anti-Oedipus*, Foucault would rightly identify a major adversary that was the target of Deleuze and Guattari's writings: fascism. "Not only historical fascism," Foucault specifies, "but also the fascism in us all, in our heads and in our everyday behaviour, the fascism that causes us to love power, to desire the very thing that dominates us."[45] For Deleuze and Guattari "there is only desire and the social, and nothing else."[46] The social is invested with and permeated by desire, even in the former's most repressive forms. It is here that we can most clearly see how Guattari united his devotion to psychoanalysis and political militancy in his analyses that brings together Marxism and psychoanalysis. For what is in question is not an anti-psychiatry nor the idea that "it's-all-society's-fault."[47] Indeed, in this sense Guattari works along similar lines to Foucault, inasmuch as "madness will not be replaced by the positivist determination, treatment, and neutralisation of mental illness, but that mental illness will be replaced by something we have not yet understood in madness."[48] In other words, it is not a question of correcting this or that deviancy, rather it is institutions that are unwell. This is why schizoanalysis is essentially institutional in that it is about the transformation of institutions rather than the correction of this or that deviant behavior. As Guattari saw it, "Psychoanalysis had indeed joined forces with the most traditional psychiatry to stifle the voices of the insane constantly talking politics, economics, order, and revolution."[49] Central to any analytic practice, then, was the necessity to challenge what Guattari saw as the affront of anti-production, saying that "the State machine and the machine of repression produce anti-production, that is to say signifiers that exist to block and prevent the emergence of any subjective process on the part of the group."[50] The capitalist system is characteristic of this anti-production, as well as what Deleuze and Guattari see as the production of lack.[51] That is to say that

> the deliberate creation of lack as a function of market economy is the art of the dominating class. This involves deliberately organising wants and needs (*manque*) amid an abundance of production; making all desire teeter and fall victim to the great fear of not having one's needs satisfied; and making the object dependent upon a real production that is supposedly exterior to desire (the demands of rationality), while at the same time the production of desire is categorised as fantasy and nothing but fantasy.[52]

From a young age, Guattari was involved with the French Communist Party, eventually growing disillusioned with the latter's reluctance to offer full support to the Algerian revolutionaries which led to Guattari and others setting up *La voie communiste*. During this time, Guattari had begun to become involved with institutional psychiatry and psychoanalysis, joining Jean Oury who had founded the La Borde clinic in 1953. Guattari was involved from the beginning, meeting Oury that same year at the age of 15, and by the age of 23 was already working with Lacan with whom he would complete his training in 1962, joining the *École Freudienne de Paris* as an analyst member in 1969.[53] While at La Borde, Guattari had founded *Federation of Groups for Institutional Study and Research* that aimed to bring together Marxism and psychoanalysis to get to grips with forces of anti-production. La Borde "lived literally to the rhythm of Lacan's seminar, the entire medical team was running to attend to it. Lacan's linguistic research and the works of Saussure and Troubetskoï were shared by the clinic's team."[54] Indeed, it was Lacan who had initially recommended Guattari read two of Deleuze's works, the *Logic of Sense* (1969) and *Difference and Repetition* (1968), inviting him to produce a review of these works.[55] Guattari's text, "Machine et Structure," which the editors refused to publish, ultimately points to the limits of structure (which Guattari came to understand through his work with patients at La Borde. For Guattari, structure is concerned primarily with the production of generality thus preventing the appearance of repetition—in a Deleuzian sense. In other words, a repetition which would not lend itself to a repetition of an original sameness but rather a repetition of difference, not identity. The task then, for Guattari, would be to imprint "the class struggle at the very heart of unconscious desire."[56] As Deleuze and Guattari put it in relation to President Schreber,

> Of course the father acts on the child's unconscious—but does he act as a head of a family in an expressive familial transmission, or rather as the agent of a machine. [. . .] Schreber's desiring-machines communicate with those of his father; but it is in this very way that they are from early childhood the libidinal investment of a social field. *In this field the father has a role only as an agent of production and antiproduction* (Emphasis in original).[57]

In other words, the wager is that, in certain analytic practices, the flows of desire (impersonal as much as personal) are captured and reduced to a "world of mental representations, where the intensities lose their steam and the connections broken."[58] An infinite process of translation occurs, where the analysand's utterances are already supposed to mean something else. Instead, a schizoanalysis begins with someone's personal utterances "and discovers their genuine production, which is never a subject but always a mechanic assemblage of desire, collective assemblages of utterance that traverse the subject and circulate within it."[59] Neither interpretation nor an operation of signification, the role of schizoanalysis rather resembles a cartography, not a history. As Deleuze said on the subject in one of his seminars at Vincennes, "If you do not find the lines that composes someone, including the lines of flight, you won't understand the problems posed nor the ones they pose for themselves."[60] Deleuze is quick to add that a line of flight is not a line of escape; it is, in the end, an act of creation. At a certain point, a line of flight can turn to a line of death, "they cannot take it any longer, it's too difficult," Deleuze says.[61] What is in question is a process, a voyage, without a predetermined trajectory or destination. The women of the Salpêtrière lived a mode of life unique to each one according to the specificities of their personal histories, but also their unique occupations, seamstresses and florists, the politics and social context too engendering numerous affectations; as either increasing or diminishing one's power to act, depending again on specific contexts. We will never know the cartographies that made up their lives and desires, collapsed instead under the generalized rubric of the psychiatric diagnosis of hysteria, nor will we know how it was that, at a certain moment, a certain point, they could not stand it any longer, *elles ne supportent plus*.

NOTES

1. Hélène Cixous, *Castration or Decapitation*, tr. Annette Kuhn, *Signs* 7, no. 1 (1981): 41–55.
2. "*Mémoire concernant les Pauvres*," in Louis Lafaist Félix and Danjou, *Archives Curieuses de l'Histoire de France depuis Louis XI jusqu'à Louis XVIII*, Series 1, Volume 15 (Paris: Membre de l'Institut Historique, 1837), 267.
3. Georges Didi-Huberman, *Invention of Hysteria*, tr. Alisa Hartz (London and Cambridge: The MIT Press, 2003), xi.
4. Michel Foucault, *The History of Sexuality, Volume I* (New York: Random House, 1978), 53.
5. Foucault, *The History of Sexuality*, 54.
6. See Michel Foucault, *Society Must Be Defended*, tr. David Macey, ed. Mauro Bertani and Alessandro Fontana (London: Penguin Books, 2004).
7. Jan Ellen Goldstein, *Console and Classify: The French Psychiatric Profession in the Nineteenth Century* (Cambridge: Cambridge University Press, 1987), 322.
8. Goldstein, *Console and Classify*, 326.
9. Didi-Huberman, *Invention of Hysteria*, 18.
10. Didi-Huberman, *Invention of Hysteria*, 19.
11. Didi-Huberman, *Invention of Hysteria*, 19.
12. Goldstein, *Console and Classify*, 326.
13. Foucault, *The History of Sexuality*, 56.
14. Cixous, "Castration or Decapitation," 49.
15. Didi-Huberman, *Invention of Hysteria*, 6.
16. Didi-Huberman, *Invention of Hysteria*, 235.

17. Didi-Huberman, *Invention of Hysteria*, 235.

18. Defert et al., "Introduction" in Michel Foucault, *Introduction to Kant's Anthropology*, 10.

19. Alenka Zupančič, "Biopolitics, Sexuality and the Unconscious," *Paragraph* 39, no. 1 (2016): 49–64.

20. This concept is often interpreted as connoting a biological character; while this can be the case, this understanding has the effect of collapsing the term, erasing its sense to convey the close relationship between life and politics in a specific sense: the multiplicity of governmental techniques of intervention and management of the human being, in turn made possible through the knowledge(s) of the human sciences, and as Foucault would later describe, statistics.

21. Michel Foucault, "Foucault répond à Sartre" in *Dits et Écrits, Volume I [1954-1968]*, ed. Daniel Defert, François Ewald and Jacques Lagrange (Paris: Éditions Gallimard, 1994), 665–666. Emphasis added.

22. I elaborate on this further in *Court of Miracles: A Genealogy of Conduct* (Forthcoming, 2022).

23. Michel Foucault, *Order of Things: An Archaeology of the Human Sciences* (New York and Oxford: Routledge, 2002), 340.

24. Foucault, *Order of Things*, 349.

25. Foucault, *Order of Things*, 352.

26. Foucault, *Order of Things*, 356.

27. Slavoj Žižek, *The Sublime Object of Ideology* (London and New York: Verso, 2008), 78–79.

28. See Guillaume Sibertin-Blanc, "Délires de langue, schizoanalyse de savoir linguistique: *lalangue*, anagramme, homophonie scénique," *Kenose: Revue Philosophique & Politique*, 0 (2013–2014): 39.

29. Foucault, *The Order of Things*, 414.

30. Foucault, *The Order of Things*, 408.

31. Foucault, *The Order of Things*, 408.

32. Foucault, *The Order of Things*, 409–410.

33. Foucault, *The Order of Things*, 410.

34. Zupančič, "Biopolitics, Sexuality and the Unconscious," 51.

35. Zupančič, "Biopolitics, Sexuality and the Unconscious," 52.

36. Zupančič, "Biopolitics, Sexuality and the Unconscious," 58.

37. Zupančič, "Biopolitics, Sexuality and the Unconscious," 58.

38. Gilles Deleuze, *Foucault*, tr. Seán Hand (London and Minneapolis: University of Minnesota Press, 2006), 73.

39. Deleuze, *Foucault*, 74.

40. Deleuze, *Foucault*, 74.

41. Hélène Cixous, *Castration or Decapitation*, 47.

42. Deleuze, "Four Propositions on Psychoanalysis" in Gilles Deleuze, *Two Regimes of Madness: Texts and Interviews 1975-1995*, ed. David Lapoujade, trans. Ames Hodges and Mike Taormina (New York and Los Angeles: Semiotext(e), 2006), 83.

43. Sigmund Freud, "New Introductory Lectures on Psycho-Analysis" (1933), Volume XXII in Sigmund Freud, *The Standard Edition of the Complete Psychological*

Works of Sigmund Freud, 1953–1975, ed. and trans. James Strachey (London: Hogarth Press and The Institute of Psychoanalysis, 1966), 58–59.

44. Foucault, *The History of Sexuality*, 150.

45. Michel Foucault, "Preface" in Gilles Deleuze and Félix Guattari, *Anti-Oedipus*, tr. Robert Hurley, Mark Seem, and Helen R. Lane (London and New York: Bloomsbury, 2013), xiii.

46. Deleuze and Guattari, *Anti-Oedipus*, 29.

47. Gilles Deleuze, "Preface: Three Group-Related Problems" in Félix Guattari, *Psychoanalysis and Transversality: Texts and Interviews 1955-1971*, trans. Ames Hodges (California: Semiotext(e), 2015), 18.

48. Deleuze, "Preface," 18.

49. Deleuze, "Preface," 10.

50. Félix Guattari, "The Group and the Person," in *Molecular Revolution: Psychiatry and Politics*, ed. and trans. David Cooper and Rosemary Sheed (London: Peregrines, 1984), 34.

51. Deleuze and Guattari, *Anti-Oedipus*, 283.

52. Deleuze and Guattari, *Anti-Oedipus*, 26.

53. Gary Genesko, *Félix Guattari: An Aberrant Introduction* (London and New York: Continuum, 2002), 5.

54. Anne Querrien, "La Borde, Guattari, Left Movements 1965-81," interviewed by Constantin V. Boundas, *Deleuze Studies* 10, no. 3 (2016): 395–416.

55. Querrien, "La Borde," 411.

56. Guattari, "Machine et Structure," *in Psychoanalysis and Transversality*, 329.

57. Deleuze and Guattari, *Anti-Oedipus*, 297.

58. Deleuze, "Four Propositions," 83.

59. Deleuze, "Four Propositions," 84–85.

60. Gilles Deleuze, *Anti-Œdipe et autres reflexions (1980)*—Enregistrement des cours de Gilles Deleuze, Cours du 27 mai 1980, Gallica, BNF. Accessed February 1, 2020. https://gallica.bnf.fr/html/und/enregistrements-sonores/anti-oedipe-et-autres-reflexions-1980-enregistrements-des-cours-de-gilles?mode=desktop.

61. Deleuze, *Anti-Œdipe et autres reflexions (1980).*

REFERENCES

Cixous, Hélène. *Castration or Decapitation.* Translated by Annette Kuhn, *Signs* 7, no. 1 (1981): 41–55.

Defert, Daniel, François Ewald and Frédéric Gros. "Introduction" in Foucault, Michel. *Introduction to Kant's Anthropology*, edited by Roberto Nigro, translated by R. Nigro and Kate Briggs, 9–12. Cambridge, MA and London: MIT Press, 2008.

Deleuze, Gilles. "Four Propositions on Psychoanalysis" in Deleuze, Gilles. *Two Regimes of Madness: Texts and Interviews 1975-1995*, edited by David Lapoujade, translated by Ames Hodges and Mike Taormina, 79–88. New York and Los Angeles: Semiotext(e), 2006.

Deleuze, Gilles and Félix Guattari. *Anti-Oedipus: Capitalism and Schizophrenia.* Translated by Robert Hurley, Mark Seem, and Helen R. Lane. London and New York: Bloomsbury, 2013.

Deleuze, Gilles. *Foucault.* Translated by Seán Hand. London and Minneapolis: University of Minnesota Press, 2006.

Deleuze, Gilles. *Anti-Œdipe et autres reflexions (1980).* Enregistrement des cours de Gilles Deleuze, Cours du 27 mai 1980, Gallica, BNF. Accessed February 1, 2020. https://gallica.bnf.fr/html/und/enregistrements-sonores/anti-oedipe-et-autres-reflexions-1980-enregistrements-des-cours-de-gilles?mode=desktop

Didi-Huberman, Georges. *Invention of Hysteria.* Translated by Alisa Hartz. London and Cambridge, MA: MIT Press, 2003.

Foucault, Michel. *The History of Sexuality, Volume I: An Introduction.* Translated by Robert Hurley. New York: Random House, 1978.

Foucault, Michel. *Society Must Be Defended: Lectures at the College de France, 1975-76.* Translated by David Macey. Edited by David Macey, Mauro Bertani and Alessandro Fontana. London: Penguin Books, 2004.

Foucault, Michel. "Foucault répond à Sartre" in *Dits et Écrits, Volume I [1954-1968].* Edited by Daniel Defert, François Ewald and Jacques Lagrange. Paris: Éditions Gallimard, 1994.

Foucault, Michel, *The Order of Things: An Archaeology of the Human Sciences.* New York and Oxford: Routledge, 2002.

Freud, Sigmund. "New Introductory Lectures on Psycho-Analysis" (1932-1936), Volume XXII in Freud, Sigmund. *The Standard Edition of the Complete Psychological Works of Sigmund Freud*, 1953-75, edited and translated by James Strachey. London: Hogarth Press and The Institute of Psychoanalysis, 1966.

Goldstein, Jan Ellen. *Console and Classify: The French Psychiatric Profession in the Nineteenth Century.* Cambridge: Cambridge University Press, 1987.

Genesko, Gary. *Félix Guattari: An Aberrant Introduction.* London and New York: Continuum, 2002.

Guattari, Félix. *Psychoanalysis and Transversality: Texts and Interviews 1955-1971.* Translated by Ames Hodges. Los Angeles: Semiotext(e), 2015.

Guattari, Félix. *Molecular Revolution: Psychiatry and Politics*, edited and translated by David Cooper and Rosemary Sheed. London: Peregrines, 1984.

Lafaist, Louis and Danjou, Félix. *Archives Curieuses de l'Histoire de France depuis Louis XI jusqu'à Louis XVIII*, Series 1, Volume 15. Paris: Membre de l'Institut Historique, 1837

Querrien, Anne. "Anne Querrien: La Borde, Guattari, Left Movements 1965-81." Interview by Constantin V. Boundas, *Deleuze Studies* 10, no. 3 (2016): 395–416.

Sibertin-Blanc, Guillaume. "Délires de langue, schizoanalyse de savoir linguistique: lalangue, anagramme, homophonie scénique," *Kenose: Revue Philosophique & Politique*, 0 (2013–2014): 38–63.

Žižek, Slavoj. *The Sublime Object of Ideology.* London and New York: Verso, 2008.

Zupančič, Alenka. "Biopolitics, Sexuality and the Unconscious," *Paragraph* 39, no. 1 (2016): 49–64.

Chapter 4

Psychoanalysis in Question

Foucault, Castel, Deleuze-Guattari

Philippe Sabot

In this chapter, I wish to address some aspects of Michel Foucault's relationship to psychoanalysis by focusing in particular on the theoretical and practical issues that lie behind *The Will to Knowledge* and that give shape to the program of a genealogy of the subject of desire. This program indeed finds in the 1976 book an important relay, even if it also goes well beyond the scope of this book. The concern for psychoanalysis and the effort to situate its dimension of rupture and innovation in the field of knowledge and social practices are present from the first investigations on "mental illness"[1] to the study of the "deployement of sexuality" with the discourse and the modes of regulation of sex which result from it, passing through the study of the asilar system and the forms of knowledge-power which support it. Such a questioning of the historical situation of psychoanalysis still unfolds, beyond *The Will to Knowledge*, from analyses devoted to the forms of confession in the West, which this time refer to the articulation of the relations between truth and subjectivity. In the course of these successive reshuffles of problematics, Foucault does not cease in a sense to return to psychoanalysis, but it must also be recognized that he approaches it most often only indirectly, to better apprehend the conditions of a rupture with the model of an empirical psychology or with the epistemological and practical expectations of asilar psychiatry, or even to approach in a critical manner the most contemporary forms of a truthful statement about oneself.[2]

The topics of psychoanalysis are thus rarely studied for themselves, but they are above all evaluated on the basis of issues that go beyond those of a simple commentary on Freud's works.[3]

This indirect approach refers to a large extent to a certain "structural ambivalence"[4] which has already been noted in Foucault's treatment of Freud's thought and which is based on the ambivalence of the theoretical and practical presuppositions of psychoanalysis itself. For example, when psychoanalysis confirms the alienation mechanism proper to asilar psychiatry by moving it out of the asylum but reconstituting it in the form of domination by the analyst,[5] or when it comes to install its power of control and regulation of sexuality at the heart of the family by capturing in its own discourse the relations of desire that pass between parents and their children,[6] or finally when psychoanalysis appears as one of the powerful relays of the procedures of confession resulting from the Christian ritualization of a formulation of truth passing by the verbalization of desire to another who claims it as a pledge of obedience as much as of access to his own identity.[7]

In the following study, I propose to take up this Foucauldian genealogy of psychoanalysis, concentrating on the confrontation, in the first half of the 1970s, of the approaches that Michel Foucault and Robert Castel proposed in support of the work they devoted to it between 1973 and 1976. This sequence corresponds, for Foucault, to the courses on *Psychiatric Power* and *Abnormal* as well as to the developments leading to the first volume of *The History of Sexuality: The Will to Knowledge*. It corresponds, for Castel, to two books offering an in-depth questioning of psychiatry and psychoanalysis: *Le Psychanalysme: L'ordre psychanalytique et le pouvoir* (1973) and *L'Ordre psychiatrique: L'âge d'or de l'aliénisme* (1976). One cannot but be struck by the converging effect that characterizes these different critical questionings on "psy" knowledge and power. In Foucault's work, particularly in the early 1970s, such questioning accompanies the project of a history of sexuality proposing to study the "*perpetual spirals of power and pleasure*" (Emphasis in original)[8] that are triggered by sex. But it is also fed by the second reception of *Madness and Civilization*, that is, by its appropriation by certain currents of anti-psychiatry (particularly Anglo-Saxon, with Laing and Cooper).[9] It is this theoretical context that led Castel to question a few years later the critical potential of anti-psychiatry in the face of what he also describes as the development of a "new psychological culture," characteristic of our contemporary era.[10] For his part, Foucault marked a theoretical departure from the presuppositions of the theoretical-practical propositions of the "anti-psy" (who, according to him, continue to think of psychiatric work and knowledge in terms of repression) while taking up the thread of a genealogy of the "Psy-function" (*Fonction-psy*).

My analysis will therefore focus on this Foucauldian theoretical proposition of the "Psy-function" to inscribe it not only in the development of Foucault's own research, in this interminable genealogy of psychoanalysis which has in fact been constantly being rewritten since the 1950s, but also in the approach that Castel himself seems to propose, even if from a different perspective. It will also be an opportunity to situate the place of Deleuze and Guattari's *Anti-Oedipus* in these intersecting questionings on the political and social function of psychoanalysis.

FROM PSYCHIATRY TO PSYCHOANALYSIS

Let us begin by reconstructing the genealogical basis of the "psy" issue as it appears in the lectures devoted to *Psychiatric Power*—before being reinvested in *The Will to Knowledge* in the form of a psychiatricization of sex and the "historical emergence" of psychoanalysis inseparable from a "generalization of the deployement of sexuality."[11] This should make it possible to effectively measure the convergences and gaps between Castel and Foucault in the apprehension of such "Psy" power-knowledge and the modalities of its application.

First of all, let us recall that from the course of 1972–1973, *The Punitive Society*, Foucault engaged in an in-depth reflection on the making of the power, envisaged simultaneously as an elaboration of the "normal" from the apparatus of sequestration that is the prison. In the 1973–1974 course devoted to *Psychiatric Power*, it is no longer the normalizing functions of the prison, with their connection to a production apparatus, that are studied, but this time the focus is on the asylum, identified as a "scene of confrontation"[12] that pits the doctor and the madman against each other in the context of a therapeutic operation envisaged above all from the point of view of power relations. One could say that it is this general program of work, which will lead, in the course of 1973–1974, to the identification of the "psy-function" and to the beginning of a genealogy of psychoanalysis.

In this respect, these analyses proposed by Foucault are both an extension of and a departure from certain theses developed by Castel since the early 1970s. They are an extension of them insofar as, in *Le Psychanalysme*, Castel also seeks to analyze the analytical situation from the angle of power relations: not therefore according to the only "scientific" criteria of a theoretical and practical truth concerning the effects of the unconscious, even if psychoanalysis would like to think and present itself as being removed from the games of power, but rather according to its extra-analytical stakes, of a social and political order, which command its practice and in reality ensure its status as truth in the social space. From this point of view, as Foucault himself points out in the roundtable discussion that follows the Brazilian conferences on "Truth and Juridical Forms" in May 1973, Castel shows that psychoanalysis, far from producing the emancipatory effects that a theory and practice of the unconscious seem to carry, "only seeks to displace, to modify, and finally to resume the relations of power that are those of traditional psychiatry"[13] and which are basically expressed in terms of normalization or the fabrication of the "normal." We recognize the Foucauldian project of a genealogy of psychoanalysis whose course on *Psychiatric Power* bears witness, particularly in its last lesson when, starting from the scene of the hysterical and the asilar off-screen, psychoanalysis finally allows psychiatry to refound itself as medical truth, once it has reoriented itself toward a new object: sexuality.

However, despite this kind of proximity, even this convergence of intention, Foucault seems to have to deviate from Castel as well, since it is not exactly in the same terms that both analyze the modalities of the exercise of these power relations. First of all, it is important to emphasize that Castel's essay develops more of a critique of psychoanalysis as it was institutionalized in his time than an exegetical study of Freudian thought. It is therefore above all a question of critically examining certain excesses of psychoanalytic practice, showing in particular

> how a method that is supposed to explore without concession the unconscious depths of subjectivity [has] at the same time become a consumer product sold on the airwaves, in the cinema, in literature, in medicine, and in marketing. How can a technique that readily boasts of being subversive be used as a crutch to improve the functioning of institutions—school, psychiatry, the army, business—which, to say the least, do not have a revolutionary aim.[14]

Moreover, according to Castel, the type of power exercised by this technique reveals what he calls "the social unconscious of psychoanalysis."[15] This means that it is necessary to go beyond the opposition between what, on the one hand, would be intra-analytical, that is to say, the rational core and the emancipatory (even revolutionary) power of psychoanalysis as a science of the effects of the unconscious, and what, on the other hand, would be extra-analytical, social, external to its own order, and as such deserving to be considered inessential, heterogeneous to the analytical truth as the analyst claims to deploy it in act and for the sole benefit of the patient in the individual treatment. Denouncing the illusory character of such an abstract opposition, Castel, on the contrary, endeavors to underline the reciprocal intertwining of the intra- and extra-analytical which, according to him, function within discourse and the analytical situation in an "ideological" manner. That is to say, the social conditions that inhabit and make possible the analytical apparatus are denied, occulted, and misunderstood, but they are also taken up, reinterpreted, and reabsorbed intra-analytically according to a procedure of recoding that is an integral part of the ideological operation of psychoanalysis or of the ideological effect produced by psychoanalysis in order to mask its own relation to power and to obscure the social and political matrix of this Psy-knowledge that functions in the social order as what organizes its reproduction.

To give an idea of this, let us note the way Castel reports the analytical situation. At first glance, this is presented according to a "convention of neutrality"[16]—that is to say, for the psychoanalyst to become a support for fantasies in the operation of transference, he or she must not be identified with any religion, any partisan commitment, and any social class. Now, this convention is clearly a delusion: so that "the political neutrality of the analyst presupposes the dimension of the social and the political, but misunderstood, that is to say present in the form of its pseudo-absence, apolitism."[17] Once this supposed "apolitism" is given for what it is, namely an ideological masking of very real and politically determined social relations, what does the comprehension of the analytical situation reveal? That it implements a "social relation characteristic of liberal societies, the relation of personalized service. It is a relationship that unites a qualified specialist with a client in a market economy."[18] Such a relationship is characterized by a structural difference in power since it actually opposes a competent specialist (and supposedly knowing) and a destitute claimant (reputed to be ignorant and suffering—suffering from this ignorance). This situation of inequality is based on the extra-analytical dimension that characterizes social relations in liberal economies (the dynamics of supply and demand organized in the form of the contract). The psychoanalyst therefore recodes it, reinterprets it, and endows it with new meanings which are now operative both in and for the analytical process and work as a condition of his own "success" on the psychic level. In short, a relationship based on the values of the market economy is recoded in the vocabulary and on the sublimated stage of an economy of desire.

However, Foucault certainly does not take up this matrix of ideological analysis of the power relations that make up the psychiatric and psychoanalytical apparatus. To put it another way, his investigation of "psychiatric power" does not seek to unmask this power, which would pass for a pure knowledge of all exteriority or all involvement in social relations. Rather, the genealogy that he proposes envisages psychiatric knowledge as one of the effects of these disciplinary type power relations, of which the asylum constitutes the privileged site but which actually irrigate the whole social space. It is here that the obvious gap between Castel's and Foucault's approaches appears in all its magnitude.

Castel develops the opposition between science and ideology and denounces the illusion of a (scientific) neutrality that would mask the reality of the power relations at work in the analytical clinic and also the effects of normalization induced by this clinic in the name of an ideal of emancipation (in terms of psychic and social life) or revelation (in terms of truth and knowledge—about oneself). Foucault rather relates these effects of normalization to the disciplinarization of behaviors, such as it is carried out within the balance of forces that is established between the psychiatrist and "his" madman, and which takes the dimension of an intensification of the real to counter the reactive will of the madman.[19] The new economy of the exercise of power that Foucault designates in his course as a "discipline" does not function therefore with ignorance, but rather with reality, with the "over-power of reality" that the psychiatrist comes to embody.[20]

THE FAMILY ISSUE

It remains to be understood, then, how the kind of extension of "psychiatric power," its migration to other disciplinary fields, which gives its basis to the "Psy-function," is elaborated from there. Foucault thus designates this instance of control of all institutions and all disciplinary apparatuses which takes the family as its referential.[21] Why does the family appear at the heart of the deployment of the "Psy-function"—according to a hypothesis whose fertility will be explored in *The Will to Knowledge* based on the analysis of the deployement of sexuality?

To understand this, it is useful to recall that Foucault does not refer the exercise of psychiatric power to the ideal disembodiment of a disciplinary power that functions optimally in the anonymity of its rules and its silent architectures of surveillance and sanction. On the contrary, he emphasizes that "one can still find in contemporary society many forms of the power of sovereignty."[22] In particular, the family, with its role as the sovereign and highly individualized authority of the father, forms such an island of sovereignty within a power regime dominated by disciplinary patterns. Consequently, it is not a question of making the psychiatrist himself a substitute of the paternal figure. But it seems more fruitful to draw a functional analogy from this analysis. In the same way that the body of the psychiatrist refers to a device of sovereignty whose crucial role is to be "the hinge, the interlocking point, which is absolutely indispensable to the very functioning" of this particular disciplinary system that is the asilar system, in the same way the family is characterized by its double function of "pinning" individuals on the disciplinary systems and of hitching them up with each other, ensuring "passage from one disciplinary system to another, from one apparatus to another."[23] What *The Will to Knowledge* will analyze as the generalization of the sexuality apparatus is thus linked to a family policy based on the regulation and control of the body and sexuality.[24]

Foucault draws from this analysis the substance of his elaboration of the "Psy-Function." This refers, on the one hand, to the "organization of disciplinary substitutes for the family" for which all "shrinks" are responsible (at school, in the army, in the hospital, in the factory), and on the other hand, to this family reference itself which guides and orients all these substitutes according to a well-established social norm, serving in a certain way as a common measure for the deployment of "Psy-oriented" discourse and practices:

> The Psy-function is, then, the agency of control of all the disciplinary institutions and apparatuses, and, at the same time and without any contradiction, it holds forth with the discourse of the family. At every moment, as psychopedagogy, as psychology of work, as criminology, as psychopathology, and so forth, what it refers to, the truth it constitutes and forms, and which marks out its system of reference, is always the family.[25]

This family, adds Foucault, thus becomes "the authority of truth on the basis of which it will be possible to describe and define all the positive or negative processes which take place in the disciplinary apparatuses."[26] It is in the name of the family, even when it is failing or lacking, in the name of family values and the hierarchy of values imposed by its model of sovereignty, that the multiple undertakings of rectification, correction, disciplinarization, and thus psychological individualization of subjects take place. We have here a double movement, which places discipline in relation to the family each time. Discipline palliates the family defect, thus returning to the family the responsibility for an indiscipline to be corrected, and in this disciplinary correction itself, it refers to the family and thus to this sovereign (and normative) truth of the family. In the lectures devoted to *Abnormal*, Foucault returns to this articulation between the family and psychoanalysis by showing how the sexualization of childhood and family relationships (through the scrupulous attention paid to child masturbation by parents) forms the concrete ground for the deployment of the psychoanalytic theory of incest.[27]

The end of the lecture of November 28, 1973 allows us to rearticulate this Foucauldian analysis of the "Psy-function" with the study of "psychoanalysis" proposed by Castel. Foucault underlines in fact that one of the effects of the circle he elaborated previously resides in the fact that psychoanalysis represents "the most 'family discourse' of all psychological discourses,"[28] in particular inasmuch as it is based on the structure of the Oedipus.[29] This means that it therefore represents that discourse, and that practice, which refers to the sovereign instance of truth that is the family. From this authority and the norms it imposes, it constitutes the raison d'être of the disciplinary apparatuses that correct and restore order to the lives of the subjects, especially with regard to their sexuality. This remark then imposes that psychoanalysis should be considered not as a critical resource to be opposed to the discipline (in all its forms and in the diversity of its applications) but on the contrary as the ultimate justification of this discipline: in the name of what and in relation to what the discipline imposes itself.

This is a way for Foucault to record the main lesson of Castel's psychoanalysis, that which refuses to "introduce a dichotomy of law between a 'pure' functioning and 'recovered' uses of psychoanalysis."[30] However, Foucault does not go so far as to treat this dichotomy in terms of a lack of knowledge of an ideological nature (i.e., linked to effects of representation) but rather interprets it from the genealogical angle of a functional, and historically constructed, articulation between family sovereignty and disciplinary apparatuses. It is therefore not because it would pass itself off as what it is not (namely, a theory and practice of unconscious effects removed from the pressure of the social and political stakes of truth) that psychoanalysis can pass itself off as a discourse of truth about the human psyche. It is because it is historically ordered to the discourse of the family and to the social and political stakes that this discourse covers (and which are fundamentally related to the conditions of the reproduction of the social order) that it participates, in a quasi-transcendental manner (it is the discourse of psychological discourses), in this continuous disciplinarization of subjects—in the name of the family, in the name of the discursive sovereignty of the Oedipus.

THE *ANTI-OEDIPUS* IN QUESTION

The Foucauldian genealogy of the "Psy-function" thus reveals its anchorage in a global strategy of refamilialization of the individual through the continuous interplay of disciplines, from psychiatry to psychoanalysis. It then seems to mobilize the resources proposed by Deleuze and Guattari in *Anti-Oedipus* in 1972. Indeed, familialism and psychoanalysis appear complementary in this analysis, which relates psychoanalysis to the discourse of the family and the family to a figure of sovereignty that subjugates the subject to the law of his desire. The last words of the lecture of November 28, 1973 echo in an obvious way the remarks made during one of the roundtable discussions that followed the lectures on "Truth and Juridical Forms." Foucault states there that, in his 1972 book, "Deleuze describes psychoanalysis as being, at its core, an enterprise of refamilialization, or of forced familialization of a desire which according to him does not have in the family its place of birth, its object and its center of delimitation."[31] In *Psychiatric Power*, Foucault says no other. But what Foucault adds in his May 1973 speech in Brazil is the idea that the family, conveniently related to the Oedipus, to the Oedipal "triangle" (Father, Mother and I), is not the instance of liberation and verification of desire, but rather, through psychoanalysis and the analytical situation, the bias by which the subject is blocked in his desire, unable to express it outside this framework, constrained and constraining, that the Oedipus imposes on him or her in the analysis in order to re-subjugate him or her to the law of his or her own desire. There thus seems to be a convergence in the comprehension of the situation and the role of psychoanalysis in this functional space where family sovereignty and disciplinary apparatuses are articulated.

However, the development proposed by Deleuze and Guattari in *Anti-Oedipus* is not limited to this critical side of the investigation, since it also includes a productive side, attached to the notion of schizophrenia.[32] Now, from this point of view, Foucault and Castel join together to express reservations about the strategy of circumventing or overcoming the Oedipus proposed by Deleuze and Guattari. During the roundtable discussion in Brazil in May 1973, Foucault preferred to remain cautious and put forward a hypothesis on the meaning of what the authors of *Anti-Oedipus* referred to as "schizophrenia":

> This notion of schizophrenia is not clear. Is schizophrenia, as Deleuze understands it, to be interpreted as the way in which society, at a certain point in time, imposes a certain number of power relations on individuals? Or is schizophrenia the very structure of non-Oedipal desire? I think Deleuze would be more inclined to say that schizophrenia, as he calls it, is non-oedipal desire.[33]

In his remarks, Foucault thus quite clearly refers Deleuze to a myth of liberation that is symmetrical to the one he denounces in his analytical recourse to the Oedipus. What Castel translates at the same time in a much more radical way when, in the last chapter of *Le Psychanalysme* (entitled "The Future of an Illusion"), he suggests that Deleuze and Guattari's book conducts a critique of psychoanalysis in the name of desire and that, from this point of view, "schizoanalysis is generalized psychoanalysis, bringing together all the powers of the unconscious. Analytical fascination can therefore be replayed and displaced, [. . .] meta-analysis in short, in the fourth, social dimension of desire."[34] This way of reading *Anti-Oedipus* amounts to restricting its critical scope, maintaining it within the limits of a repressive conception of "psychic" power, considered as that which deprives the subject of his desire by recoding it in the reactionary and familialist structure of the *Oedipe*.

Now, in relation to this undertaking of a critique of psychoanalysis that would exploit its own presuppositions in order to turn them against it and hope thus to invest, or even liberate the productivity of the desiring machines in the social field, the approach proposed by Castel is in line with Foucault's analyses of the "Psy-function" and also of psychoanalysis.[35] This approach consists of a series of statements where the fracture line that separates them from Deleuze is drawn.

It must certainly be recognized that psychoanalysis is not only, contrary to what some psychoanalysts have been able to claim, a discourse of truth, but that it is above all a social practice, that is to say, one that is connected to the social and to social relationships. The major contribution of *Anti-Oedipus* from this point of view is to show "how psychoanalysis reiterates, systematizes, displaces ('reterritorializes') in the sphere of private existence a fundamental anthropological structure whose genesis must be sought on the side of the *socius*."[36] Let us recall that Castel, unlike Foucault, interprets this reterritorialization in ideological terms, therefore according to the logic of an inversion of real relationships into imaginary or illusory relationships, destined in any case to be misunderstood. It is in the "pinning" of the disciplinary on the sovereign dimension of the family that Foucault sees for his part the knotting of the "Psy-function" and its variety of applications that psychoanalysis in a way caps with its discourse of truth and verification of desire.

However, where Foucault joins Castel, and in turn separates himself from Deleuze, is that he does not oppose the operation of capturing desire in the Oedipus and of redoubling this capture in the analytic enclosure, the liberating dimension of a return to non-Oedipalized desire, which would also signify the promise of social emancipation. *The Will to Knowledge* marks a definitive end to the definitive nonacceptance of any avatar of Freudo-Marxism,[37] whose specter also haunts certain developments in anti-psychiatry.

PSYCHOLOGICAL CULTURE OR CULTURE OF CONFESSION?

Under these conditions, what function and what scope should be given to a critical analysis of the "Psy-function"? Castel's answer to this question is important and provides the general framework for his own further research:

> It remains to measure from this place that psychoanalysis has come to occupy in the social structure, the powers that it deploys in it. It is one thing to denounce the shadow cast by psychoanalysis because of the ignorance it orchestrates. It is another thing to account for the positivities that it deposits and that constitute its trace in history.

This project is of a sociohistorical nature and does not quite overlap with the program of a genealogy of psychoanalysis. To carry it out, Castel proposes to investigate the following question:

> What has arisen, imposes itself and produces its effects in the name of psychoanalysis, under its guarantee, according to its criteria, thanks to its prestige, from the device it has invented, through the channels it has set up, within the institutions it controls or infiltrates?[38]

In a sense, this questioning echoes the type of analysis proposed by Foucault in the 1973 lectures and again in the lectures on *Abnormal*, with the study of the emergence of psychiatric expertise and the connection of the "Psy-function" to the law, which marks a new extension of his field of intervention.

But, for Castel, he above all opens up a new avenue of study devoted to what he calls, in the last chapter of *La Gestion du risque*, the "post-psychoanalysis" (*l'après-psychanalyse*), by which he does not mean the end or the overcoming of psychoanalysis, its scientific and social expiration, but rather "the end of psychoanalysis's control of the process of diffusion of psychological culture in society."[39] This "psychological culture" is now taken into account at all levels of individual, professional, and social life, with a view to producing the adherence of supposedly normal subjects to behaviors and ways of being that optimize their performance while relying on their autonomy and creativity. The analysis of this "new psychological culture," supported by the development of a neoliberal governmentality, thus seems to be a continuation of Foucault's studies, at the end of the 1970s, on neoliberalism and the constitution of an individual who is an "entrepreneur of oneself."

But, while this is undoubtedly an interesting extension that Castel proposes to the analyses that he himself had begun in the early 1970s, Foucault's study of "psychiatric power" and of the extension and generalization of the "Psy-function" (based on the genealogical matrix of a critique of psychoanalysis) will have constituted an important relay; it should also be recalled that, in the latter, subsequent developments around the "Psy"-issue are not limited to the sociohistorical analysis of the neoliberal individual's life-forms. Rather, they are extended into long-term genealogical questioning, which brings to light the way in which psychoanalysis itself, after having reproduced, by displacing it, the alienation apparatus peculiar to nineteenth-century psychiatry, it also renews and even reinforces the injunction to discover and tell—to another—the truth about oneself that has accompanied the development of Christianity, focused on the "confessions of the flesh" and animated by the ever deeper questioning of the imputability of desire to the subject under the dizzying horizon of a "fallen will."[40] The genealogy of psychoanalysis, the centerpiece of Foucauldian reflections on the "Psy"-issue, thus takes its place in an ethical and political history of the relationship between subjectivity and truth which is fundamentally that of the "mechanism of perpetual confession connected to permanent obedience."[41]

NOTES

1. The work published in 1954 under the title *Maladie mentale et personnalité* (*Mental Illness and Personality*) includes a first part devoted to the "Psychological Dimensions of Illness," in which the contribution of "analytical psychology" is established, particularly in the transition it makes from a psychology of evolution

to a psychology of genesis—or of individual history. Foucault Michel and Basso Elisabetta, "Un manuscrit de Michel Foucault sur la psychanalyse," *Astérion*, no. 21 (2019). http://journals.openedition.org.ressources-electroniques.univ-lille.fr/asterion/4410. In order to account for Foucault's interest in the place of psychology in contemporary knowledge and in the power relations that cross and animate it, we must therefore go back to the early 1950s, when Foucault himself became involved in a training course in psychology and elaborated his first theoretical reflections on the epistemological status and historical situation of psychology (in relation to the treatment of "mental illness"). On Foucault's relationship between psychology and phenomenology, see Basso Elisabetta and Bert Jean-François (dir.), *Foucault à Münsterlingen. À l'origine de l'Histoire de la folie* (Paris: EHESS, 2015).

2. On the sequence of these problematizations of psychoanalysis in Foucault's thought, see Lagrange Jacques, "Versions de la psychanalyse dans le texte de Foucault," *Incidence*, no. 4–5 "Foucault et la psychanalyse" (2008–2009): 11–54, Basso Elisabetta, "Foucault entre psychanalyse et psychiatrie. 'Reprendre la folie au niveau de son langage,'" *Archives de Philosophie*, no. 79 (2016): 27–54, Frédéric Gros, "Freud, l'évité de Foucault au Collège de France," in *Freud au Collège de France 1885-2016*, ed. Antoine Compagnon et Cécile Surprenant (Paris: Collège de France, 2018): http://books.openedition.org/cdf/5660, Laurie Laufer, and Amos Squvever (dir.) *Foucault et la psychanalyse. Quelques questions analytiques à Michel Foucault* (Paris: Hermann, 2015), and Laurent Dartigues, "La question de psychanalyse chez Michel Foucault," *Astérion*, no. 21 (2019). :http:// journals.openedition.org.ressources-electroniques.univlille.fr/asterion/4278. The latter provides a fairly complete review of the work devoted to the question of the relationship between Foucault and psychoanalysis (Laurent Dartigues, "La question de la psychanalyse chez Michel Foucault," note 10).

3. Yet it is obvious that Foucault had a firsthand knowledge of Freudian work, to which he devoted a large number of reading notes and notes, whether in the preparation of his first book, *Mental Illness and Personality*, or in the course of his teachings over a period of 15 years. The archives of the Fonds Foucault housed at the Bibliothèque nationale de France contain a large number of manuscripts that bear witness to Foucault's in-depth study of Freud's work. Boxes Nr. 38 and 46 contain notes and preparatory manuscripts for the 1954 book (notes on "Illness and Personality in Freud") and for lessons no doubt given at the ENS (notes on "Freud's Anxiety," "The Unconscious in Psychoanalysis," "The Notion of Psychoanalytical 'Milieu'" based on the example of "The Wolf Man"). Boxes Nr. 51 and 78 contain the manuscripts of the courses of Clermont-Ferrand (1964) and Vincennes (1969), devoted to sexuality. See Michel Foucault, *La sexualité. Cours donné à l'université de Clermont-Ferrand. 1969*—suivi de *Le Discours de la sexualité. Cours donné à l'université de Vincennes. 1969* (Paris: Le Seuil-Gallimard, coll. "Hautes études," série "Cours et travaux de Michel Foucault avant le Collège de France," 2018).

4. Frédéric Gros, "Freud, l'évité de Foucault au Collège de France," 3–4.

5. See Foucault Michel, *Madness and Civilization: A History of Insanity in the Age of Reason*, trans. Richard Howard (London: Routledge, [1961] (1972) 1988), chapter 4, "Birth of the Asylum"; Michel Foucault, *Psychiatric Power. Lectures at*

the Collège de France 1973-1974, trans. by Graham Burchell (New York: Palgrave MacMillan, 2006), 1–18.

6. Michel Foucault, *Abnormal. Lectures at the Collège de France 1974-1975*, trans. Graham Burchell (London: Verso, 2003), 263–290.

7. See Michel Foucault, *The History of Sexuality. Volume I: An Introduction. The Will to Knowledge*, trans. Robert Hurley (New York: Pantheon Books, 1978), 63–70. This relationship between the scrupulous examination of one's own desires, the ritualization of the confession, and obedience to another constitutes one of the threads of volume 4 of *The History of Sexuality 4. The Confessions of the Flesh*, trans. Robert Hurley (New York: Pantheon Books, 2021). See also Gros Frédéric, "Freud, l'évité de Foucault au Collège de France," 6–13.

8. Michel Foucault, *The History of Sexuality. Volume I: An Introduction.* p. 45. This topic of the "*perpetual spirals of power and pleasure*" is at the center of Derrida's lecture "Au-delà du principe de pouvoir," *Rue Descartes* 82 ([1985] 2014): 4–13.

9. This context is very well captured in Mario Colucci, "Hystériques, internés, infâmes: Michel Foucault et la résistance au pouvoir," *Sud-Nord* 20 (2005): 123–145.

10. Robert Castel, *La Gestion des risques. De l'antipsychiatrie à l'après-psychanalyse* (Paris: Éditions de Minuit, coll. "Le sens commun," 1981), Chapter 4.

11. Michel Foucault, *The History of Sexuality. Volume I: An Introduction*, p. 129.

12. Michel Foucault, *Psychiatric Power*, 9.

13. Michel Foucault, "La vérité et les formes juridiques," in *Dits et écrits*, vol. II (Paris:Gallimard, coll. "Bibliothèque des sciences humaines," 1994), 639. I translate: the American edition of *Dits et Écrits* does not include the exchanges that followed the Rio lectures. This resumption, of the order of a (simple) displacement, thus signs the limit of the emancipatory gesture of psychoanalysis: "Psychoanalysis can appear—and has often appeared—as an escape, an exit from psychiatric hell and its deleterious effects. The psychoanalyst presents himself without walls, without straitjackets. But for Foucault, this depsychiatrization produced by psychoanalysis, effective and spectacular, nevertheless misses the essence of the alienating system. Indeed, psychoanalysis maintains the relationship with the doctor as intact and decisive. This depsychiatrization is not the same as a demedicalization. The caretaker may be without a hospital, his power of domination is rather concentrated in the silence and the gaze of the analyst suspended above the analyzer" (Gros 2018, p. 6; my translation).

14. Robert Castel, *Le psychanalysme. L'ordre psychanalytique et le pouvoir* (Paris: Maspéro, coll. "Textes à l'appui/Série: Psychiatrie," 1973), back cover (I translate).

15. Robert Castel, *Le psychanalysme*, Chapter 1.

16. Robert Castel, *Le psychanalysme*, Chapter 2.

17. Robert Castel, *Le psychanalysme*, 54 (I translate). On this supposed "apolitism" of psychoanalysis, see Laufer 2010, p. 95–110. The question may arise as to whether this neutrality is passive (and, as Castel seems to indicate, the effect of an ideological instrumentalization) or whether it is the result of active abstention, remaining at the initiative of the analyst—which leads us to consider other analytical practices than those which concentrate Castel's criticisms.

18. Robert Castel, *Le psychanalysme*, 69 (I translate).

19. It is undoubtedly possible to measure in this way a shift in Foucault's position, from his *Lectures on the Will to Know* to *Psychiatric Power*. In the first course at the Collège de France, Foucault still analyzes the history of Oedipus as the myth of a power based "on a truth that is accessible only on guarantee of purity," whereas in reality it was constituted "from a class struggle, a shift of power, an interplay of alliance and transaction." Michel Foucault, *Lectures on the Will to Know: Lectures at the Collège de France 1970-1971*, trans. Graham Burchell (New York: Palgrave MacMillan, 2013, 193). The universality of the Oedipus complex promoted by Freud is thus related to a structure of misunderstanding whose foundation is political and whose stake concerns a certain relationship between the subject and the truth.

20. See Philippe Sabot, "Discipliner et guérir. La 'réalité' comme enjeu du pouvoir psychiatrique chez Michel Foucault," in *La pensée politique de Foucault*, ed. Orazio Irrera et Sandro Vaccaro (Paris: Kimé, 2017), 157–170.

21. Michel Foucault, *Psychiatric Power*, 79–87.

22. Michel Foucault, *Psychiatric Power*, 79.

23. Michel Foucault, *Psychiatric Power*, 81.

24. See on this subject Rémi Lenoir, "Famille et sexualité chez Michel Foucault," *Sociétés & Représentations* 22 (2006):189–214.

25. Michel Foucault, *Psychiatric Power*, 86.

26. Michel Foucault, *Psychiatric Power*, 87.

27. This circularity between family norms and social norms is analyzed by Jacques Donzelot, who sees it as one of the keys to the development of the Freudian psychoanalytic approach. Jacques Donzelot, *La Police des familles*, suivi de *L'ascension du social* par Gilles Deleuze (Paris: Les Éditions de Minuit, coll. "Critique," 1977).

28. Michel Foucault, *Psychiatric Power*, 88.

29. Michel Foucault, *Abnormal*, 273. To contextualize Foucault's intervention on this point, it should be remembered that Foucault deals here above all with psychoanalysis as practiced by Freudian psychoanalysts at the time he wrote. Indeed, Lacan proposes, for his part, a critique of the question of the Oedipus well before 1973.

30. Robert Castel, *Le psychanalysme*, 277 (I translate).

31. Michel Foucault, "La vérité et les formes juridiques," 623 (I translate).

32. See on this point Guillaume Sibertin-Blanc, *Deleuze et l'Anti-Œdipe. La production du désir* (Paris: PUF, coll. "Philosophies," 2010), 55sq.

33. Michel Foucault, "La vérité et les formes juridiques," 624 (I translate).

34. Robert Castel, *Le psychanalysme*, 273 (I translate).

35. See in particular on this subject Michel Foucault, *The History of Sexuality. Volume I: An Introduction*, end of Chapter 4.

36. Robert Castel, *Le psychanalysme*, 275 (I translate).

37. On Freudo-Marxism and its critique by Foucault, see Charles Boyer, "Du « freudo-marxisme » au « freudo-libéralisme » ?," *Le Philosophoire*, 38, no. 2 (2012): 229–249.

38. *Ibidem.*

39. Robert Castel, *La Gestion des risques*, 151 (I translate).

40. Michel Foucault, *Confessions of the Flesh*, 266–276, on the "libidinization of the sexual act."

41. Michel Foucault, *On the Government of the Living. Lectures at the Collège de France 1979-1980*, trans. Graham Burchell (New York: Palgrave MacMillan, 2014), 308. On this "circle of hermeneutics of self and obedience to another," see Frédéric Gros, "Freud, l'évité de Foucault au Collège de France," 13.

REFERENCES

Basso Elisabetta, "Foucault entre psychanalyse et psychiatrie. 'Reprendre la folie au niveau de son langage,'" *Archives de Philosophie,* no. 79 (2016): 27–54.

Basso Elisabetta and Bert Jean-François (dir.), *Foucault à Münsterlingen. À l'origine de l'Histoire de la folie*. Paris : EHESS, 2015.

Boyer Charles, "Du « freudo-marxisme » au « freudo-libéralisme » ?," *Le Philosophoire*, 38, no. 2 (2012): 229–249.

Castel Robert, *Le psychanalysme. L'ordre psychanalytique et le pouvoir*. Paris: Maspéro, coll. « Textes à l'appui/Série : Psychiatrie », 1973.

Castel Robert, *L'Ordre psychiatrique. L'âge d'or de l'aliénisme*. Paris: Éditions de Minuit, coll. « Le sens commun », 1976.

Castel Robert, *La Gestion des risques. De l'antipsychiatrie à l'après-psychanalyse*. Paris : Éditions de Minuit, coll. « Le sens commun », 1981.

Colucci Mario, "Hystériques, internés, infâmes : Michel Foucault et la résistance au pouvoir," *Sud-Nord* 20 (2005): 123–145.

Dartigues Laurent, "La question de psychanalyse chez Michel Foucault," *Astérion*, no. 21 (2019). http://journals.openedition.org.ressources-electroniques.univ lille.fr /asterion/4278.

Deleuze Gilles et Guattari Félix, *Anti-Oedipus. Capitalism et Schizophrenia*, trans. Robert Hurley, Mark Seem, and Helen R. Lane. Minneapolis: University of Minnesota Press, 1983.

Derrida Jacques, "Au-delà du principe de pouvoir," *Rue Descartes* 82 ([1985] 2014): 4–13.

Donzelot Jacques, *La Police des familles*, suivi de *L'ascension du social* par Gilles Deleuze. Paris: Les Éditions de Minuit, coll. « Critique », 1977.

Foucault Michel, *Maladie mentale et personnalité*. Paris: PUF, coll. « Initiation philosophique », 1954.

Foucault Michel, *The History of Sexuality. Volume I: An Introduction. The Will to Knowledge*, trans. Robert Hurley. New York: Pantheon Books, 1978.

Foucault Michel, *Madness and Civilization: A History of Insanity in the Age of Reason*, trans. Richard Howard. London: Routledge, [1961] (1972) 1988.

Foucault Michel, "La vérité et les formes juridiques," in *Dits et écrits*, vol. II, 538–646. Paris: Gallimard, coll. « Bibliothèque des sciences humaines », 1994.

Foucault Michel, *Abnormal. Lectures at the Collège de France 1974-1975*, trans. Graham Burchell. London: Verso, 2003.

Foucault Michel, *Psychiatric Power. Lectures at the Collège de France 1973-1974,* trans. Graham Burchell. New York: Palgrave MacMillan, 2006.

Foucault Michel, *Lectures on The Will to Know. Lectures at the Collège de France 1970-1971*, trans. Graham Burchell. New York: Palgrave MacMillan, 2013.

Foucault Michel, *On the Government of the Living. Lectures at the Collège de France 1979-1980*, trans. Graham Burchell. New York: Palgrave MacMillan, 2014.

Foucault Michel, *La Sexualité. Cours donné à l'université de Clermont-Ferrand. 1964* – suivi de *Le Discours de la sexualité. Cours donné à l'université de Vincennes. 1969*. Paris: Le Seuil-Gallimard, coll. « Hautes études ,» Série « Cours et travaux de Michel Foucault avant le Collège de France », 2018.

Foucault Michel, *The History of Sexuality 4. Confessions of the Flesh*, trans. Robert Hurley. New York: Pantheon Books, 2021.

Foucault Michel and Basso Elisabetta, "Un manuscrit de Michel Foucault sur la psychanalyse," *Astérion*, no. 21 (2019). http://journals.openedition.org.ressources-electroniques.univ-lille.fr/asterion/4410.

Gros Frédéric, "Freud, l'évité de Foucault au Collège de France," in *Freud au Collège de France 1885-2016,* ed. Antoine Compagnon et Cécile Surprenant. Paris : Collège de France, 2018) : http://books.openedition.org/cdf/5660 [consulté le 8 juin 2019].

Lagrange Jacques, "Versions de la psychanalyse dans le texte de Foucault," *Incidence,* no. 4–5 « Foucault et la psychanalyse » (2008–2009): 11–54.

Laufer Laurie, "Psychanalyse hors case : un exercice politique," *Cliniques méditerranéennes* 81 (2010): 95–110.

Laufer Laurie and Squvever Amos (ed.), *Foucault et la psychanalyse. Quelques questions analytiques à Michel Foucault.* Paris : Hermann, 2015.

Lenoir Rémi, "Famille et sexualité chez Michel Foucault," *Sociétés and Représentations* 22 (2006): 189–214.

Sabot Philippe, "Discipliner et guérir. La 'réalité' comme enjeu du pouvoir psychiatrique chez Michel Foucault," in *La pensée politique de Foucault*, ed. Orazio Irrera et Sandro Vaccaro, 157–170. Paris : Kimé, 2017.

Sibertin-Blanc Guillaume, *Deleuze et l'Anti-Œdipe. La production du désir.* Paris : PUF, coll. « Philosophies », 2010.

Chapter 5

The Christian Invention of the Sexual

In Pursuit of Psychoanalysis

Frédéric Gros (translated from French by Edward McGushin)

Numerous publications have taken on the problem of Foucault's relation to psychoanalysis. The number of articles, dissertations,[1] collections, and special issues has continued to grow for several decades. It seems like we will never *be done* with this subject. And yet explicit declarations, direct statements, and well-articulated theses from Foucault are rare. The latter is largely content with suggestive formulations and enigmatic claims. For example, to give only three of the most striking and remarkably mutually contradictory cases:

> Freud [. . .] freed the patient from that asylum existence to which his "liberators" had condemned him, but he failed to spare him the essential components of that existence. He concentrated its power, stretched them to the limit, and placed them in the hands of the doctor. He created the psychoanalytic situation, where, in the short circuit of a stroke of genius, alienation became disalienating because, in the doctor, it became subject. The doctor, as an alienating figure, remains the key to psychoanalysis.[2]

> It is to the political credit of psychoanalysis—or at least, of what was most coherent in it—that it regarded with suspicion (and this from its inception, that is, from the moment it broke away from the neuropsychiatry of degenerescence) the irrevocably proliferating aspects which might be contained in these power mechanisms aimed at controlling and administering the everyday life of sexuality.[3]

> You don't have to be Oedipus, unless, of course, an amusing mind tells you: but yes, yes you do! If you are obliged to tell the truth it is because, without

knowing it, despite everything, there's a bit of Oedipus in you too. But you see that the person who tells you this in the end does no more than turn the glove inside out, the glove of the Church.[4]

No doubt at this point what has been written about Foucault's relation to psychoanalysis greatly surpasses what Foucault was able to say or write about it—even if the archive at the Bibliothèque nationale might still have some surprises in store for us.[5]

At the same time, this simple fact invites (*reçoit*) an explanation. The statements, as our examples above show, are most often paradoxical, ambiguous, and vague. In *History of Madness*, Foucault says of Freud, on the one hand, that he resuscitates an experience of madness which grasps it as language ("Il faut être juste avec Freud . . .") and, on the other hand, that in the dispositif of listening that he proposes, Freud concentrates all the powers of silent alienation of the doctor: same critical contradiction in *History of Sexuality Volume 1*, where psychoanalysis is, at one and the same time, praised for breaking from a psychiatry of degeneration which fosters fascism and criticized for having reestablished very old schemas of domination.

This back and forth prevents us from establishing a univocal position of Foucault. Having already tried, in two previous articles, to describe the winding path of the *énoncés*, I am not going to make yet another attempt to synthesize them. Rather in the following I will seize upon the last volume of *History of Sexuality: Confesssions of the Flesh*,[6] in order to show the outline of a secret archaeology of psychoanalysis traced in it, as if Foucault's interest in Christian practices of subjectivation (what he also calls "acts of truth"[7]) was largely motivated by this genealogical aim.

Confessions of the Flesh, a work devoted to the first centuries of Christianity, essentially developed through the works of the Church Fathers—from Tertullian to Cassian passing by way of Augustine—is composed of three chapters. The first focuses on the procedures of baptism, penance, and monastic direction. The second studies, in its chronological development, the increasing valorization of virginity in Christian ethics. Finally, the last chapter examines the constitution of a doctrine of marriage, from John Chrysostom to Augustine. Characterized in this way, these three chapters seem unlikely to shed light on the founding concepts of psychoanalysis. I would like to show that this is far from the case and that, however erudite, these patristic studies nevertheless bring into focus the horizons within which the psychoanalytic edify will inscribe itself.

The first section of *Confessions of the Flesh* examines the establishment of rituals and procedures of baptism, penitence, and the direction of conscience in the Christianity of the early Church Fathers (second to fifth centuries). This study, astonishingly detailed for a book devoted to sexuality, is preceded by an introductory look at Clement of Alexandria. It is mainly a matter for Foucault here to illuminate briefly a Christian doctrine of sexuality still suffused by Hellenism. The work of Clement of Alexandria, Christian Father born in Athens in the middle of the second century CE, stands at a crossroads. On the one hand, it breaks with the teaching of the ancients by constituting, for example, the sexuality of the married couple as an autonomous, separate, and specific domain. Up until this point, when this subject was examined, it was taken as a simple intersection of a matrimonial art of living with a medical hygiene of the sexual act—or even of a philosophy of the pleasures. What one could learn from Hippocrates could intersect (depart with, cut across) with the recommendations one might get from Xenophon, but in neither case would conjugal sexuality form a separate chapter the way it does for Clement. At the same time, the latter is able to continue to reflect on the sexual act as participating in the mystery of Creation, the power of the Logos. It has not yet passed through the filter of the Augustinian concept of libido.

It's only after this scansion, destined especially to make manifest a *difference*, at the very heart of the destiny of Christianity, that Foucault develops three patient studies of baptism, penitence, and the direction of conscience.[8] Baptism and penitence taken together form a first pair to be studied. Besides, theologically—and this is the knot that Foucault is trying to untie—the two terms tied together in the early Church: elements of penitence support the preparation for baptism and establishing a ritual of penance poses the problem of the possibility of a second baptism. It is impossible to enter into these debates in detail here and I will retain only one point: the importance given to Tertullian, *De Baptismo*.

Up until Tertullian, baptism was seen as an ontological leap: abrupt illumination, complete subjective transformation, and sudden access to an other being, an other world, and other knowledges. The power of the ritual, the interiorization of the creed, was taken as transformative. Tertullian, to the contrary, emphasized the preparation, the labor on the self, the continual asceticism enabling and prolonging the effects of baptism, a fear propped up against the facile illusions of the total remission of sin obtained upon baptism—at this time, and for a long time to come, baptism was essentially for adults.

All these themes are the occasion for Foucault to open up and problematize a dimension of subjectivity that he will amplify in his Greek and Latin explorations—but which he would have discovered in Christianity[9]—and which will give rise to the famous neologism, much repeated after, "subjectivation." The subject is no longer grasped as transcendental nucleus nor as a separate spiritual essence, a principle of permanence, or even as an existential project. It is the volume sustained by an exigence of transformation, deployed by techniques, imposing all at once work, text (*épreuve*), and examination (*examen*).

Certainly, one might conclude, if one thinks especially of Lacan, that this subjectivity has little in common with that which the latter claims as "subject of science" (*sujet de la science*), which be the subject of psychoanalysis. One could then object that it is a complete misunderstanding and that the "self," object of techniques of existence, the elaboration of which Foucault seeks in Hellinistic and Roman (especially Stoic) wisdom, remains far afield of the Cartesian-Lacanian subject, which is in question, for example, in Lacan's Seminar XI devoted to the four fundamental concepts of psychoanalysis. But the texts of Lacan are sufficiently diverse and open that we should remember at least this lesson: without a doubt psychoanalysis presumes a subject for whom the truth comes with a certain price; even more precisely, a truth which demands, in order to gain access to it, a certain number of subjective transformations; finally, a truth which is not so much the confirmation of the subject's cognitive capacities as that which shakes (*fait trembler*) its very being. And the subject who addresses the analyst harbors in itself, in its demand, the need (*l'exigence*) for its own transformation.

In some deliberately suggestive remarks published in *Corriere della sera*,[10] on the occasion of Lacan's death, Foucault recalls two things: first, Lacan is the one who would have re-asked the question of the subject ("he sought in [psychoanalysis] not a process of behavioral normalization, but a theory of the subject"), in order to escape from the simple alternative of either "free" subject of philosophy or the "conditioned" subject of the human sciences; second, the obscurity of his parole is an occasion given to the subject of desire to labor on itself and not fall prey to the illusion of an ineffective and counterproductive "I understand!" (Lacan wanted "the labor necessary to arrive at real comprehension to be a labor of self-realization").

In this way, Foucault situates the work of Lacan neatly within the perspective opened up by Tertullian with respect to baptism: the subject is not a transparent agency of "awareness," but the volume where an active and painstaking relation of the self unfolds ("elaborandum est"). Let's not forget that this homage was written precisely at the moment when Foucault was drafting *Confessions of the Flesh*. Some months later, at the Collège de France, he reiterated this point: "Lacan was, it seems to me, the only one since Freud to recenter the question of psychoanalysis around the question of the relation between the subject and truth."[11] He asserts at the same time that for psychoanalysis to rediscover itself, it will have to reposition itself "along the historical axis of the existence of spirituality and its requirements."[12]

Still in this first chapter of *Confessions of the Flesh*, Foucault describes first foundations of what Gregory of Nanzianze calls "the art of arts" (*teckné teknôn*)[13]: the direction of souls. The latter develops and gains strength in a precise context: the founding of the first monasteries and the emergence of the first cenobitic communities in the West. To perfect these organizations, a whole project of regulating life in common was necessary. The work of John Cassian (360–435) was determinative because it was the first to provide a detailed collection of monastic ordonnances to prescribe, and Foucault is particularly attentive to the way these prescriptions structure relations between older and younger monks. Two passages in particular are frequently cited, exploited, and examined.

The first (*Institutions*, IV, 9) requirement of the monk obligates him to keep nothing that could occur to him—such as thoughts and agitations—hidden from his director, to immediately verbalize them for himself before repeating them orally. This principle (which I call "discursive redoubling of representations") calls for the projection of everything that occurs to me into a verbal framework. I constitute myself as a subject to the extent that I make of my "I" the referent of a discourse addressable to an Other.

The second passage (*Conferences*, I, 20) requires of each one that put "the quality of his thoughts" to the test (*épreuve*) by probing their origins rather than by verifying their objectivity or pertinence. The truth of a representation is no longer evaluated according to its adequation to an external reality or the validity of its internal logic but according to its psychic origin: From whence did it come to me? From myself, or was it secretly inspired in me *by an Other*? For example, if a monk decides to go on a fast in order to purify himself, he must search for the authenticity of this desire within him and verify it with his elder. In effect, even if a fast is in itself a good thing, it could be that the devil inspired the asceticism in me precisely in order to weaken and then assail me. The effort to reach the truth must, therefore, no longer sustain itself as a demand for coherence or external verification but as a permanent suspicion: To what extent am I the one who thinks or wants, or instead is it the devil who is tempting me? It is a matter of turning the interior scene inside out: examine the underbelly (*l'envers*) of one's representations.

These two principles (exhaustive redoubling and radical suspicion) constitute powerful matrices of subjectivity which psychoanalysis will know how to take hold of. Let's recall the image chosen by Freud to illustrate his fundamental rule: that one imagines oneself a passenger on a train, seated by the window, who describes to a traveling companion seated behind, what one sees as the countryside rolls by. It is very much a discursive discipline that he imposes. Isn't it the analyst who perpetually dangles before the analysand the possibility that everything the analysand believes she thinks, desires, or imagines could in fact be thought, desired, or imagined by *an Other*?

By fastening these two principles interiorly, we see at last that Christian subjectivation operates under the condition of a double alterity: verify *by way of an Other*, by means of a continuous verbalization of your representations, that that which you think is not thought *by an Other*! It is this folding together of these two alterities that psychoanalysis reactivates in its method of listening.

But Foucault adds one more thing that will come to act as a source of concern for psychoanalysis. Cassian says very clearly that if the monk must redouble what occurs to him by through its implicit inscription in a verbal framework addressable to an Other, *it is in order to become as obedient as possible*. One will object that what we have here is a specific historical synthesis and that Freud detaches the techniques from their primary aim in order to use them according to medical imperatives. Nevertheless, one notices that Freud does not establish these two elements (examination of self and obedience) according to simple order of juxtaposition but rather systematically intertwines them very tightly. In so doing he raises some questions: Up to what point does the hermeneutics of the self represent a form of obedience? To what point does searching for the truth of one's desire constitute a strategic move in a general tactic of submission to the other? To what point does the question "Who am I, truly?" take down the path of alienation? This "art of arts" (the direction of souls which organizes and justifies systems of listening), which for Foucault is a distinctive characteristic of Christianity, leads him to forge his concept of "governmentality." The Christian pastorate enables him to comprehend the level of intervention that was interesting to him in what he had previously called "power," a concept that was certainly far too general and vague. What Foucault calls "governmentality" is a rational technique for "conducting the conduct" of individuals, of tracing, in the heart of subjects, the arc of a consent. Pastoral governmentality, as a bond of dependence, is a manner of governing the other by getting the other to produce the truth of himself verbally.

This principle of concern must not however conceal a limit to this side of the Foucauldian critique of psychoanalysis: the deployment of listening, insofar as it is rooted in the Christian technique, remains a machine of power. It is as such—and this can be verified in his manuscript for *Le chair and le corps*—that Foucault maintained a unilaterality in the relationship of listening (penetrating, dominating, and culpabalizing) and remained absolutely impermeable to a logic of transfer, which transforms this relation into a reciprocal exposition of vulnerabilities. Decidedly, for Foucault, the *dispositif* of listening is an instrument of power.

The second long chapter of *Confessions of the Flesh*[14] is composed of an examination of several treatises on virginity, from the second to the fifth century, from Cyprian to Basile [of Ancyra], and from Methodius to Gregory of Nyssa. This study, again extremely in depth, might appear surprising. After all, one might be astonished that Foucault endeavors to grasp a Christian sexual ethic by studying the valorization of a choice of existence based on the exclusion, the rejection of all carnal relations. We should state here the main themes of the second chapter, the central support beam of *Confessions*, in order to be able to tease out what is at stake in it. Foucault carefully describes a number of developments: how one goes from treatises describing circles of women to the project of organizing communities of men; how one goes from virginity as a simple status, defined negatively (*absence* of carnal relations) to virginity as a plenitude of being, an entire art of life, a state of spiritual and physical wholeness. Trace of a lost paradisial innocence, promise of a future heavenly purity, vibrant permanence of baptismal grace received: virginity plays its part in a general economy of salvation.

But mostly virginity is less and less described as a state of serenity, a happy stability, than as a permanent struggle, a ceaseless battle which provokes its enemies—in a double sense: puts them on guard and brings them to life. It's this latter development that interests Foucault.[15] This is what enables one to understand what could be called the Christian invention of the "sexual" as that which exceeds the genital. Paradoxically—but this paradox is without a doubt the genius of Christianity—the point of emergence of this invention is in the art of virgin life. By sexual, one intends here a desire which functions as a concrete metaphor for an orgasmic referent. In other words, it concerns a suspicion that the underlying principle of the "innocent" pleasures (reading, nourishment, etc.) would be reproductive jouissance (*la jouissance génésique*). However, if chastity is a combat, that is to say, less an accomplished fullness than a dynamic of self-conquest, then it requires that the one who seeks it track down the offshoots, disguises, and substitutes of a sexuality blocked from its classic anatomical aim. Without this hunt, Christian virginity would be almost indistinguishable from the Roman Vestal Virgin. Overcoming sexual acts would have no sanctifying value unless it involved an eradication far more complex than a merely physical one: that of diverted gratifications.

Accordingly, beginning with the texts of Basil of Ancyra or John Cassian, Foucault shows the deployment of an arsenal of punctilious self-interrogations, sustained controls, and systematic suspicions. This arsenal forms a powerful spiritual and institutional equipment, like a tracking device: unearthing, hunting down everything, among the many temptations, which might take shape as an expedient form of genital jouissance. At the same time, and according to the logic exposed in *History of Sexuality Volume 1*, the tracking itself arouses: let's not forget that the central thesis of the first volume of *History of Sexuality Volume 1* bears on the productivity of power that one fails to understand if one only considers the mechanisms of prohibition, repression, and the law of castration. Sexuality (*le sexuel*) multiplies, takes form, volume, and consistency, by way of the very operations that presume to eradicate and censor it. The metaphorization of genital pleasure in the infinite flowering of the "sexual" is not first of all a psychic mechanism, described by Freud, of sublimation-displacement of an unspeakable origin. The overflowing of the genital by the sexual, which the first statements of the *Three Essays* of Freud certainly represent, is a cultural matrix established by the Christian arts of virginity. From this alone (*rien qu'en cela*) it is impossible to characterize Christianity as a religion founded on the contempt, disgust, rejection, and condemnation of the sexual, because, on the contrary, Christianity has invented it.

The third part of *Confessions* bears entirely on the Christian doctrine of marriage such as the Christian Fathers constituted it—principally John Chrysostom and St. Augustine. The construction is meticulous and the scholarly work colossal. I will take up especially the final developments concerning Augustine, because it's here, in a form pure and fundamental, that the theme less of a libidinal subjectivation than of libido as the principle of subjectivation *as such* takes shape.

In order to understand this thesis in all its fullness, it is necessary to recapture some point of the theological debates that might seem strange, or even a little zany, to us. Foucault takes into consideration the doctrinal evolution of Augustine over the course of several decades,[16] but here we will focus mainly on the theses that take shape in book XIV of *The City of God*. The Christian exultation of virginity, taken to the extreme, could represent a danger. How could humanity prosper and multiply as commanded in Genesis (1:28)? One must not reduce marriage to nothing more than a pitiful consolation destined to the vast majority of Christians incapable of perfect chastity. Augustine endeavors to define for marriage a regime for its own proper perfections, comparable to the state of virginity, which is going to require a reevaluation of the sexual act. It is in this context that he constructs a theoretical framework around libido, which Foucault says will inspire the official sexual doctrine of the Church in the West for centuries. First of all, it involves postulating the existence of sexual relations between Eve and Adam in paradise while discovering in this some irreducible points (*points d'irreductibilité*). We can see very well the alternative before which Augustine finds himself: by postulating nothing but pure, ethereal relations without carnal intercourse between the first man and the first woman, one makes sexuality a result of original sin, one sees it only in light of sin, and one offers the state of virginity as the only possible path to salvation; by admitting sexual relations in paradise, without saying anything more about it, one grants it an intrinsic innocence that is hard to reconcile with conjugal restrictions.

Augustine is going to trace an original and powerful third way that will, to say it one more time, inform the sexual doctrine of Western Christianity. He begins by admitting the existence of sexual relations in paradise but in order to immediately argue that the mechanism is irreducible to that which humanity subject to the law of sin knows. The sex organs were under the complete control of their bearers so that Adam and Eve could use them a little like the way they used their hands or limbs: by submitting them completely to their will. The sexual act, in its accomplishment, did not introduce any involuntary passivity and remained under the absolute control of each partner. One must believe that the pleasure was mild, measured, and in no way orgasmic.

What is original sin in the teaching of Augustine? First of all, an act of disobedience against God, the expression of a revolt, and an act of the excessive pride of a creature who believes he can break away from his ontological dependence. We know the two principal penalties levied against humanity for this foolish transgression: suffering and death. But it is the third which interests Foucault: the introduction of involuntary sequences into the sexual process. Irrepressible excitation, unruly intercourse, sexuality includes elements largely beyond voluntary control, escaping all authority. These centers of the involuntary—the libidinal element of sexuality—are like the inverse echo of the willful pride of Adam. We disobeyed God; our sexuality bears the trace of it. It is that within us that disobeys: stirring up uncontrollable excitations, crowning the act of coitus, which defies all mastery. Sexuality is that within us which disobeys, as we disobeyed our Lord at the moment of sin: repetition-punishment of the original fall.

Does that simply mean that thereafter brief irruptions of uncontrollable violence traverse and wound our sexuality, which we must accept as the stigma of our finitude? But Augustine is going to develop, to the contrary, a detailed inventory of the relationship of the self to its libido (uncontrollable element of our sexuality), which complicates this model of resignation by introducing juridical qualifications and by the permanent casuistic edification of the subjective relationship to the sexual involuntary. It is not possible to recreate the complex and precise detail of the Foucauldian demonstration. We present only the result of it here, by never forgetting that it is always at the same time a matter of preserving the possibility of reasonable and legitimate sexual relations in the marriage and of giving oneself the criteria in order to be able to distinguish the "good" and the "bad." The responsibility of the sexual partner is going to take hold in the manner by which, at the moment of the sexual act, he situates himself with respect to the uncontrollable element: by accepting it, but not surreptitiously giving oneself over to it. I accept the automatic excitement that the naked body of my partner produces in my sexual organs; I accept the orgasm that the act leads to, while never giving in to them through a clandestine complaisance, without ever taking it as an opportunity to intensify the objective pleasure mechanically produced by the friction of two fleshy bodies with a guilty jouissance.

Clearly the principle of regulation is no longer based in the relational structure of the act. In order to judge the legitimacy of the act, one can no longer be content to ask "With whom? When? In what position?" It would be necessary to interrogate the relationship each one takes to his own desire. Here one could repeat Lacan's formula ("there is no sexual relation"), since the Augustinian libido makes the sexual relation disappear in favor of the solitary relation to one's desire. The subjectivation of desire signifies that it is the relationship of self to self, before, during, and after the act, which determines the quality of one's desire, but never the "sexual relation" itself, gravitating around the existence of a partner and the taking into account of their pleasure.

Referring to the "subjectivation of desire" it is not enough merely to say, the subject, in addition to its other activities, must concern itself with and interrogate its relationship to its own desire. One must go further: the interrogative matrix delimits and invents a level of being of desire, and it is the desire brought to life here which produces the subject-form (*la forme-sujet*). More precisely, the subject-form is established by a juridical claim on desire, since in effect it makes each one responsible for the degree of their acceptance of it. Desire is no longer, as it was in the ancient notion of the aphrodisia, a scansion in a dynamic interaction of pleasure and act naturally prone to get carried away. Augustine makes us accountable to ourselves and before God for our inner relation with our libido—and more concretely before an Other (the director of conscience). This *dispositif* creates the subject. The "subject" is a cultural form brought into being by a sexual desire no longer tied to an act by the dynamic of a natural force that can be mastered through the wisdom of proper use. Christianity invents the subject of desire, but not by adding to the familiar subjective performance yet another scene (every subject will be *also* a subject of desire), but by impressing on desire, by the *dispositif* of its juridical grip and its provocation, the shape of the subject-form. Each one, because he or she must give and account to an Other, in a determinate game of truth (speaking and listening), of the form of his consent to his own desire, becomes *subject of desire*. And every subject takes its one being from this form of a desire provoked by the law—that is to say, he or she must give an account of it by "telling the truth" of it before an Other. It is this knot of truth, sex, and law that Christianity weaves, and it is not completely impossible to think that on the platform, once secularized, psychoanalysis will take its stand.

From the feverish metaphor of Freud (verbalize for an Other all that comes to mind) to the biting statement of Lacan ("there is no sexual relation"), passing by way of the principle that the sexual exceeds the genital, Foucault, in meticulously studying in the work of the Christian Fathers the value of the rites of baptism, penitence, and the organization of the direction of souls; in rereading the treatises on virginity; and in explicating the doctrine of marriage, weaves the genealogical threads that require psychoanalysis to face its own history, in order to see itself as the heir of this powerful cultural matrices which forged, in the West, the figure of the subject of desire.

NOTES

1. The site that tracks dissertation defenses in France (these.fr) reports more than a dozen. There are innumerable articles. Regarding volumes of collected essays, I will just cite the two most recent: Laufer Laurie et Amos Squverer (ed.), *Foucault et la psychanalyse* (Paris: Hermann, 2015); Basso Elisabetta et Laurent Dartiques (ed.), "Foucault à l'épreuve de la psychiatrie et de la psychanalyse." *Astérion*, no. 21 (2019). doi: 10.4000/asterion.4074.
2. Michel Foucault, *History of Madness*, trans. Jonathan Murphy and Jean Khalfa (London and New York: Routledge, 2006), 510–511.
3. Michel Foucault, *History of Sexuality vol. 1: An Introduction*, trans. Robert Hurley (New York: Vintage Books, 1990), 150.
4. Michel Foucault, *On the Government of the Living, Lectures at the Collège de France 1979-1980*, trans. Graham Burchell (New York: Picador), 312.
5. For a general overview see Michel Foucault, *Sexuality. The 1964 Clermont-Ferrand and 1969 Vincennes Lectures*, trans. Graham Burchell (New York: Columbia University Press), 2021.
6. Michel Foucault, *History of Sexuality vol. 4, Confessions of the Flesh* (New York: Pantheon, 2021).
7. Foucault, *On the Government of the Living*, 81.
8. Section 2, section 3, and the first part of section 4 of *Confessions of the Flesh*, 37–110.
9. On this point, cf, Arianna Sforzini, "L'autre modernité du sujet, Foucault et la confession de la chair: les pratiques de subjectivation à l'âge des Réformes," *Revue de l'histoire des religions*, n. 235 (2018): 485–505; Arianna Sforzini, "Foucault et les Pères (1977-1984). Brève généalogie des *Aveux de la chair*," *Foucault, le Pères, le sexe, Paris*, ed. Philippe Büttgen, Philippe Chevallier, Agustín Colombo and Arianna Sforzini (Paris: Éditions de la Sorbonne, coll. "La philosophie à l'œuvre," 2021).
10. Michel Foucault, "Lacan, 'libérateur' de la psychanalyse," in Michel Foucault *Dits et écrits* vol. 1 (Paris: Gallimard, 2001), 1023–1024.
11. Michel Foucault, *L'herméneutique du sujet. Cours au Collège de France 1981-1982* (Paris: Seuil/Gallimard, 2001), 31.
12. Cf. see Jean Allouch, *La psychoanalyse est-elle un exercise spirituel?* Paris: Epel, 2007.
13. *Oratio*, II. 16.
14. Foucault, *Confessions of the Flesh*, "Being Virgin," 111–189.
15. Foucault, *Confessions of the Flesh*, "Virginity and Self-Knowledge," 158–189.
16. Foucault, *Confessions of the Flesh*, "The Good and the Goods of Marriage," "The Libidinization of Sex," 221–285.

REFERENCES

Allouch, Jean. *La psychoanalyse est-elle un exercise spirituel?* Paris: Epel, 2007.

Basso Elisabetta et Laurent Dartiques (ed.). " Foucault à l'épreuve de la psychiatrie et de la psychanalyse." *Astérion*, no. 21 (2019). doi: 10.4000/asterion.4074

Foucault, Michel. *History of Madness*. Translated by Jonathan Murphy and Jean Khalfa. London and New York: Routledge, 2006.

Foucault, Michel. *History of Sexuality vol. 1: An Introduction*. Translated by Robert Hurley. New York: Vintage Books, 1990.

Foucault, Michel. *History of Sexuality vol. 4, Confessions of the Flesh*. New York: Pantheon, 2021.

Foucault, Michel. "Lacan, 'libérateur' de la psychanalyse," in Foucault, Michel *Dits et écrits* vol. 2, 1023–1024. Paris: Gallimard, 2001.

Foucault, Michel. *L'herméneutique du sujet. Cours au Collège de France 1981-1982*, edited by Frédéric Gros. New York: Palgrave McMillan, 2001.

Foucault, Michel. *On the Government of the Living, Lectures at the Collège de France 1979-1980*. Translated by Graham Burchell. New York: Picador, 2016.

Foucault, Michel. *Sexuality. The 1964 Clermont-Ferrand and 1969 Vincennes Lectures*. Translated by Graham Burchell. New York: Columbia University Press, 2021.

Laufer Laurie et Amos Squverer (ed.). *Foucault et la psychanalyse*. Paris: Hermann. 2015.

Sforzini, Arianna. "Foucault et les Pères (1977-1984). Brève généalogie des *Aveux de la chair*." in *Foucault, le Pères, le sexe*, ed. Philippe Büttgen, Philippe Chevallier, Agustín Colombo, and A. Sforzini. Paris: Éditions de la Sorbonne, coll. "La philosophie à l'oeuvre,", 2021.

Sforzini, Arianna. "L'autre modernité du sujet, Foucault et la confession de la chair: les pratiques de subjectivation à l'âge des Réformes." *Revue de l'histoire des religions*, no. 235 (2018): 485–505.

Chapter 6

Phantasms and Their Vicissitudes

Laura Hengehold

When, in *Civilization and Its Discontents*, Freud referred to the palimpsest of Roman ruins as a possible analogy for the layers of displaced and condensed meaning in the unconscious, he was aiming for a reductio ad absurdum, for he believed no such analogy could be sustained.[1] And yet by presenting us with this image, he allows us to think about what it is we cannot imagine or say in a unified spectacle or text. He also encourages us to reflect on the ways in which visualization and other forms of imagination fill in the gaps between discursive thoughts and about how discourse emerges to elaborate, investigate, or cover up experiences that confuse, rather than complete, the body's ability to anticipate sensation.

Throughout his career, Freud's overall goal remained a scientific study of psychic life and its variations or misfortunes,[2] as well as an effective and authoritative therapeutic practice. This meant that the place of images in human thought and experience in his work was subordinated to biological images of the human body and to the role of vision and imagination in late nineteenth-century science. But Freud's disavowed analogy to Rome could also be read as referring to the different "imaginal" forms that intersect in psychic life. To be sure, dreams are included here, but so are the wishes and drives dreams are said to represent, the "hypnoid state" or daydream of the hysteric, and so-called primal scenes and primitive phantasms that persist in adult life as forgotten stepping stones on the infant's path to distinguishing self from other.[3] Moreover, these would be interwoven with waking perception and even the histories of the arts that teach us how to see and feel, including those left to us by ancient Rome.

Freud's image of Rome seems to refer exclusively to the past, even as it insists on the nonlinear nature of memory. But in truth, this analogy is really about the "landscape" of thinking as an act or process that ceaselessly connects human bodies to other realities—including those in emergence. According to Jean Laplanche, Freud's discovery that neurosis was a matter of a patient's "psychic reality" never dissuaded him from pursuing "actual" historical events that would have shaped that reality—real traumas and disappointments.[4] Freud wanted to *add* the realit(ies) of fantasy to those of the "real world" while acknowledging that the very idea of fantasy was also a way of accounting for the temporal complexity of our involvement with that world. We take this landscape of thought for granted, in part because it is so difficult to articulate and its elements are so elusive to straightforward cognition.

This chapter explores Foucault's and Deleuze's interaction with the corpus or body of psychoanalysis as an intervention in the history of images and imagination. By treating the phantasm and the dream as uninterpretable monuments and/or set of forces, Foucault and Deleuze give psychoanalysis itself "multiple beginnings" rather than tracing it to a single origin. They also suggest several exits from psychoanalysis that preserve the dream's existential importance for patients without imprisoning them in a single "will to know." Foucault's genealogies reveal Freud's dependence on the techniques for seeing and saying in medicine and (religious) confession, while Deleuze's proclamation that "the brain is the screen" resituates Freud's determination to trace the dream to neural processes in a larger ontology of time. Finally, both Foucault and Deleuze decenter the body known by phenomenology with respect to its empirical form, turning the artist's and viewers' corporeality into deliberately creative simulacra.

DREAMING

Ordinary language may not distinguish between the "dream" and the "phantasm," but they represent two different, though interlocking, levels of psychic analysis. According to Freud, the dream was the expression of a wish.[5] Its imagistic and affective components could be translated into verbal forms. However, these did not obey the logical principles of ordinary propositional discourse; indeed, they were the product of associations, visualizations, and recontextualizations that Freud attributed to the interaction of conflicting agencies within the psyche: for example, a repressed agency and a "censor."[6] Freud believed that it was more difficult to repress the imagistic aspect of troubling wishes or memories than their verbal form, but images were also harder to interpret, enabling them to bypass the "censor" when decontextualized and presented in a quasi-hieroglyphic form by dreams.[7] Such constitutive inhibitions meant that a dream's meaning could only be approached by observing which themes appeared repeatedly at varying levels of association.[8]

Though Freud claimed that all characters in the dream represent the dreamer himself or herself and that the real "core" of the dream is a childhood wish, he also refers to a fundamentally obscure spot in every dream, a "navel."[9] The navel is inaccessible because the dream does not simply present a wish or drive but represents, in displaced form, the first signs or indicators of those wishes as the psyche distinguished itself from the body's own impulses or sensations and the resistance of a surrounding world. These signs or indicators are phantasms—coherent but preverbal and/or unacceptable wishes whose early repression or seemingly irrational expression in later behavior gives rise to dreams, among other symptoms.[10] Unlike dreams, which usually happen only when the dreamer is immobilized by sleep, and daydreams, which are at least partly voluntary, phantasies or phantasms are compatible with waking life and often shape what it occurs to us to notice, think, or say rather than providing us with conscious intentional contents. But their powers must also be inferred from the repetition of waking symptoms and dreams; they cannot be directly observed like the latter. Their powers, in other words, are the presignifying correlate of any "meaning" that interpretation might find in the dream.[11]

Like dreams, then, phantasms also have a fundamental relationship to repetition. In one sense, they are simply a visual way of talking about the *drives* Freud posited behind and within psychic phenomena. Drives (*Trieben*, translated as *Instincts* in Strachey's English) are neither purely biological nor purely psychological motivators or forces but confuse the distinction between the two, because their multiplicity preexists the unity of childhood self-awareness.[12] They convey something about an individual's unique way of relating to his or her physiology and to the "external" world from which he or she is physically distinct. In "Instincts and Their Vicissitudes," Freud hypothesized that seeing and being seen, speaking and being spoken to, and touching or being touched (partial drives) were the building blocks of personality and intersubjective apprehension that could also, under extreme circumstances, be points of vulnerability or psychic catastrophe.[13]

MULTIPLE BEGINNINGS

In France, where turn of the twentieth-century psychology was strongly biological, psychoanalysis arrived by way of surrealism, an artistic and social movement that attempted to harness creative forces associated with chance and the unconscious through mechanisms such as automatic writing and controlled daydreaming.[14] Jacques Lacan was a member of the surrealist circle before turning into the most celebrated representative of French psychoanalysis and then its most infamous exile. Thus it is not surprising that his understanding of the Freudian drive(s) was drawn from cinema and visual art—montage and collage.[15]

For Lacan, following Austrian/British analyst Melanie Klein, the phantasm is an arrangement of partial drives, but also a way of keeping them under control such that the psyche can anticipate the satisfaction of desire, particularly through discursive intersubjectivity. In his early theory, Lacan reconceived of Freud's first topography of the ego, the unconscious, and the preconscious in terms of three simultaneous dimensions through which psychic life and interaction could be approached: the Imaginary, the Symbolic, and the Real.[16] He associated the Imaginary with the undifferentiated symbiosis between infant and caretaker that provided a basis for selfhood; the Symbolic with the differentiations between self and others that provided a basis for intersubjectivity and propositional thought or discourse, as well as social institutions; and the Real with whatever remained obscure but urgent and disturbing in each of the other dimensions.

But we must not imagine that the imaginal is equivalent to the Imaginary. First, the domain of "visualization" is not closed: a Symbolic "gaze" can be distinguished from the Imaginary "eye."[17] For example, art theorist Steven Levine points to Lacan's reworking of Freud's case study of Leonardo da Vinci.[18] Where Freud believed the Italian master repeatedly painted (and thus recreated) the adoring gaze between mother and son, to the point of leaving many projects and works open-ended or unfinished, Lacan pointed to the fact that *The Virgin and Christ with Saint Anne* also depicts the infant Christ playing with a lamb in an allusion to the Symbolic destiny that would eventually take him from Mary's embrace. In other words, the Symbolic introduces a cut and turns our potentially limitless "imaginary" sensory experience and production into a "work."[19] Second, the world of images must not be imagined as *static*, nor the visible as a timeless "picture," whether painted, photographed, or imagined.

Freudian psychotherapy famously prioritized "talk," but the concepts of "sublimation" and "working-through" connected it to other artistic media, including theater and social activism (e.g., in the case of Freud's early patient Anna O.).[20] The presence of psychoanalysis in the work of late twentieth-century French philosophers was mediated by Jacques Lacan but also by a reaction against phenomenology and an engagement with thinkers on the border of philosophy, literature, and the arts such as Pierre Klossowski.

In 1954, the year Lacan was giving his second seminar on the ego and the Imaginary, Merleau-Ponty was also lecturing at the Collège de France on "institution" and "passivity" in psychic life where he spoke of an "oneiric consciousness" whose domain would extend further than that of intentional consciousness.[21] In *Phenomenology of Perception* (1945), Merleau-Ponty had put forward a theory of language as the expression of a fundamentally embodied human (inter)subjectivity. Drawing on Husserl's unpublished manuscripts, he rooted both the medical understanding of perception and the philosophical-psychological understanding of subjectivity in existential ontology. As his career progressed, Merleau-Ponty was influenced by Ferdinand de Saussure, but continued to regard linguistic structure (langue) as secondary to expressive speech (parole)—unlike "structuralists," who conceived of subjectivity and meaning as secondary effects of structures that in themselves could not be considered "meaningful."[22]

To the extent that structuralists were empiricists, they prioritized evidence of statistical and syntactical regularity over evidence of psychological or communicative expression. The publication of Deleuze's *Empiricism and Subjectivity* in 1954 contributed to this discussion, as did Foucault's first essay that same year on existential psychoanalyst Ludwig Binswanger's *Dream and Existence* (1930).[23] Foucault's introduction largely explores implications of Freud's unsatisfied desire to reduce the dream image to language and Husserl's unsatisfied desire to reduce *meanings* to image-like instances of intuition, which, in Platonic fashion, he referred to as "essences."[24] Foucault distinguishes *imagination* from the *image* and places the dream on the existentially expansive side of imagination, while (like Freud) he associates the image with the limited manifest content of the dream and (as for Lacan) with the existentially deadening or limiting dimension of the Imaginary.[25]

But unlike Lacan, Foucault reminds us that Western tradition also gave dreams another function, one that is fulfilling as well as disappointing. For Binswanger, the dream's "navel" is not birth but death, and the work of imagination is to spatially represent the drama of the individual's confrontation with mortality.[26] Because both imagination and the image are associated with death, the true opposition is not between Imaginary and Symbolic but between an image which, like Heidegger's idle talk, avoids anxiety regarding death and one in which death is anticipated as fulfillment (in the sense that Aristotle says no man can be called happy until he is dead). In Lacanian terms, Foucault's point is not that the meaning of existence is given by the Imaginary rather than the Symbolic but that the decisive (even heroic) experience of death is associated with an image that is Symbolic rather than one that is merely Imaginary. It is this that implicitly allows for a transition from "madness" to the "work" of one's life. Following Binswanger, who was himself strongly influenced by Heidegger, Foucault refers to this problematic as "anthropological."[27]

In *The Order of Things* (1966), Foucault made a place for Lacan's structuralism (and Levi-Strauss's anthropology) not because he was particularly committed to the truth of psychoanalysis, whose power relations he had already examined in *History of Madness*, but because it seemed capable of resisting the "anthropological" problematic associated with phenomenology.[28] Despite

Merleau-Ponty's optimism, Foucault suspected that language and perception did not naturally produce an orderly world of interpretable experience, or what Deleuze would call "good sense" and "common sense."[29] Indeed, Merleau-Ponty could only imagine that he inhabited a world that was naturally expressive and perceptive in its intertwining with the human because he could trust his readers to draw on an image of "man" that made multiple spaces of imagination associated with discourse, architecture, and the arts cohere.[30]

Just as Foucault's essay on Binswanger expressed skepticism for the *image* by comparison to *imagination*, then, *The Order of Things* suggests that Kant's awakening from his dogmatic slumber was only a "dream within a dream." "Man," to follow Freud's model, would be the image sustaining the dreamer's wish while allowing him to remain in the existentially satisfying "anthropological sleep," both oriented toward and evading death: one of modernity's most powerful phantasms.[31]

Foucault's analysis of medical perception as well as the different forms of disciplinary knowledge in *The Order of Things* highlighted the discrepancy between what we can name and what we can see or imagine, drawing attention not only to lacunae within each medium but also to the backdrop against which they were differentiated. This discrepancy reflects Foucault's growing understanding of consciousness as a secondary and *contingent* effect of linguistic and/or perceptual conditions that do not resemble consciousness until combined under specific conditions.[32] For Deleuze, the conditions for phenomenological experience "make sense" only as a result of their combination with an "aleatory" or nonsignifying element.[33] In place of the "dogmatic image of thought" underwriting representation, Deleuze insisted that what gave rise to sense and thought was anomaly rather than a measured desire for order and homogeneity.[34] This shock or minimal difference, a multiplicity which can also be conceived as a *motion* or *affect*, inhabits and mobilizes every still and apparently unified image.

Implicitly, therefore, these thinkers sidestepped the phenomenological and existential aspect of psychoanalysis to emphasize the understanding of signs—visual and verbal—that allowed psychoanalysts to think of their work as *interpretive* and the scientific understanding of perception as *representative* of a unified world, a phenomenological experience. For Freud, the oneiric relationship between seeing and saying had to be organized in an interpretable way, just as the dream itself was thought to be an *interpretation* of the drive.[35] To Foucault, however, this approach not only consolidated the dream around the dreamer's ego (a unity Freud himself admitted was modeled on the perceptual unity of the body); it also consolidated psychoanalytic discourse around the authorial subject—the doctor celebrated in artistic, photographic, and verbal depictions as witness to and redeemer of the mad.[36]

Lacan's hope, at least in the early years, was that the energies associated with the drives (and conceptually indicated with the idea of *phantasm*) would be freed from the false or stultifying repetition of the Imaginary and channeled through linguistically and socially approved paths of desire, perhaps breaking some new paths of their own through creative sublimation. Pierre Klossowski, who translated *The Gay Science* into French and strongly influenced the environment in which Foucault and Deleuze engaged with Nietzsche, thought that the unified subject of discourse was no less an illusion than the ego.[37] Both directly and in the words and predicaments of his literary characters, Klossowski contends that phenomenological and psychological experience result from conflicts between phantasms, understood as pure intensities or forces that do not resemble the ideas or representations they produce (whether visible or articulable, bodily or existential).

For Klossowski, there is never just one phantasm or "primal scene," even for a single aspect of the drive like watching or grappling and being overpowered. Indeed, the unity of the ego (modeled on and serving as a model for the unity of the body) is not just an object of consciousness as for Sartre or the imaginary scene par excellence as for Lacan; it is both a phantasm and the simulacrum or mask manifesting a host of phantasms within the world. Klossowski also considers at least some phantasms collective: his characters grapple with the possibility that some spirits possess more than one body at a time or over time. Such phantasms can only be interpreted through *dramatization*—not through *commentary*, which makes them seem static and fixed in an organic whole. They are simulacra related only to one another; to be interpreted, they must first be organized into a world of signs and referents. Deleuze explicitly connects the idea of the simulacrum to resemblances that cannot be assimilated to exemplars of a Platonic Idea.[38] Because they elude thought, simulacra *provoke* both thought and the processes of sensory seeking/reception which look to thought and its transcendental for phenomenological coordination.

Thus where Merleau-Ponty and Freud both took the unity of the body for granted (without denying its intercorporeality or imbrication with other bodies), for the characters in Klossowski's novels, as in Deleuze's reading of Nietzsche, the question is always *which one* (spirit, lover, phantasm) a disunified body is manifesting theatrically at any given moment. According to Klossowski, the phantasm's resistance to generality is best communicated through ambiguous *gestures* that seem to both solicit and repel, affirm and deny, and attract the gaze and express a desire to see without being seen. Such gestures leave room for the subject to be active or passive (as for Freud's *Trieben*) but also, as in Lacan's account of the *pulsions*, for the subject to solicit or hide from them. Toward the end of his life, Klossowski dedicated himself to producing life-size paintings, sculptures, and (with the aid of others), films enshrining the gestures he had described in his novels as "tableaux vivants"—threatening and promising violence and pleasure at the same moment.[39]

Readers of Foucault and Deleuze—and anyone who has experienced even everyday mood swings, much less shifts in sexual orientation or gender identity or the personality changes that come with migration, life in a second language, or massive economic dislocation—must ask themselves whether this account is not actually *phenomenologically* more faithful to the swings of experience than the "natural" unity and progression of Merleau-Ponty's "transcendental-empirical doublet" with its "good sense" and "common sense." Might it not also allow us to better see the sanity in or even learn from those considered mad?

DREAM AND PHANTASM BEYOND THE "TRANSCENDENTAL-EMPIRICAL" DOUBLET

Following Nietzsche, Klossowski implies that the unities of psychoanalytic theory—the ego, the unconscious, and the body—are all products of a certain arrangement of social forces, among which he gives religious ideals great weight.[40] Freud and his psychoanalytic successors could only imagine the landscape of thought as a repressed or censored counterpart to perception and cognition, largely sexual, which became the "signified"—that which we *cannot enact*. In other words, the highly charged sensory, verbal, and affective elements that played a role in the child's distinction of self from other, and which were subsequently connected with one another by neural processes inaccessible to consciousness, shaped waking experience but *could not participate* in that experience, for neurological reasons as well as because they represented morally uncomfortable urges. In the words of J. B. Pontalis, the (linguistic) unconscious was an "other scene," and not as phenomenology might suggest, merely an "other side."[41]

But phenomenology, as we have seen, imagined even that "other side," the landscape of pre-personal or proto-expression, on the model of empirical perception and its unified, signifying world. Timothy Mooney points out despite its rich engagement with seeing and saying, Merleau-Ponty's philosophy seems to be unaware of those moments when these two dimensions conflict and either are produced by or produce nonsense in their turn. Nor does Merleau-Ponty grapple with those instances, perhaps unavoidable, when the surge of expressive perceptual human existence feels existentially threatened by ambivalence.[42] Gary Shapiro notes the priority of language over sensibility even in Merleau-Ponty's most eloquent engagements with the nonverbal world (a problem, he notes, that was also motivating to Lyotard).[43]

As a result, Merleau-Ponty's transcendental repeats the empirical and encourages thought to produce new empiricities on the model of those it has already encountered/selected.

What attracts Foucault in the imaginal realm, as revealed by both the arts and the history of discourse, is precisely the *uninterpretable* aspect of this regime, which reveals the shock and struggle beneath the waters of interpretation ("the endlessly repeated play of dominations") just as what attracts Deleuze is the combination of *forces* it expresses.[44] In works after *The Order of Things*, Foucault traces the "institutional" stability of discourse, architecture, painting, and the other arts to a power struggle rather than a natural expression or progressively sedimented institution. Indeed, both Deleuze and Foucault eventually concluded that psychoanalysis itself results from such a power struggle over the management of, respectively, the biopower of populations and the capture of desiring-production.[45]

The archeological analysis of discourse in terms of *enoncés* or "statements"—which Foucault characterized as turning interpretable documents into mute "monuments"—was important not only because it challenged the natural unity of seeing and saying proclaimed by phenomenology.[46] It was also important because it allowed for a focus on the *event* of discourse itself rather than on events as "contents" represented or manifested by discourse. In parallel, the *event* of painting—and of a particular painterly strategy—became as important as whatever was seen or portrayed within a painting. For Foucault, the priority of eventfulness over meaning was one of Deleuze's most important challenges to phenomenology, at least in its Merleau-Pontyan version.[47] According to Catherine Soussloff, the painting's resistance to interpretation provided Foucault with a model for an anti-hermeneutic approach to discourse.[48]

Foucault tried applying the principles of archeology to painting as a historical institution during his stay in Tunisia. His essays on the surrealist poet Raymond Roussel and the painter René Magritte were steps along the way. In *This Is Not a Pipe* (1968), he considered the inclusion of words within paintings, such those employed by the surrealist René Magritte, as visual artifacts rather than signifying discourse.[49] Just as he had once championed imagination against the image in his Binswanger essay, here Foucault championed *similitudes* against *resemblance*'s power to bind multiplicity to an "original" or essential meaning.[50] By contrast, he argued, Manet treated elements of painting that had become accepted as mimetic or "simply" representative, such as the relation between light and dark, the depth of perspective, and the portrayal of the mirror within the canvas—as genuine signifying elements.[51] Thereby Manet reintroduced viewers to the event from which the "representative destiny" of painting had been chosen—and pushed that destiny in a different direction.

In a later essay (1975) on the figurative painter Gérard Fromanger, Foucault showed how painting and photography could be combined to unpack and prolong an event, rather than to extend representational painting.[52] Fromanger projected photographs of street scenes, often taken during political protests, onto the canvas like a hallucination or "latent content" shaping the work invisibly from without, and then painted himself into the picture, with or without other figures who "occupied" the imaginative space thereby produced. Like other indexical traces of a singular moment or *haecceity*, something *in* the photo survived like a phantasm in the way Fromanger organized the "manifest" elements of the final work.

> Images that the spectator does not see come from the depth *(fond)* of space, and through an obscure force succeed in springing from a single photo, only to spread out in different paintings each of which in turn could give rise in turn to a new series, a new dispersion of events.[53]

Like Klossowski, Fromanger pushes the image closer to a *performance* which is both visually recorded and verbally documented.

Thus Foucault's explorations of the *enoncé* and similitudes in *The Archeology of Knowledge* and his essays on art suggested that neither words nor images needed to be approached as interpretations or as representations. Later in his career, studying the prison but also, in *The History of Sexuality Volume 1*, the therapeutic session and its debt to the Catholic practice of confession, Foucault went into greater detail regarding the "sites of subjectivation" and "correlate domains" accompanying the deployment of an *énoncé*.[54] A text conceived as a representation and a hermeneutic puzzle, like the dream and the drive/phantasy which it both interpreted and reproduced, tended to be a fertile target for power relations. At the same time, power relations (such as the repressive hypothesis in politics and psychology) were often at work when a field of signs was closed on itself so that some statements were referred to others as interpretations. From a Freudian standpoint, Foucault simply added "power" (to move and be moved) to the objects of the drives which he had already studied and sought to reconceive: the gaze (to see and be seen) and voice (to hear and be heard).

Over the course of his own career, Deleuze began stating with increasing boldness that pragmatics preceded linguistics, which had mistakenly limited the whole of signification to language.[55] He claimed that words were merely selections from a wide range of forces or power-laden signs extending through all of social and perhaps nonhuman reality. For the *form* and *content* of language taken as a universal, Deleuze substituted Hjelmslev's more expansive taxonomy of *content* (with a form and substance) and *expression* (with a form and substance).[56] The form of conventional linguistic signs remained; that is, recognizable vocalizations and written figures, as well as nonverbal gestures, but the *material* from which they were cut—pure vocal sound, the flow of ink, the circulation of papers and books, and above all the *affects* produced and caused by language—were given new significance. All of these, like the gestures, images, and verbal simulacra of Klossowski, are signs around which subjectivity and subjectivities can coalesce. Like the objects of the Freudian or Lacanian drive, moreover, all of these signs are forces with which one can ally or to which one can respond.

The "eventfulness" of the image and its appearance at the crossroads of repetition is treated differently in Deleuze's writings on cinema than in early works like *Difference and Repetition*.[57] Here, the distinction between the representative "movement-image," which signifies temporal change through measurable movement in space, and the "time-image," whose unexpected qualities indicate to the viewer that time has elapsed or is elapsing during his or her encounter with a film, is a purely visual version of the distinction between the proposition and the *enoncé*.[58] Bergson, on whom Deleuze relies at first, noted the limitations on experience imposed by calculative intelligence, the demands of action, and the "spatialization" of time—for example, in the series of still images which gives the illusion of motion in cinema.[59] The stillness of the time-image, and the way it is set off from its surrounding action by surprising or seemingly illogical cuts, indicates to the viewer motion not within the space of the film but between the film and the viewer—time as *emotion*.

Branching out beyond the op-sign and the son-sign (of which images and words are only approximations or simulacra), Deleuze tries to develop a taxonomy of all the ways in which film auteurs connected up the moving elements of a fictional and factual world.[60] In this way, he comes closer to populating the empty zones of the visible and the articulable toward which Foucault had pointed. These are the gaps in the inchoate landscape of our thought, provoked by distraction and sensation as much as by the incipient senselessness of our own words. Signs, including dreams and drives and their components, can be sensed or reflectively analyzed only through their repetition. Only in a certain "regime of signs" are signs presented as obscure intentions to be interpreted or as invitations to develop an interior subjectivity.[61] Psychoanalysis participates in a signifying regime, which is associated with the institutions of state societies, as well as in a postsignifying regime, in which such institutions have lost self-evident legitimacy and are sustained by the emotional conviction of their members.

The analysis presented in the cinema books and in *A Thousand Plateaus* leads Deleuze (and in the latter, Guattari) to challenge not only the importance of the dream but the very idea of the Imaginary—as employed by Lacanians, as well as theorists building on Marx and/or Bachelard such as

Castoriadis and Durand. In "Doubts about the Imaginary," Deleuze contends that the very concept is ill-formed and really refers to the event of confusion between the real—defined here as elements that contribute to ongoing continuity—and the unreal, or virtual and discontinuous elements (think of Descartes's identification of waking life with perceptual continuity).[62] What is often called "imagination" is simply the work of connecting those unreal (but virtual) elements to real ones—by building with brick and stone what we have envisioned—or, conversely, of actualizing the virtual. Such actualization is neither true nor false but generates elements that might be linked in a system admitting of truth:

> There are two systems of images: a system one might call organic, that of the movement-image, which is based on rational cuts and linkages and itself sets forth a model of truth (truth is the whole . . .) and then a crystalline system, that of the time-image, based on irrational cuts with only relinkings, and substituting for the model of truth the power of falsity as becoming.[63]

Subjectivity, too, is a complex heterogeneous flow which has been separated from its environment and divided into content and expression (with associated forms—such as dreams, tics, and symptoms—and corresponding substances—affects, drives, and inhibitions). In its encounter with the film image, the aspect of our existence can best be visualized as the brain encounters something virtual and organizes these flows to produce a world to match its shift in affect.[64] The whole world "changes completely" and abruptly from one mood to the next.

CONCLUSION

For Deleuze, the Lacanian Imaginary resembles a "movement-image" through which real thoughts and real perceptions are connected as partial perspectives on a presumptive whole. Despite contributing to a series which appears to move, the movement-image is still, frozen, unless it is put in relation to a time-image which reveals its affective connections—which turns it into a crystal. "To imagine is to make the image behave like a crystal."[65] The "cut" or castration associated with the Symbolic is always a start to some other new becoming; this generativity is as important or more important than the capacity to finish a "work" or close a door on the past.

The psychoanalytic phantasm is a way of conceptualizing an affective limit, an intensity that would be traumatic and soul-destroying if approached too directly or completely actualized rather than left, as Deleuze says, in the "virtual." Psychotherapies and many artistic practices try to give that limit a tolerable form, turning its anxiety into energy for creative and thoughtful responses. In this sense, they continue the work of embodying and dramatizing phantasms that therapeutic practices have always played in human cultures, long before the era of Western anthropology. Deleuze's work suggests we might think of phantasms as points of tension and stabilization in the psyche—as well as in a given body and its ecosystem—whether over time or in regularly repeated but intermittent continuities. These points of tension and uncertainty could be expressed in images or statements, through symbols or through raw cries, as well as performances and cinematic images, that convey the open passage of time rather than representing self-contained events.

In this model, trauma would be the result of an assemblage's distention and disintegration due to incompatible speeds—the degree zero of a body without organs, which, like Klossowski, we could conceive both as a single phantasm and the product of conflicting phantasms. But we should note that trauma would also result if the phantasm(s) were frozen or deprived of becoming. As a point where processes of subjectivation are provoked in the social collective, the phantasm is the dream insofar as it connects the dreamer to society and the cosmos, and not just to the dreamer's own biological body or existential anthropology. The phantasm, as noted earlier, may mark the division between inner and outer, a separation from the world under the threat of an "order word" felt to be disempowering (castrating).[66] So too it may be the only site on which those two domains can begin to reconnect. For Deleuze, the challenge is not to organize man and world in a hermeneutic whole but to measure the *speed* with which various sound, imaginal, and other signs connect, repeat, differentiate, or disconnect from one another so that the psyche is capable of recognizing itself *at least in part* from one event to the next, without getting "frozen" or entering an endless feedback loop.

If Freud's image of ancient Rome were a time-image subtending the narrative history of psychoanalysis as well as a given patient's life, with what affect would it suffuse psychoanalytic theory and the working through of actual transference? Recognizing the phantasm behind a dream, a symptom, or a habit not only allows new images to be added to the series but also reveals the dreamer in the midst of an action in which he or she can discover a kind of fate. Perhaps this is also the sense in which Binswanger's dream gives a Symbolic function to the image, one associated with fulfillment and destiny. When it connects the dreamer to the world, prior to any biological understanding of the body or existential psychological schema, you don't spend the morning interpreting a dream; you wake up with an idea or reach for the phone, ready to take a walk.[67]

NOTES

1. Sigmund Freud, *Civilization and its Discontents* (1930). In Volume 21 of *The Standard Edition of the Complete Psychological Works of Sigmund Freud*, ed. and trans. James Strachey (London: Hogarth Press, 1953-74), 69–71.

2. Sigmund Freud, *The Interpretation of Dreams* (1900), in Vol. 4–5 of *The Standard Edition*, 35–39.

3. The "imaginal" is a concept from Chiara Bottici, following Henry Corbin, that refers to imagistic elements of experience considered prior to or apart from the distinction between the real and the fictitious. Unlike "imagination" which, in the history of philosophy, is presumed to be individual, and the "Imaginary" which is held to be social by thinkers such as Castoriadis or Bachelard, the imaginal can play on both registers. See Bottici, *Imaginal Politics: Images Beyond Imagination and the Imaginary* (New York: Columbia University Press, 2014), 6–7.

4. Laplanche, Jean and J. B. Pontalis, "Fantasy and the Origins of Sexuality" (1964), in *Formations of Fantasy*, ed. Victor Burger, James Donald, Cora Kaplan (London: Methuen, 1986), 5–34.

5. Freud, *The Interpretation of Dreams*, 133, 155–160.

6. Freud, *The Interpretation of Dreams*, 177, 269–270.

7. Freud, *The Interpretation of Dreams*, 312, 343–344, 347, 352–355.

8. Freud, *The Interpretation of Dreams*, 341–342, 371.

9. Freud, *The Interpretation of Dreams*, 358, 592, 564.

10. The etymology of "Phantasy," "Fantasy," and related terms in several languages is discussed by Jean Laplanche and J. B. Pontalis, in *The Language of Psychoanalysis*, trans. Donald Nicholson-Smith (New York: W. W. Norton, 1973), 314–319. In French, the term has connotations related to the "phantom" or supernatural apparition, upon which Klossowski plays in his novels.

11. It should be noted that Freud's interpretive strategy, at least initially, seems more a matter of "decoding" the visual and verbal elements of the dream than the kind of holistic approach we find associated with hermeneutics, yet Freud defined himself in opposition to the classical cryptographic approach associated with "dream books." Freud's position with respect to multiple meanings of "interpretation" has been widely discussed and goes beyond the scope of the present chapter.

12. Freud also uses the term *Instinkt* to refer to "psychic pressures" with a clearly biological basis. *Trieb* does not have a clear object, which is why its aim can be reversed or one object substituted for another. See Laplanche and Pontalis, *The Language of Psychoanalysis*, 214.

13. Sigmund Freud, "The Instincts and Their Vicissitudes" (1915/1925), in Vol. 14 of Freud, *The Standard Edition*, 109–140.

14. Sherry Turkle, *Psychoanalytic Politics: Jacques Lacan and Freud's French Revolution*, 2nd edition (New York/London: The Guilford Press, 1992), 5.

15. Jacques Lacan, *Four Fundamental Concepts of Psychoanalysis*, trans. Alan Sheridan. Book 11 (1964) of *The Seminar of Jacques Lacan*, ed. Jacques-Alain Miller (New York: W. W. Norton. [1973] 1981), 169.

16. For example, Jacques Lacan, *The Ego in Freud's Theory and in the Technique of Psychoanalysis*, trans. Sylvana Tomaselli with John Forrester. Book 2 (1954–55) of *The Seminar of Jacques Lacan*, ed. Jacques-Alain Miller (New York: W. W. Norton, [1978] 1988), 36.

17. Steven Z. Levine, *Lacan: A Guide for the Arts Student* (London: I. B. Tauris, 2008), 11.

18. Levine, *Lacan: A Guide*, 4–7, 23–30. Lacan's discussion is found in his 1956–1957 seminar on object relations (*La Relation d'object*). Levine, *Lacan: A Guide*, 23.

19. The relationship between the rationality or literary significance of the "work" and its excluded preconditions forms the theme of several Foucault essays of the 1960s, including "Introduction to Rousseau's *Dialogues*" (1962), trans. Robert Hurley, in *Aesthetics, Method, and Epistemology*, ed. James Faubion. Vol. 2 of *Essential Works of Foucault 1954–1984* (New York: New Press, 1998), 33–52; and "Madness, the Absence of Work" (1964), trans. Peter Stastny and Deniz Şengel, in *Foucault and His Interlocutors*, ed. Arnold Davidson (Chicago: University of Chicago Press, 1997), 97–104.

20. Freud, *Civilization and its Discontents*, 97; Sigmund Freud and Josef Breuer, *Studies in Hysteria* (1895), Vol 2 of *The Standard Edition* (London: Hogarth Press, 1895).

21. Lacan, *The Ego in Freud's Theory;* Maurice Merleau-Ponty, *Institution and Passivity: Course Notes from the Collège de France (1954-1955)*, trans. Leonard Lawlor and Heath Massey (Evanston, IL: Northwestern University Press, 2010).

22. James Edie, "Forward" to *Consciousness and the Acquisition of Language*, trans. Hugh J. Silverman (Evanston: Northwestern University Press, 1979).

23. Ludwig Binswanger, *Dream and Existence* (1930), trans. Forrest Williams; ed. Keith Hoeller, *Review of Existential Psychology and Psychiatry*, special issue 19, no. 1 (1986): 81–105.

24. Michel Foucault, "Dream, Imagination, and Existence" (1954), trans. Forrest Williams; ed. Keith Hoeller, *Review of Existential Psychology and Psychiatry*, special issue 19, no. 1 (1986): 35–41; see also Gary Shapiro, *Archaeologies of Vision: Foucault and Nietzsche on Seeing and Saying* (Chicago: University of Chicago Press, 2003), 201–207.

25. Foucault, "Dream, Imagination, and Existence," 45–47.

26. Foucault, "Dream, Imagination, and Existence," 51–55.

27. Foucault, "Dream, Imagination, and Existence," 56–57.

28. Michel Foucault, *The Order of Things: An Archaeology of the Human Sciences* (1966), trans. Alan Sheridan (New York: Random House, 1970), 379–382.

29. Gilles Deleuze, *Difference and Repetition* (1968), trans. Paul Patton (New York: Columbia University Press, 1994), 224–227.

30. Foucault, *The Order of Things*, 378.

31. Foucault, *The Order of Things*, 340–342.

32. Michel Foucault, "Nietzsche, Genealogy, History" (1971), trans. Donald F. Bouchard and Sherry Simon, in Foucault, *Aesthetics, Method, and Epistemology*, 374.

33. Gilles Deleuze, *Difference and Repetition*, 145; "How Do We Recognize Structuralism?" (1972), in *Desert Islands and Other Texts: 1953-1974*, ed. David Lapoujade; trans. David Paul (Cambridge, MA: MIT Press/Semiotext(e), 2004), 203.

34. Deleuze, *Difference and Repetition*, 131–141.

35. Freud, *The Interpretation of Dreams*, 628.

36. For example, in Michel Foucault, *History of Madness* (1961), trans. Jonathan Murphy and Jean Khalfa (London: Routledge, 2006) and "What Is an Author?" (1969), trans. Josué V. Harari, in Foucault, *Aesthetics, Method, and Epistemology*, 205–222. Georges Didi-Huberman addresses the role of photographic and painterly images in Charcot's psychiatric practice, which was eye-opening for Freud, while Shapiro discusses the analogy between the painter and the author in Foucault's work. See Didi-Huberman, *The Invention of Hysteria: Charcot and the Photographic Iconography of the Salpêtrière*, trans. Alisa Hartz (Cambridge, MA: MIT Press, 2003), and Shapiro, *Archaeologies of Vision*.

37. See Shapiro, *Archaeologies of Vision*, for a discussion of how Nietzsche's idea of *recurrence* influenced the French reception of Freudian *repetition*.

38. Gilles Deleuze, *Logic of Sense* (1969), ed. Constantin V. Boundas, trans. by Mark Lester with Charles Stivale (New York: Columbia University Press, 1990), 256–257.

39. For a detailed discussion, see Hervé Castanet, *Pierre Klossowski: The Pantomime of Spirits*, trans. Adrian Price and Pamela King (Oxford: Peter Lang, 2014). One is also reminded of the "parade des fous" in which the patients of the asylum at Münsterlingen circled the town in costume during Foucault's 1954 visit and Artaud's efforts to integrate Native American and Balinese ritual directly into theater. On the former, see David Macey, *The Lives of Michel Foucault* (London: Random House UK, 1993), 61–62.

40. See Pierre Klossowski, *Nietzsche and the Vicious Circle* (1969), trans. Daniel W. Smith (Chicago: University of Chicago Press, 1998); for a synthetic interdisciplinary overview of these themes, see Pierre Klossowski, *La Ressemblance* (Marseille: Editions Ryôan-Ji, 1984).

41. Jean-Bertrand Pontalis, "The Problem of the Unconscious in Merleau-Ponty's Thought," trans. Wilfried Ver Eecke and Michael Greer, in *Review of Existential Psychology and Psychiatry* 18 (1982–83), 83–96.

42. Timothy Mooney, "Repression and Operative Unconsciousness in *Phenomenology of Perception*," in *Unconsciousness between Phenomenology and Psychoanalysis*, ed. Dorothée Legrand and Dylan Trigg (Cham, Switzerland: Springer. 2017), 72–73.

43. Shapiro, *Archaeologies of Vision*, 200–203. In many respects, the present research was inspired by Catherine Malabou's gorgeous article, "An Eye at the Edge of Discourse," trans. Carolyn Shread, *Communication Theory* 17 (2007): 16–25, which deals with Lyotard and for whose discovery I am indebted to Chris Whittey.

44. Foucault, "Nietzsche, Genealogy, History," 377; Deleuze, *Difference and Repetition*, 131–132.

45. This claim was foreshadowed in *History of Madness* and expanded in *The History of Sexuality Volume 1* as well as in Deleuze and Guattari, *Anti-Oedipus*.

46. Michel Foucault, *The Archeology of Knowledge and the Discourse on Language* (1969 and 1971), trans. A. M. Sheridan Smith (New York: Vintage Books, 1972), 79–86.

47. Michel Foucault, "Theatrum Philosophicum" (1970), trans. Donald F. Bouchard and Sherry Simon, in Foucault, *Aesthetics, Method, Epistemology*, 351.

48. Catherine M. Soussloff, *Foucault on Painting* (Minneapolis: University of Minnesota Press, 2017), 11.

49. Michel Foucault, *Manet and the Object of Painting*, trans. Matthew Barr (London: Tate Publishing, 2009).

50. Michel Foucault, "This Is Not a Pipe" (1968), trans. James Harkness, in Foucault, *Aesthetics, Method, Epistemology*, 187–203; Soussloff, *Foucault on Painting*, 29–31, 69–95.

51. Foucault, *Manet and the Object of Painting*.

52. Michel Foucault, "La peinture photogénique" (1975), in Vol. 2 of *Dits et Écrits (1970–1975)*, ed. Daniel Defert and François Ewald (Paris: Gallimard, 1994), 707–715.

53. Foucault, "La peinture photogénique," 714.

54. For example, see Foucault, *The Archeology of Knowledge*, 92–100.

55. Gilles Deleuze and Félix Guattari, *A Thousand Plateaus* (1980), trans. Brian Massumi, Vol. 2 of *A Thousand Plateaus: Capitalism and Schizophrenia* (Minneapolis: University of Minnesota Press, 1987), 75–79.

56. Deleuze and Guattari, *A Thousand Plateaus*, 92, 43–45, 85–86.

57. Gilles Deleuze, *Cinema 1: The Movement-Image* (1983), trans. Hugh Tomlinson and Barbara Habberjam (Minneapolis: University of Minnesota Press, 1986); Gilles Deleuze, *Cinema 2: The Time-Image* (1985), trans. Hugh Tomlinson and Robert Galeta (London: Athlone, 1989).

58. Deleuze, *Cinema 1*, 8, 29; Deleuze, *Cinema 2*, 34–35.

59. Paola Marrati, *Gilles Deleuze: Cinéma et philosophie* (Paris: Presses Universitaires de France, 2003).

60. Gilles Deleuze, "Doubts About the Imaginary" (1986), in *Negotiations, 1972–1990*, trans. Martin Joughin (New York: Columbia University Press, 1995), 67.

61. Gilles Deleuze, "On Philosophy" (1988), in *Negotiations*, 112–115.

62. Deleuze, "Doubts About the Imaginary," 67.

63. Deleuze, "Doubts About the Imaginary," 67.

64. Deleuze, "On Philosophy," 149.

65. Deleuze, "Doubts About the Imaginary," 66.

66. Deleuze and Guattari, *A Thousand Plateaus*, 75–85.

67. Thanks to Brent Adkins for helpful comments and the Case Western Reserve University Baker-Nord Center for the Humanities for financial support during the research and writing of this chapter.

REFERENCES

Arnaud, Alain. *Pierre Klossowski*. Paris: Seuil, 1990.

Binswanger, Ludwig. "Dream and Existence" (1930). Translated by Forrest Williams, edited by Keith Hoeller *Review of Existential Psychology and Psychiatry,* special issue 19, no. 1 (1986): 81–105.

Bottici, Chiara. *Imaginal Politics: Images Beyond Imagination and the Imaginary.* New York: Columbia University Press, 2014.

Castanet, Hervé. *Pierre Klossowski: The Pantomime of Spirits.* Translated by Adrian Price and Pamela King. Oxford: Peter Lang, 2014.

Deleuze, Gilles. *Cinema 1: The Movement-Image.* Translated by Hugh Tomlinson and Barbara Habberjam. Minneapolis: University of Minnesota Press, 1986 [1983].

———. *Cinema 2: The Time-Image.* Translated by Hugh Tomlinson and Robert Galeta. London: Athlone, 1989 (1985).

———. *Difference and Repetition.* Translated by Paul Patton. New York: Columbia University Press, 1994 (1968).

———. "Doubts About the Imaginary" (1986) In *Negotiations, 1972–1990.* Translated by Martin Joughin, 62–67. New York: Columbia University Press, 1995.

———. "How Do We Recognize Structuralism?" In *Desert Islands and Other Texts: 1953-1974,* edited by David Lapoujade; translated by David Paul, 170–192. Cambridge, MA: MIT Press/Semiotext(e), 2004 (1972).

———. *Logic of Sense.* Edited by Constantin V. Boundas; translated by Mark Lester with Charles Stivale. New York: Columbia University Press, 1990 [1969].

———. "On Philosophy" (1988). In *Negotiations, 1972–1990.* Translated by Martin Joughin, 135–155. New York: Columbia University Press, 1995.

Deleuze, Gilles, and Félix Guattari. Vol. 2 of *A Thousand Plateaus: Capitalism and Schizophrenia.* Translated by Brian Massumi. Minneapolis: University of Minnesota Press, 1987 (1980).

Didi-Huberman, Georges. *The Invention of Hysteria: Charcot and the Photographic Iconography of the Salpêtrière.* Translated by Alisa Hartz. Cambridge, MA: MIT Press, 2003.

Edie, James. "Forward" to *Consciousness and the Acquisition of Language.* Translated by Hugh J. Silverman. Evanston: Northwestern University Press, 1979.

Foucault, Michel. *Aesthetics, Method, and Epistemology*, edited by James Faubion. Vol. 2 of *Essential Works of Foucault 1954–1984.* New York: New Press, 1998.

———. *The Archeology of Knowledge and the Discourse on Language.* Translated by A. M. Sheridan Smith. New York: Vintage Books, 1972 (1969 and 1971).

———. *Birth of the Clinic: An Archaeology of Medical Perception.* Translated by A. M. Sheridan Smith. New York: Vintage Books, 1994 (1963).

———. "Dream, Imagination, and Existence" (1954). Translated by Forrest Williams; edited by Keith Hoeller. *Review of Existential Psychology and Psychiatry,* special issue 19, no. 1 (1986): 29–78.

———. *History of Madness.* Translated by Jonathan Murphy and Jean Khalfa. London: Routledge, 2006 (1961).

———. "Introduction to Rousseau's *Dialogues*" (1962). Translated by Robert Hurley. In Foucault, *Aesthetics, Method, and Epistemology,* 33–52. New York: New Press, 1998.

———. "La peinture photogénique" (1975). In Vol. 2 of *Dits et Écrits (1970-1975)*, edited by Daniel Defert and François Ewald, 707–715. Paris: Gallimard, 1994.

———. "Madness, the Absence of Work" (1964). Translated by Peter Stastny and Deniz Şengel. In *Foucault and His Interlocutors*, edited by Arnold Davidson, 97–104. Chicago: University of Chicago Press, 1997.

———. *Manet and the Object of Painting*. Translated by Matthew Barr. London: Tate Publishing, 2009.

———. "Nietzsche, Genealogy, History" (1971). Translated by Donald F. Bouchard and Sherry Simon. In Foucault, *Aesthetics, Method, and Epistemology*, 369–391.

———. "Structuralism and Post-structuralism" [1983]. Translated by Jeremy Harding. In Foucault, *Aesthetics, Method, and Epistemology*, 433–458.

———. *The Order of Things: An Archaeology of the Human Sciences*. Translated by Alan Sheridan. New York: Random House, 1970 (1966).

———. "Theatrum Philosophicum" (1970). Translated by Donald F. Bouchard and Sherry Simon. In Foucault, *Aesthetics, Method, and Epistemology*, 343–368.

———. "This is Not a Pipe" (1968). Translated by James Harkness. In Foucault, *Aesthetics, Method, and Epistemology*, 187–203.

———. "What is an Author?" (1969). Translated by Josué V. Harari. In Foucault, *Aesthetics, Method, and Epistemology*, 205–222.

Freud, Sigmund, *The Standard Edition of the Complete Psychological Works of Sigmund Freud.* 24 volumes. Edited and translated by James Strachey. London: Hogarth Press, 1953–74.

———. *Beyond the Pleasure Principle* (1920). In Vol. 18 of Freud, *The Standard Edition*, 1–64.

———. *Civilization and its Discontents* (1930). In Vol 21 of Freud, *The Standard Edition*, 59–148.

———. "The Instincts and Their Vicissitudes" (1915/1925). In Vol. 14 of Freud, *The Standard Edition*, 109–140.

———. *The Interpretation of Dreams* (1900). Vol. 4–5 of Freud, *The Standard Edition.*

Freud, Sigmund, and Josef Breuer. *Studies in Hysteria* (1895). Vol 2 of Freud, *The Standard Edition.*

Klossowski, Pierre. *La Ressemblance.* Marseille: Editions Ryôan-Ji, 1984.

———. *Nietzsche and the Vicious Circle*. Translated by Daniel W. Smith. Chicago: University of Chicago Press, 1998 [1969].

Lacan, Jacques. *Four Fundamental Concepts of Psychoanalysis.* Translated by Alan Sheridan. Book 11 (1964) of *The Seminar of Jacques Lacan,* edited by Jacques-Alain Miller. New York: W. W. Norton, 1981 (1973).

———. *The Ego in Freud's Theory and in the Technique of Psychoanalysis.* Translated by Sylvana Tomaselli with John Forrester. Book 2 (1954-55) of *The Seminar of Jacques Lacan,* edited by Jacques-Alain Miller. New York: W. W. Norton, 1988 (1978).

Laplanche, Jean and J. B. Pontalis. "Fantasy and the Origins of Sexuality" (1964). In *Formations of Fantasy*, edited by Victor Burger, James Donald, Cora Kaplan, 5–34. London: Methuen, 1986.

———. *The Language of Psychoanalysis.* Translated by Donald Nicholson-Smith. New York: W. W. Norton, 1973.

Levine, Steven Z. *Lacan: A Guide for the Arts Student.* London: I. B. Tauris, 2008.

Macey, David. *The Lives of Michel Foucault.* London: Random House UK, 1993.

Malabou, Catherine. "An Eye at the Edge of Discourse." Translated by Carolyn Shread. *Communication Theory* 17 (2007): 16–25.

Marrati, Paola. *Gilles Deleuze: Cinéma et philosophie.* Paris: Presses Universitaires de France, 2003.

Merleau-Ponty, Maurice. *Institution and Passivity: Course Notes from the Collège de France (1954-1955).* Translated by Leonard Lawlor and Heath Massey. Evanston, IL: Northwestern University Press, 2010.

Mooney, Timothy. "Repression and Operative Unconsciousness in *Phenomenology of Perception.*" In *Unconsciousness Between Phenomenology and Psychoanalysis,* edited by Dorothée Legrand and Dylan Trigg, 61–74. Cham, Switzerland: Springer, 2017.

Phillips, James. "Merleau-Ponty's Nonverbal Unconscious." In *Unconsciousness Between Phenomenology and Psychoanalysis,* edited by Dorothée Legrand and Dylan Trigg, 75–92. Cham, Switzerland: Springer, 2017.

Pontalis, Jean-Bertrand. "The problem of the unconscious in Merleau-Ponty's thought." Translated by Wilfried Ver Eecke and Michael Greer. *Review of Existential Psychology and Psychiatry* 18 (1982-83): 83–96.

Shapiro, Gary. *Archaeologies of Vision: Foucault and Nietzsche on Seeing and Saying.* Chicago: University of Chicago Press, 2003.

Soussloff, Catherine M. *Foucault on Painting.* Minneapolis: University of Minnesota Press, 2017.

Turkle, Sherry. *Psychoanalytic Politics: Jacques Lacan and Freud's French Revolution,* 2nd edition. New York/London: The Guilford Press, 1992.

Chapter 7

Sex(uality) as State of Exception

Cindy Zeiher

Language uses us as much as we use language. As much as our choice of forms of expression is guided by the thoughts we want to express, to the same extent the way we feel about the things in the real world governs the way we express ourselves in these settings.[1]

Desire is more than merely a concept of perpetual subjective crisis. It is something which actually does trouble the subject and its orientation in the world, perhaps because its obvious counterpart, sex, has historically been regarded with suspicion. Yet, for psychoanalysts, especially those from the Freudian and Lacanian traditions, it is clear that desire has its foundation in the libidinal drives and is thus a source of anxiety. What then can be said about desire? On the one hand, it is a somewhat vague, umbrella term, on the other, a very precise one lying within the lexicon of everyday life. Furthermore, understood as a cluster of temporal symptoms and interrogations manifesting their own psychic power, desire is resistant to symbolic homogenization. Because it is a ubiquitous term for both Foucault and Lacan, in order to read desire we have to first unpack what keeps it contained. Freud held that because we are always living beyond the means of our desire, we are therefore bound to repress it while at the same time living alongside its pervasive force. So in order to live a tolerable life which is able to encompass desire, we have to be living simultaneously in perpetual denial of it: this is Freud's "life instinct" (1920).[2] In addition, for Freud psychoanalysis has an ethical duty to point out the psychic cost to this instinct, namely that knowing desire is from the very beginning simply an illusion.

The process of unpacking desire is confusing because when we are driving toward something, someone, or somewhere we tend to think of this as a manifestation of desire rather than a will to jouissance. Yet this tendency is intrinsically irrational because desire is already, always, unthinkable. Nevertheless what we do is to displace desire in favor of some person, thing, cause, and so on. Yet this procedure, appearing to establish for the subject a rational link or actuality with desire, is no more than a psychic defense against the intangibility and irrationality of desire, whose sovereignty is just too much for the subject to bear. However, for those of us oriented by psychoanalysis, whether theoretically and clinically, psychoanalysis has the tools and muscle to take a deliberately ambivalent stance toward desire and thereby to assess whether we are facing the thing we really want or something else standing in as a placeholder. So although we might think of desire as a concept in perpetual crisis, it is more correctly a crisis lying within our subjectivity.

In attempting to read desire, the subject of psychoanalysis must be cautious not to fall into the delusion that one knows what one's desire is. This is precisely the crisis of desire psychoanalysis provokes the subject to take up. The way both into and out of this crisis is via language which for Lacanians is the only viable tool we have for such a traversal. Therefore, rather than dismissing language because of its limitations, we need to use it carefully, with thought and procedure.

Foucault's ontology of discourse emanates from the cultural and social conditions which, he contends, are imposed upon us. He understands discourse as an ordering of everything (people, attitudes, values, and so on) as they emerge and reproduce within different discursive fields such as sex, science, or history. For him, the subject emerges from a composition of many discourses, all of which carry political investment. Thus for Foucault the body is a text which can be read discursively, having already itself produced a politics of discourse. Such discourse can be thought of as language in action, one which vehemently rejects all notions of self-knowledge, sovereignty, narrative, agency, and so on, because, claims Foucault, these are already generated for us and we either take them up or not.[3]

Although Lacan agrees with Foucault that discourse emerges from the subject in terms of working rules, for Lacan discourse is neither so conscious nor so political as Foucault claims. For Lacan because there is no "true sex," desire has to be interpreted as lying within the manifestation of symptoms which *are* methodologically examinable on the psychoanalytic couch, where any lack of agency a subject might experience through alienation, destitution, and melancholy can be restored to dignity. For the analysand, the analyst grants complete freedom to say anything, anytime, and without judgment: libidinal desire is always what envelopes the subject and formalizes the procedure of analysis. Although the technique of free association has no discourse (there is no ulterior motive or pressure for the analysand to make any sense), nevertheless whatever transpires is still discourse, namely the analyst's discourse regarding the formation of a subject as an analysand. As many Lacanians well know, in addition to being committed to the analytic procedure, the analysand has to do other things: look after children, be in an intimate loving relationship, get along with colleagues at work, pay bills, nurture friendships, and so on. For Lacan, these are all also symbolically discursive experiences and activities in so far as, from the inane to the jubilant, they all hinge on knowledge which discourse has enveloped them in. Whereas for Foucault discourse speaks via operating fields of activity, for Lacan it speaks via the subject. These differing positions on discourse have implications for desire: either as a Foucauldian rationality which is egoic, consistent, and stable or as a Lacanian inaccessible problem which makes one's life nearly impossible to decipher.

Lacan theorizes four distinct but related discourses from which desire can be read: these being discourses of Master, University, Hysteric, and Analyst (figure 7.1).

In order to specularize the movement between these related discourses in a way which he thought bypasses confusions in ordinary language, Lacan devises a formalized language of mathematical typology whose symbols stand for the sources of agency and effect in each discourse: S1 is the master signifier; S2 is the chain of signifiers (all knowledge); $ is the split subject barred by the signifier; *a* is the *object a* cause of desire.

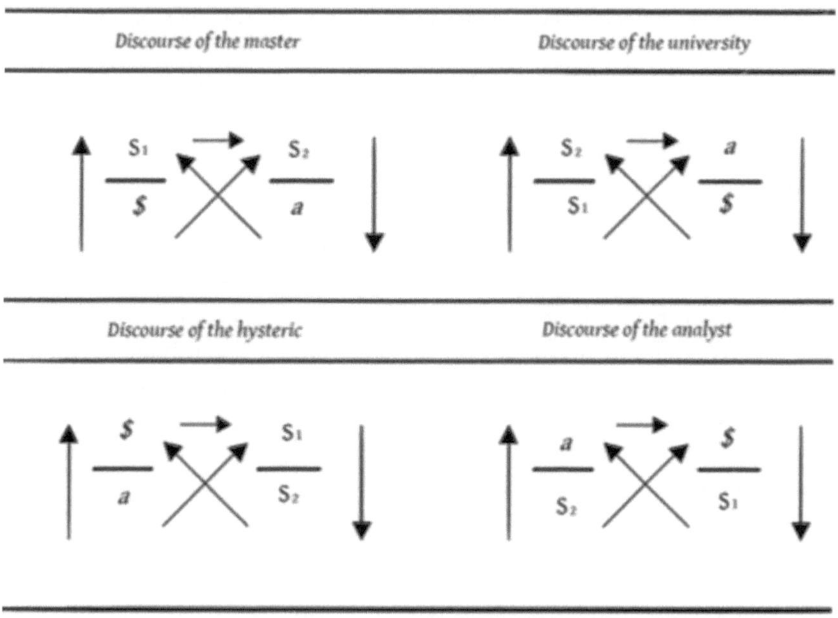

Figure 7.1 Lacan's Four Discourses. *Source*: Adapted and drawn by the author.

Lacan theorizes that as the subject circulates within and between these discourses via ordinary language, desire is generated and reproduced. Each discourse implies a unique signifying process whose product is *objet a*, the object cause of desire and surplus enjoyment, which is at the same time representative of the lost object and lack in both the subject and the Other. For Lacan discourse is, through language, responsible for all social relationship: "I can say until I'm blue in the face that the notion of discourse should be taken as a social link [*lien social*], founded on language."[4] His theory of discourse presents different discursive subject and their particular ways of enjoyment, for example, a dedicated academic within the university discourse might regard knowledge as a prime source of enjoyment whereas hysterics would enjoy simply through the persistence of symptoms unique to them (hence the Lacanian catchphrase, "Enjoy Your Symptom!"). The dominant position held in a given discourse (top left hand) is the agent who takes up the unique enjoyment of that discourse. In each discourse the subject functions as the object of the Other's desire; yet because no one symptom can provide never-ending enjoyment, new symptoms are unconsciously created by the subject in order to perpetuate the cycle of enjoyment.

Regarding the unconscious, in *Encore* Lacan states,

> The unconscious is not the fact that being thinks, though that is implied by what is said thereof in traditional sciences, the unconscious is the fact that being, by speaking enjoys [*jouisse*] and, I will add, wants to know nothing more about it.[5]

Although both Lacan and Foucault respect the singularity of the subject who enjoys and endures anguish amid competing discourses, the effects of this enjoyment and anguish are handled differently by them: for Foucault, it is via political intervention whereas for Lacan it is, first and foremost, via subjectivity which may or may not involve a politics to come. Nevertheless it seems both thinkers accept desire as the state of exception intrinsic to the joy and anguish of subjectivity. Furthermore, insofar as desire is entwined within discourse, their respective examinations of it enable a study of how discourse is produced at an intersection of the subject and the social bond. Certainly, for both thinkers desire is libidinal and lies at the origin or singularity of subjective truth.

Foucault and Lacan recognize that the relation between truth and knowledge is tenuous. Foucault suggests that truth emerges and operates like a *regime*:

> Each society has its *régime* of truth, its "general politics" of truth: that is, the types of discourse which it accepts and makes function as true; the mechanisms and instances which enable one to distinguish true and false statements, the

> means by which each is sanctioned; the techniques and procedures accorded value in the acquisition of truth; the status of those who are charged with saying what counts as true.[6]

Such truth is for Foucault a historical construction and inevitably, therefore, one organized by discourse about how sex and pleasure can be discussed and practiced. This gives the truth of sex and pleasure an empirical bodily presence which for Foucault is problematically interpellated within essentialism:

> "Sexuality": the correlative of that slowly developed discursive practice which constitutes the *scientia sexualis*. The essential features of this sexuality are not the expression of a representation that is more or less distorted by ideology, of a misunderstanding of taboos; they correspond to the functional requirements of a discourse that must produce its truth. Situated at the point of intersection of a technique of confession and a scientific diversity [. . .] sexuality was being defined "by nature."[7]

Truth structures fantasies, forms relationships, hides secret obsessions, and is at the root of consciousness. Being libidinal in character, it is from a Lacanian perspective situated both within and beyond discourse. Given this position we can consider Foucault's claim that power is both strategizing and itself a strategy. On the couch, where one is attending directly to desire, language alone provides a strategy to speak to this. During transference the analyst is not attempting to be inside or outside a power relation. Insofar as the psychical life of the analysand is what counts regarding the desire of the analyst to be evoking symptoms in the analysand, any power there might be remains with the analysand. Moreover, in discovering what form desire might take, the analysand shows willingness to undergo transference by turning the volume up on their symptom. Here neither the analyst nor the analysand is speaking (or staying silent) from a position of power but rather from one of truth. Only in this way can desire be seriously put to work. For all their differences, Foucault and Lacan agree that more time should be spent on deciphering or, as Joan Copjec puts it, "reading our desire." In doing this we might attain a different knowledge and theory of what it is to be a subject in the world.

Regarding the relation between discourse and desire, Foucault and Lacan agree (although for different reasons)[8] that sex presupposes discourse founded on the promise and possibility of truth. Different truths may be yielded but in the end desire is situated similarly, outside discourse, notwithstanding that its interpellation and traversal is ultimately needed when attending to desire. For Foucault discourse frames desire as itself a discourse which entraps the subject, thereby enabling relations of authority to be perpetually reproduced and circulated. In this scenario desire is understood against the backdrop of already existing power relations. Desires are taken up because they appear already structurally *desirable* to the subject. An example of this given by Foucault is how the sexed subject is constructed within the dominant ideology of heteronormativity in which the body speaks, but only via power relations brokered by an authoritative voice within discourse.

To understand what Foucault means by the emergence of discourse as it pertains to the sexed body, we must include his conception of power as referring to which are historically, strategically constructed:

> Power is not a thing, an institution, an aptitude or an object. Power describes relations of force, and as such is a nominal concept: One needs to be nominalistic, no doubt: power is not an institution, and not a structure; neither it is a certain strength we are endowed with; it is the name one attributes to a complex strategical situation in a particular society.[9]

For Foucault power consists of the wider social body interwoven with institutions and activities which bring about knowledge including sex and sexualities. What frames power as *power* are the resistances which initially motivated its hegemony, yet such is its ultimate inherence it can appear to be neutral—this is a hallmark of Foucault's account of power. For him, although power is not tangible, it has tangible institutional effects and articulations in every facet of human activity: sex, family, education, medicine, punishment, and so on. In deciphering power Foucault claims that, being invested in the body as an object to be desired, power negates or cancels the potential to discover the self because as subjects we always perceive ourselves in relation to the power already invested within us by discourses of authority. We only have the ability to recognize ourselves only in ways which speak to or resist imprisoning power structures. Within this circulation of power truth for the subject is determined solely by institutional, cultural, and historical phenomena. Thus Foucault's radical position portrays the effect of power as historical, historicizing, and totalizing.

Here Foucault's theory of the subject takes an interesting turn regarding its implications for desire. In his famous dialogue with Noam Chomsky, moderated by Fons Elders, Foucault does not discount the existence of human nature but insists that it emerges from specific cultural and historical practices (1974).[10] In the same interview Foucault then also argues against creativity, universal values, justice, idealism, and so on. What makes this interview so memorable and important today is not so much its confounding of Chomsky and Elders as the strength of Foucault's conviction—that defining the self in terms of a human nature (whatever that might be) merely endorses existing underlying social, historical, cultural, and political universals. The problem, states Foucault, is that these are not universal at all but simply attributes of social life and nothing more. Furthermore, since these supposed universals may be used to support oppressive hegemonies they should be argued against. He gives the example of the university tasked with inventing disciplines to prop up some rules while negating others.[11] Foucault is not here being cynical—rather, he is pointing out that it is precisely the role of an institution to be tasked to provide the content required by the power it has been set up to serve.

On this Foucault and Lacan are in only partial agreement. It is well-known that Lacan was dismissed from the IPA because of his unorthodox clinical practices, thus prompting him to set up his own clinical seminar and training pathway, only to quash when realizing that this hinted at institutional methods which spoke to the master of the university discourse. For Lacan, the aim has always been for psychoanalysis to be socially viable and acceptable, whereas for Foucault, the goal is critical thinking: both remained skeptical that the university could reliably undertake these important tasks.

Where does this leave their respective positions on desire? While both thinkers were privileged intellectuals, they certainly stood with conviction in the name of something bigger than themselves. Foucault has a documented history of political struggle in the area of same-sex rights in France and Lacan paid the price for practicing a more experimental psychoanalysis. Foucault and Lacan certainly put desire directly to work and in so doing ask the question "How does desire provoke the subject—'what does desire, *desire*?'"

An important if enigmatic aspect to Lacan's theory of desire is its working of desire via the *objet a*, where in reaching toward truth desire and drive don't need to be always antagonistic. For Lacan, it is the hard work of speaking one's unconscious in the clinic which constitutes a creative moment, without which desire cannot be read. In this experience of desire pleasure is sustained in part through the experience of displeasure. For Foucault however, desire is simply a production of pleasure locatable through language. In the dialogue between Foucault and Chomsky, Foucault makes the poignant claim that creativity cannot contribute toward the emergence of truth. Desire which propels creativity cannot reveal truths because these are already politicized forms of social, cultural, and historical practice. Thus, for Foucault there is nothing essential about desire for creativity because it is already constructed and invested, as is the truth which it signifies.

These two approaches to reading desire are not as disparate as they might appear, they are simply *situated* differently. Foucault situates his reading of pleasure and desire in the Symbolic, whereas for Lacan, desire lies very much in the realm of the Real from which the symptom infiltrates the consciousness of the subject, thereby permitting a reading of desire. In psychoanalysis interrogation of the symptom—putting it to work—allows a specific entry into the Real and hopefully relieves the analysand at the point where "unpleasurable pleasure" becomes unbearable. For Lacan the praxis of psychoanalysis is an entry into subjective truth via a different kind of knowledge which the analysand can take up in relation to desire. Foucault however simply rejected psychoanalysis as a passing fad, as itself an unrelieved symptom of vast and unrelenting desire. The theories of both are still very much contested today.

Thus far desire has been interrogated via the conduit of pleasure. If we allow that there is pleasure in the question of desire thereby presenting desire as the cause of itself—that is, desire *desires* desire—we arrive at an enigma complex enough without throwing Foucault into the mixture. For Foucault, desire is understood in the masters discourse, the one offering knowledge, whereas for Lacan desire sits within the analysts discourse, the one in which desire is unconscious *savior*. Put this way, desire is given a troublingly inconsistent name.

Yet for both Lacan and Foucault there exists a duty to desire, that it be commanded by the law thereby enabling its traversal. From the perspective of the neurotic desire is a transgression, a desire for unlawfulness, which inevitably leads to guilt. As Braunstein puts it,

> Inverting the Freudian formula, one can say the Oedupis complex (a dream, according to Lacan) is heir to the superego, the primitive and ferocious superego that proffers the unacceptable and impossible order to *jouir*.[12]

Joan Copjec's 1994 reading of desire mediates Foucault and Lacan by proposing that desire challenges the possibility of multiple positions, not merely subjective choices. For example, the "guilty versus useful" pleasures binary provides for the subject a classification from which desire can be oriented and thus read as part of an architecture of desire. Guilt and usefulness enable a "dressing" of desire, cloaking it so as to (initially at least) make it functional. For Copjec (as for Foucault and Lacan) duty is what renders desire an ethical procedure for the subject in which desire is not necessarily a useful *thing* because not everything that is useful is pleasurable. Yet the utility of desire certainly has its uses. What Copjec is getting at here regarding desire as an ethical procedure is that even under the superego imperative of utility, even if for a moment attention to one's desire is absolutely for the common good, one can still interrogate it in Lacanian terms. It is at this conjuncture that Copjec's Lacan becomes Foucauldian:

> The position of psychoanalysis is often the reverse of the way people ordinarily think of it. I'm thinking at the moment of Foucault, specifically, who is of course no ordinary person but donned the mask of one in his *History of Sexuality* to criticise psychoanalysis not on the level of what Freud or Lacan actually said, but on the level of doxa, that is, of what others have said psychoanalysis said. Throughout *the History of Sexuality* Foucault focuses on the "repressive

> hypothesis" of psychoanalysis and argues that Freud colludes in the modern attempt to "out" sexuality, to make subjects "confess" it, as though sex were a secret identity that had to be openly declared and thus easily monitored. The first problem is that Foucault pays no attention to primary repression and builds his whole argument on the far less radical idea of secondary repression. If one begins from the premise of primary repression, it is impossible to suppose that sex can be "outed," that it can be revealed. Sex is, rather, a negativity; it cannot therefore found a subject's positive identity. More, Foucault makes psychoanalysis out to be a kind of "culturist" theory, that is, a theory of the way cultural or social forces "make up" or produce people.[13]

Knowing what one needs to sacrifice or support is crucial in seeking an ethical pleasure-identity. However, as Copjec rightly states, "the psychoanalytic subject, in short, being subject to a principal *beyond* pleasure, *is not driven to seek his own good*" (1994, 87; emphasis in original). Copjec is revealing something in ourselves of both Foucault and Lacan: desire is not an index for the common good but rather one for invention or discovery of a new knowledge. Here Copjec, like Foucault and Lacan, inevitably comes up against the sexed subject of desire as one who deliberately disrupts the stability of sex and sexual difference via their singular desire:

> We could put it this way: *male and female, like being, are not predicates, which means that rather than increasing our knowledge of the subject, they qualify the mode of the failure of our knowledge.*[14]

It is in the failure of our ability to properly grasp language that our knowledge of the sexed subject of desire falls short. In his controversial summation of this missed encounter Lacan claims that *there is no sexual relation* (*il n'y a pas de rapport sexuel*)[15] and later that "through the mediation of masks, the masculine and the feminine meet in the most acute, most intense way."[16] Here Lacan is bringing together the sexed body with the fantasy of the sexual encounter as an enigma: it is not so much a matter of sex which brings people together but rather the fantasy that it can, which sets up desire and compels us to take up the question of desire as a fantasy of the Other: *I have to imagine what the other wants from me in order to orient my desire in such a way that I am desirable.* For Lacan "between male and female human beings there is no such thing as an instinctive relationship because all sexuality is marked by the signifier."[17] For him, sex will always lure desire and simultaneously miss the mark, but this failure neither prevents nor subdues the will toward subjective desire for being in the position of the Other's longing. The sexed subject is always—and should be—vacillating between ambivalence and the desire to naturalize the category of sex. In this way the subject ensures that sex always "sticks" to the subject; it is always "sticking as a category of being intrinsic to subjectivity".

We cannot be indifferent to sex as a signifier. As Alenka Zupančič points out, being used in so many different ways and contexts, sex is a signifier which gets played around with all the time; it is *nonsense* as well as jouissance.[18] For Zupančič sex provides the much needed short circuit the subject craves: it is both a way in and way out of the ontological conundrum of naturalization. Yet it is the very signifier which causes so much anxiety (because in the end jouissance can't be denaturalized) and returning trauma of disavowal. Sex is the perfect exception which allows for a subject's unconscious repeating of the symptom. For Zupančič sex can be ontologized within varying layers of repression and denial where it is opposed to any intellectual meaning. Zupančič's ontology is in some ways a return to Freud—sex being the foundation of the death drive which, via the momentary release of repression, allows a tolerable life.[19] That is, because of the antagonism or opposition between the ego (death instincts) and sex (life instincts), we may try to die on our own terms all the while knowing that we can't even live on them. It is specifically this anxiety which enables us to revisit the question of desire as also a question of sovereignty. Desire being situated the other side of inertia of being satisfied, contributes to the crisis of the subject and sex is the signifier upon which this crisis hinges.

What then can be said about desire in relation to the trajectory of the ontology of sex starting with Freud via Lacan and Foucault to Copjec and Zupančič? We have on the face of it, two competing discourses. For Foucault the act of sex and the negotiation of sexuality are settled wholly through the function of knowledge of desire and pleasure. By contrast Lacan determines that what structures the sexed subject and sexuality is a will to the jouissance of fantasy, notwithstanding that this is a non-relation. Furthermore, the sticky matter of sex is a troubling signifier of desire which, like it or not, the subject must grapple with. Sex plays a role in orienting the discursive flow of desire in which it *is* the discursive event whose "truth" underlies all conventions and hegemonies.

Given these contrary positions how can the problematic of sex, designated a category of sexuality, be addressed? Not as is currently the case where sex within the social bond is oriented through collective agency and identity politics, but perhaps rather as a space which is libidinally driven toward the unknowability of sex. As Lacan makes abundantly clear, sex is a bodily and psychic ontology which extricates itself from jouissance into desire. The order of desire is a question of how one takes up the Phallus in discourse. For the divided subject such a state of exception beckons desire as an ontological question yet at the same time signals an ultimate impasse: we are stuck with sex. Copjec and Zupančič make sex the exception for such a reading of desire, the very state upon which we can not only think desire itself but also consider desire an extimate space. It is both inside and outside the subject, intrinsic to being yet already socially and politically set up. This location of sex is like the bug crawling on the Möbius strip of desire; sex makes us lose our way and forget where we are while trying to see beyond the obvious. Sex is the discursive eruption from which desire emanates, momentarily revealing itself and only then thrusting the subject back into a discursive flow of trying to make sense of the self in the world. Being a sexed subject of desire is no easy task even when sex is considered as the state of exception which nevertheless marks desire.

NOTES

1. Robin Lakoff, *Language and Women's Place* (New York and Toronto: Colophon, 1975): 3.
2. Sigmund Freud, *Beyond the Pleasure Principle*, translated by James Strachey (New York and London: Norton, 1920).
3. It is important to note that for Foucault it is the very interpellation of discourse which allows for collective social and political transformation. Interestingly, this conviction can be said to be foregrounded by none other than Ferenczi who also claimed that nothing serves to resist inevitable change because it is the phantasy of difference that provides the foundation of the drive. Luis Izcovich offers a more in-depth discussion of Ferenczi's idealism in Luis Izcovitch, *The Marks of a Psychoanalysis* (London: Karnac, 2015).
4. Jacques Lacan, *Le Séminaire. Livre XVII. L'envers de la psychanalyse*, 1969-1970, ed. Jacques-Alain Miller (Paris: Seuil, 1991): 17.
5. Jacques Lacan, "Conférence à Genève sur le symptôme." Les *Block-Notes de la psychanalyse* (Brussels, 1975).
6. Michele Foucault, "Truth and Power," *The History of Sexuality*, Power/Knowledge, trans. Robert Hurley (London: Allen Lane, 1979), 131.
7. Michele Foucault, "The Will to Knowledge," *The History of Sexuality* (London: Penguin, 1976), 68.
8. Whereas for Foucault the sexed body is interpellated within a dominant ideology, Lacan's position is that we are all subjects of jouissance which, because of our stake in the social bond, needs to be repressed.
9. Foucault, *The History of Sexuality*, 93.
10. Fons Elders, *Reflexive Water: The Basic Concerns of Mankind, "Human Nature: Justice versus Power"* (London: Souvenir Press, 1974).
11. Lysenko's bogus theory of genetics in Stalinist Russia is a perfect example.
12. Nestor Braunstein, *Jouissance. A Lacanian Concept*, trans. Silvia Rosman (New York: SUNY Press, 2006), 246.
13. Joan Copjec, *Read My Desire. Lacan against the Historicists* (Cambridge and New York: MIT Press, 1994), 190.

14. Copjec, *Read My Desire*, 212 (emphasis in original).

15. Jacques Lacan, *Le Séminaire. Livre XVII. L'envers de la psychanalyse*, 1969-1970, ed. Jacques-Alain Miller (Paris: Seuil, 1991), 134.

16. Jacques Lacan, *Encore: The Seminar of Jacques Lacan Book XX: On Feminine Sexuality, The Limit of Love and Knowledge*, 1972-1973, trans. Bruce Fink (London: Norton, 1991), 107.

17. Jaques Lacan, "Conférence à Genève sur le symptôme."

18. Alenka Zupančič, *What Is Sex?* (Cambridge: MIT Press, 2017).

19. See Freud, *Beyond the Pleasure Principle.*

REFERENCES

Braunstein, Nestor. *Jouissance. A Lacanian Concept*, trans. Silvia Rosman. New York: SUNY Press, 2006.

Copjec, Joan. *Read my Desire. Lacan Against the Historicists*. Cambridge and New York: MIT Press, 1994.

Copjec, Joan and Chubbs, Colby. "Psychoanalysis and Consequences," *CHIASMA*, 6, no. 1 (2020): 189–203.

Elders, Fons. *Reflexive Water: The Basic Concerns of Mankind, 'Human Nature: Justice versus Power.'* London: Souvenir Press, 1974.

Foucault, Michel. "The Will to Knowledge," *The History of Sexuality*. London: Penguin, 1976.

Foucault, Michel. "An Introduction," *The History of Sexuality,* trans. Robert Hurley. London: Allen Lane, 1979.

Foucault, Michel. "Truth and Power," *The History of Sexuality*, Power/Knowledge, trans. Robert Hurley. London: Allen Lane, 1979.

Freud, Sigmund. *Beyond the Pleasure Principal*, trans. James Strachey. New York and London: Norton, 1920.

Izcovich, Luis. *The Marks of a Psychoanalysis*. London: Karnac, 2015.

Lacan, Jacques. "Conférence à Genève sur le symptôme." Les *Block-Notes de la psychanalyse*. Brussels, 1975.

Lacan, Jacques. *Encore: The Seminar of Jacques Lacan Book XX: On Feminine Sexuality, The Limit of Love and Knowledge*, 1972-1973, trans. Bruce Fink. London: Norton, 1991.

Lacan, Jacques. *Le Séminaire. Livre XVII. L'envers de la psychanalyse*, 1969-1970, ed. Jacques-Alain Miller. Paris: Seuil, 1991.

Lacan, Jacques. *The Four Fundamental Concepts of Psycho-analysis*, 1973, trans. Alan Sheridan. New York: Routledge, 2018.

Lakoff, Robin. *Language and Woman's Place*. New York and Toronto: Colophon, 1975.

Zupančič, Alenka. *What is Sex?* Cambridge: MIT Press, 2017.

Chapter 8

Twisted (A Tribute)

Foucault, Deleuze, and the Rhizomatic Book

Lynne Huffer

Chacun envoie sa flèche dans la cible de l'autre.
Each one sends their arrow into the target of the other.
—Gilles Deleuze, 1985

As for the "*Envois*" themselves, I do not know if their reading is bearable.
—Jacques Derrida, 1980

ENVOI (FOR ALEXA)

Alexa Cucopulos was my student: a brilliant poet-scholar who passed away, suddenly, on April 25, 2020. She was 25 years old, a doctoral student at Duke, dying unexpectedly, in the midst of thought, alone in her apartment in Durham. As an undergraduate philosophy major at Emory, Alexa wrote an honors thesis about death, *poiesis*, and mise en abyme in Foucault. Alexa wrote, "The shard of Foucault I am reading here is Foucault the poet and Foucault the reader of poetry."[1] She found in Foucault's poetic writing an ethics of transformation: "The experience of one's own epistemic limits forces a subject to split from oneself, or more aptly, within oneself, and look back on oneself as strange."[2] Alexa saw *The History of Sexuality Volume 1* as a "poem-life" of the species body where the "constant undoing and remaking of the self is an ongoing resistance to biopower."[3] She explored that resistance from the perspective of death and mourning, citing, for example, Eve Kosofsky Sedgwick's obituaries for her friends lost to AIDS. For Alexa, time was twisted. Writing about *Sexuality One*, she already knew, wiser than her years, that "we are made to mourn ourselves in the future anterior perspective the book provides in its last pages."[4]

Advising us to mourn ourselves "while we are still alive,"[5] Alexa opens her readers to "the possibility of something that is other than us."[6] Proleptically describing her own mourning by others, she leaves us "undone," our "bodies folded over in madness, in grief, in vigil."[7] And yet, she reminds us on the very last page, this mourning "leaves a space open for our remaking, and undoing again. This recursive, spiraling process is a constant resistance to life as bios, a constant process of seeing life otherwise."[8]

Reading through their grief, people have told me they hear Alexa in my writing. Her voice, murmuring, becomes a mirror. Is this what Alexa meant when she wrote about "looking back on oneself as strange" and "seeing life otherwise"?

Deleuze wrote *Foucault* (1986) as a homage to his friend in the wake of his friend's untimely death. Mirroring Deleuze, I write this chapter as a homage to Alexa. In "Language to Infinity," Foucault describes writing as an age-old defense against death: "Headed toward death, language turns back upon itself; it encounters something like a mirror."[9] We might compare this description to what Iddo Dickmann calls a "static mirror."[10] But "from the depths of [that] mirror," Foucault writes, "another language can be heard."[11] That other language is the dynamic mirror whose language is the speech of the "bard":[12] a poetic speech that doubles the mirror to infinity. As I read Alexa, I hear that speech in the same way Foucault's Ulysses hears, in *The Odyssey*, a story about himself in the mouth of a stranger. Like Ulysses, I receive Alexa's words as a mise en abyme, "in the gesture of a woman to whom the dead body of a hero is brought after a battle."[13]

From the Latin *inviare*—to send on the way—this is my *envoi*: like a kick-off, an *envoi de lettres*, a dedication at the end of a ballad.[14] *Chacun* envoie *sa flèche dans la cible de l'autre*.[15] This *envoi* as a sending of arrows, crossing: a Deleuzian whale line, twisting like Foucault.

The whale line doubles back, catching me in its coils.

Mise en abyme

"*Chacun envoie sa flèche dans la cible de l'autre*."[16] Each one sends an arrow into the target of the other, Deleuze says in his 1985 course on Foucault, a tribute to his friend following Foucault's death from AIDS in 1984. Deleuze calls this exchange of arrows *le plus beau*—the most beautiful thing in Foucault. What is this exchange, and what are its stakes? How are we to read these *envois* between a still living Deleuze and his recently departed friend? Does death make their reading unbearable? Or might reading the exchange activate something other than longing for a life without loss, something other than desire for that which is always already lost? Is the possibility of another desire—desire as affirmation—what Deleuze means by *le plus beau*?

I explore these questions here through the lens of mise en abyme, a narratological concept with ontological implications. Specifically, thinking *en abyme* opens what Foucault calls "the thought of the outside," where thinking refers to something other than the bringing of concepts into the interiority of the mind.[17] Writing about Foucault, Deleuze calls that extroversion of the thinking subject "the *twisting line of the outside* spoken by Melville."(Emphasis added)[18] This line of the outside is a mise en abyme that transforms psychoanalytic desire-as-lack into the Nietzschean eternal return of eros's arrow, what Dickmann calls a mobile mirroring. Importantly, in both Foucault and Deleuze the eternal return includes empirical readers in its "complicated coils, twisting and writhing . . . in almost every direction."[19] To submit oneself to that almost-unbearable reading is an "ontological decision"[20] to access other-than-psychological ways of thinking or, as Alexa put it, "to look back on oneself as strange."[21]

But what exactly is a mise en abyme? In its most familiar literary form, the mise en abyme is a work's interior, self-replicating mirror; it denotes "a segment of [a] work that resembles, mimics or is even identical to the literary work of art as a whole."[22] Well-known examples include *Hamlet*'s play within a play, *1001 Nights*, the *Decameron*'s nested tales, Russian matryoshka dolls, and the Dutch Droste cacao powder tin (figure 8.1).

In 1893, in one of his journals, André Gide famously illustrated this static conception of mise en abyme with the image of embedded heraldic shields (figure 8.2).

As Lucien Dällenbach explains in his classic work on the topic, *The Mirror in the Text* (1977), this structure is lacunary: "A's acceptance of the ability to be reproduced produces *a lacuna* within the identity of A. . . . The addition of B to A in fact *subtracts* from it."[23] Each shield in the series "can only take on the form the previous shield prescribes for it by incorporating a new shield, which, in turn, makes a hole in it."[24] In my previous work on the stylistic dimensions of Foucault's writing I have brought out this lacunary conception of mise en abyme. In a 2012 essay, I described *The History of Sexuality Volume 1* as a nested set of reported speech acts that stage the instability of the subject who speaks by exploiting the ventriloquisms of free indirect discourse.[25] In *Foucault's Strange Eros* (2020), I focused specifically on the chiastic structure of mise en abyme in Foucault to describe the "I" as a temporally contingent, embedded set of connections rather than as a substance. Undone by the self-hollowing subtractions of the *abyme*, the subject dissolves into the endless murmur of language reflecting itself.

How does this focus on mise en abyme help us to read desire in the Foucault-Deleuze exchange? As a narratological concept, mise en abyme is most

Figure 8.1 Mise en abyme in Cacao Powder Tin. *Source*: Public domain.

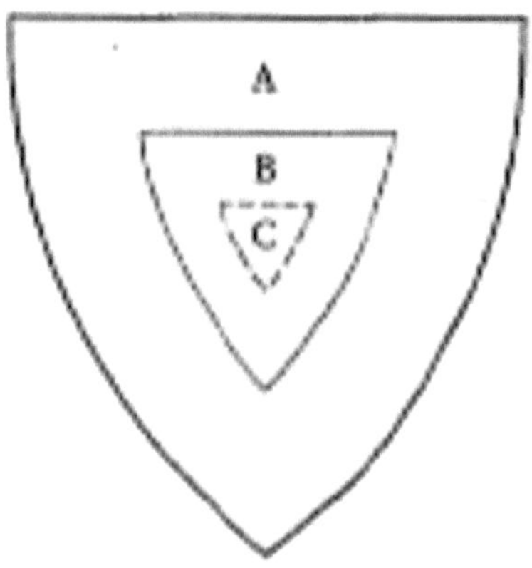

Figure 8.2 Mise en abyme in Gide's Shields. *Source*: Public domain.

strongly associated with the French New Novel of the 1950s and 1960s. In *The Little Crystalline Seed*, Iddo Dickmann draws on that literary legacy to show how continental philosophy took up mise en abyme during the same period to develop a post-Heideggerian ontology. Dickmann convincingly argues that this ontology finds its most radical expression in Deleuze, a thinker who explores "a type of Being which Heidegger's account does not have a grasp of."[26] If the classic mise en abyme structure is that of the static mirror we find in Gide's shields—a story within a story or an image within an image that hollows it out from within—Dickmann demonstrates how Maurice Blanchot, Wolfgang Iser, and especially Deleuze transform the static mirror into a "mobile mirroring" that replaces Gide's heraldic, lacunary conception. Dickmann draws on the new New Novel of the 1970s and 1980s and the Klein form of mathematical topology to describe an "exchangeability of narrative levels"[27] that does away with the static "ground" of lacunary introversion. Importantly, mobile mirroring and the Klein bottle imply "a radical extroversion . . . that characterizes the 'rhizomatic book'"[28] as an "assemblage with the outside." If that assemblage is a mirror—a mise en abyme—its true object of reflection is neither the subject gazing at the mirror nor the subject's specular reflection as an object, but the very "middle" between them, their juxtaposition.[29]

Chacun envoie sa flèche dans la cible de l'autre.[30] Deleuze's book, *Foucault*, written in the wake of Foucault's death, is rhizomatic: a mise en abyme in the dynamic sense described by Dickmann. There has been much debate about whether or not Deleuze's book offers a "faithful" representation of Foucault. But such debate misses the fact that mobile mirroring has nothing to do with a logic of representation. "Representation fails to capture the affirmed world of difference," Deleuze writes in *Difference and Repetition*.[31] Writing is not a representational act but an experiment in relation: "writing as a form of thinking rather than a form of representation."[32] Thus the nonrepresentational "object" of *Foucault* is neither Foucault nor Deleuze but the very "middle" between them: an exchange of arrows at the point of their crossing. As in the Klein bottle, that point of crossing is not an edge: the exchange happens in a fourth dimension we cannot experience even though we know it's there.[33] In the ontological register of the rhizomatic book whose "narrative level overlaps with the empirical world," Deleuze's *Foucault* does not "represent" Foucault but constructs Foucault as "a real that is yet to come," "a new type of reality."[34] We are urged in *Foucault*, as in all Deleuze's writing, to "make a rhizome":[35] Captain Ahab *is* Melville who *is* Deleuze who *is* Foucault becoming whale.

This chapter is also an experiment in writing-as-thinking rather than a representation of philosophers and their concepts. It is driven by desire—for understanding, for something lost, for the voice of a dear student now gone—even as desire (not a Foucauldian word) dissipates at the point of our crossing. Inspired by Deleuze's flat ontology and Oulipian practices of "generative" writing, my chapter tracks the "interplay between sentences, words, and even letters"[36] as the mobile mirroring of mise en abyme. As a rhizomatic book, *Foucault* offers a mirror where I can see myself "as [an] open-ended system always on the verge of becoming-other."[37]

In reading *Foucault* as an open-ended being, I too risk "becoming-whale."[38] "We are all too familiar with the dangers of the line of flight, and with its ambiguities. The risks are ever-present."[39] The arrow is a harpoon point at the end of a whale line that twists and coils, catching me, reading, in its recursive flight. I bear this reading, this eternal return, however unbearable it might be. I receive its arrows. Eros undoes me into a different listening. Making rhizomes, I hear Alexa: mise en abyme of a speech after death.

Foucault (Ad Hoc Encounter with a Sentence)

Deleuze's line in *Foucault* is twisted: he identifies a recursive, twisting movement in the trajectory of Foucault's thought. This twisting of the line puts Deleuze's reading out of sync with typical periodizations of Foucault's work that insist on a developmental chronology of early, middle, and late phases. Instead, Deleuze presents Foucault as a thinker who returns, picking up earlier threads but from different angles, through different lenses, heading off on different paths. This retroaction describes a movement of recoil, with the ethical valence Charles Scott gives it in his book on ethics in Nietzsche, Foucault, and Heidegger.[40] In Scott, as in Foucault, there is a kind of questioning—a recoil—that puts in question the body of values that led to the questioning: the questioning is dependent on the very thing it questions. The relation between that thing and the questioning constitutes the groundless ground of ethics. Ethics begins, again and again, in this juxtaposition: in the middle of ethics as a question.

In line with such an ethics, here I read Deleuze's *Foucault* by starting in the middle, on page 43 (51 in the French original), at the end of Part One of a book that is split in two. Part One, "From the Archive to the Diagram," includes "A New Archivist (*The Archeology of Knowledge*)" and "A New Cartographer (*Discipline and Punish*);" Part Two, "Topology: 'Thinking Otherwise,'" indirectly invokes the Klein bottle of mathematical topology as well as the Foucauldian "otherwise" at the end of Alexa's thesis. Part Two includes three chapters: "Strata or Historical Formations: The Visible and the Articulable (Knowledge)," "Strategies or the Non-Stratified: The Thought of the Outside (Power)," and "Foldings, or the Inside of Thought (Subjectivation)." *Foucault* also includes an appendix "On the Death of Man and Superman."

Starting in the middle, at the end of Part One, my method is inspired by Deleuze's approach to Foucault in his course, a method he describes as *tâtonnement*. *Tâtonnement*, from *tastoner*, to touch or caress, is what we do when we feel our way through a dark space: a slow, hesitating, tactile, ad hoc thinking that bumps into obstacles, gently retreats, hovers over details, moves on again, returning to more ad hoc encounters. Deleuze reads Foucault's texts through a method of *tâtonnement*, linking this tactile, tentative approach to a kind of fidelity: a trust in the author. "*Faire confiance à l'auteur, ça veut dire la même chose que tâtonner*," he says. "To trust the author means the same thing as *tâtonner*." Deleuze contrasts this tactile trust with "the voices of objection" we, philosophers especially, tend to hear in our heads. We must quiet those voices in ourselves, he says. We must silence the voices that want to say, too quickly: "Oh, but there, there's something that doesn't work." He wants us, like Nietzsche, to ruminate: to chew our cud, to slowly turn things over, attending to those things that only strike us after lingering with them for a while: the frequency of words, the style, the author's obsessions. All of this, Deleuze tells his students, is *tâtonnement*: a twisted, tactile, trusting method.

In *Foucault*, Deleuze writes in a mise en abyme of his own writing that "the book and its outside can only encounter upon a ground made up of their ad hoc encounter."[41] *My tâtonnement*, an ad hoc encounter, starts in "the very middle" of *Foucault* with a single sentence toward the beginning of the last paragraph of "A New Cartographer." Here is the sentence: the history of forms, archive, is doubled by a becoming of forces, diagram.[42] This ad hoc encounter with a sentence in the middle is my doubled *envoi*, repeating my earlier *envoi* for Alexa: it sends me on the way, again, offering me the beginning of a line, again, that will twist and double back, as whale lines do. Deleuze invokes, later in the paragraph, the *twisting line of the outside* spoken of by Melville.[43]

In the radical exchange of narratological levels that characterizes the rhizomatic book, the whale line simultaneously guides me through *Foucault*, captures the whale in *Moby Dick*, and opens to the thought of the outside. As Melville writes in *Moby Dick*, "The whale-line folds the whole boat in its complicated coils, twisting and writhing around it in almost every direction" (page number). It drags harpooners and readers overboard to their death. It drags their corpses through the water.

My line through the paragraph twists, recoiling back from Melville to my original sentence: "The history of forms, *archive*, is doubled by a becoming of forces, *diagram*."[44] On a first reading this sentence seems to neatly "capture" the theme of Part One as the sentence repeats the major elements of Part One's title: "From the *Archive* to the *Diagram*." But to read the sentence in this whale-capturing way would be to miss its rhizomatic function. As one point of crossing in the dynamic line of a mobile mirror, this sentence is already twisting and writhing in different directions.

Let me start with the most obvious twist in the line: the parallel, double structure of the sentence, reflecting the action of the verb, "to double," which divides the sentence in two. "The history of forms, archive, is *doubled* by a becoming of forces, diagram."[45] The double structure speaks both to the sentence's symmetry and to doubling as a kind of mirroring that allows us to see the sentence as the static mirror, a mise en abyme of Part One's overall theme: history, forms, and archive on one side and becoming, forces, and diagram on the other, with the first half taken up and reflected back by the second. But in that reflective structure within the sentence—a mise en abyme of the sentence as mise en abyme of Part One—something apparently static—history, forms, archive—is made dynamic—becoming, forces, diagram. On the level of the text itself, the self-doubling repetition within Part One and within a single segment of Part One that also mirrors Part One as a whole (my starting sentence) produces a qualitative shift.

How are we to understand such a qualitative shift, from archive to diagram, as ontological? Throughout *Foucault*, Deleuze offers terms to describe the diagram: "an abstract machine," "a spatiotemporal multiplicity," and "no longer an auditory or visual archive but a map, a cartography that is coextensive with the whole social field."[46] He gives the plague model and the leper model in Foucault as examples of diagrams. Dickmann explains how maps and diagrams are rhizomatic. "Any rhizome," Dickmann writes, citing Deleuze,

> comprises a peculiar "map" that is "itself a part of [that] rhizome," reflecting its very reflection, a *mise en abyme*. Being incommensurable, lacking a presupposed shared ground, the book and its outside can only encounter upon a ground made up of their ad hoc encounter.[47]

As a rhizomatic book, *Foucault* is generative in this specific sense. The leaps between levels are both ad hoc and ontological because they generate openings in the literal encounter between reader and book.

Recoiling back to the sentence that immediately precedes my starting sentence, the line finds such an opening in Foucault: "Nothing in Foucault is really closed off."[48] Juxtaposed with my starting sentence, along with what readers "know" about Foucault, this "preceding" sentence is startling. The assertion that nothing in Foucault is really closed off disregards common wisdom about Foucault as a thinker of closure and confinement: not just physical, bodily confinement, but the confinement of our thinking. From the Great Confinement and the Cartesian *ratio* in *History of Madness* to the panoptical subjection that is our carceral rationality in *Discipline and Punish* to the cruel debunking of an anti-repressive conception of sexual freedom in *The History of Sexuality Volume 1*, it is hard to find a "way out" in Foucault. Indeed, how can there be a "way out" when, as Foucault puts it in *Discipline and Punish*, "there is no outside"?[49] Whether as asylum or panopticon or modern sexual subjectivity, Foucault's prison-forms feel like lockdown.

But "nothing in Foucault is really closed off,"[50] Deleuze tells us, *tâtonnant*. Unlike most readers of Foucault, Deleuze's *Foucault* generates in Foucault a thought of openings: a thought, in Foucault, of Melville's *twisting line of the outside*. As Dickmann explains, in the logic of mise en abyme as a dynamic mirror, the outside *is* an opening. The rhizomatic book "marks a radical case of extroversion."[51] It "'transcodes' rather than encodes—it signifies in a yet to come code for yet to come recipients."[52] Thus, Deleuze writes in *Foucault*, "the outside is always an opening on to a future."[53] Even more provocatively, the outside offers "the possibility of 'resistance.'"[54] "*Resistance comes first*":[55] Alexa's Foucauldian word, "resistance,"[56] in the last sentence of her thesis, returns here, *en abyme*, in this Foucault-Deleuze crossing. Deleuze writes, "The final word on power is that *resistance comes first* (Emphasis in original), to the extent that power relations operate completely within the diagram, while resistances necessarily operate in a direct relation with the outside from which the diagrams emerge."[57]

If Foucault is a diagram, Alexa is "the outside" from which that diagram emerged. Such resistance triggers another twist of the whale line, a circling back to my starting sentence: "The history of forms, archive, is doubled by a becoming of forces, diagram."[58] Twisting and writhing, that starting sentence will return again and again in different permutations across *Foucault*'s pages, generating new diagrams and new outsides. To take one instance of such permutations within the rhizomatic book, in Part Two's "Strategies, or the Non-Stratified," the starting sentence on page 43 is repeated on page 85, with a difference, in condensed, reversed, and italicized form: "*There is a becoming of forces that doubles history.*" (Emphasis in original)[59]

Circling back from page 85 to the starting sentence, in their repetition the two sentences cross, each segment sending an arrow into the target of the other (figure 8.3).

As this new diagram makes clear, in repeating the starting sentence on page 43, the new sentence on page 85 generates a particular kind of mise en abyme: chiasmus. "The word 'chiasmus,'" Alexa wrote in her thesis, "stems from the Greek word for 'crossing,' and the Greek letter 'chi,' written as 'X.' It is the literal image of a criss-cross."[60] The inverted parallelism of chiasmus—AB, B'A'—creates a configuration whose "parts at once depend upon and negate one another."[61]

This chiastic structure appears, at first glance, to repeat the lacunary (desire as lack) conception of mise en abyme we saw in Gide's shields. Based in

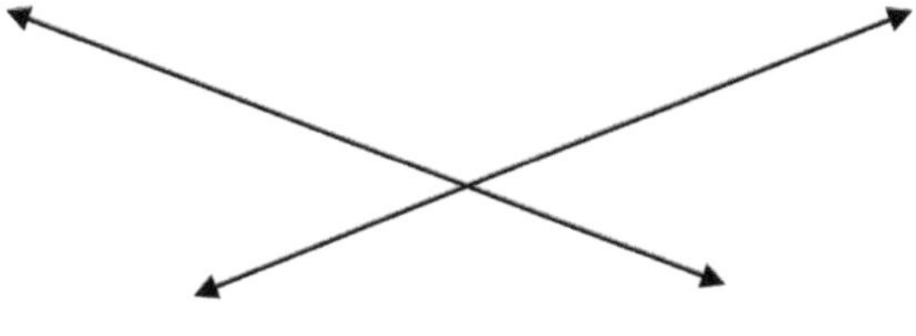

There is a becoming of forces that doubles history. (85)

Figure 8.3 Adapted and drawn by the author based on Deleuze's *"Foucault"*, p. 85.

sameness and negating inversion, chiasmus in this mode performs the operations of the static mirror. But to simply locate chiasmus as a static conception of lacunary repetition in *Foucault*, as I have done here, citing Alexa as the diagram's outside, would be to miss the extroverting movement of eternal return: return that differs. There is no equivalency here between chiasmus in Alexa and chiasmus in *Foucault*. As Deleuze puts it in *Difference and Repetition*, "Nothing is equal."[62] The eternal return is not the return of the *same* but a repetition of difference "shown *differing*." (Emphasis in original)[63] "Eternal return relates to a world of differences implicated one in the other."[64] With eternal return we find ourselves in "a complicated, properly chaotic world *without identity*" (Emphasis in original) [65] where "everything bathes in its difference, its dissimilarity and its inequality, even with itself."[66]

If we read *Foucault* as rhizomatic, we can track this transformation of mise en abyme as lacunary chiasmus (desire as lack) into an ontology of difference (and desire) as affirmation. As suggested by my parenthetical additions, this transformation describes an ontological shift from psychoanalytic desire-as-lack into a Deleuzian affirmative desire where nothing is lost. The fact that such a transformation occurs in *Foucault* is not a betrayal of Foucault but a "faithful" *tâtonnement* attentive to the reverberations of two arrows crossing.

The next sentence in *Foucault*, another mise en abyme of my starting sentence, generates the shift I've just described from lacunary to yes-saying crossing: "There is a becoming of forces not to be confused with the history of forms, because it operates in another dimension."[67] If the previous two sentences on pages 43 and 85 described an exchange of arrows seemingly arrested as an X—a negating, lacunary relation between history/form and becoming/force—here in the new sentence on page 86 the previous sentences return with the movement of becoming. In *another* mise en abyme, the rhetorical movement generated by the sequencing of the three repeated sentences themselves mirrors the "content" of the new sentence, where "a becoming of forces" differentiates itself from "the history of forms." The chiasmus is transformed by that movement of becoming from a "form" to a "diagram" in the Deleuzian sense; it becomes a diagram through the effects of doubling that constitute both the content and the expression of the previous sentences on pages 43 and 85. Each of the two previous sentences is "about" doubling; at the same time, in the book's expression, the starting sentence is "doubled" by the subsequent sentence.

These transformations on the level of both content and expression expose doubling in *Foucault* as effects of "double articulation," a linguistic concept borrowed from the Danish linguist Louis Hjelmslev, invoked by Deleuze at the beginning of Part Two in *Foucault*. Hjelmslev's double articulation refers to the sign function as composed of both "content" and "expression," inseparable as "functives" of the sign function. In *Foucault*, Deleuze borrows "contents and expressions" from Hjelmslev but "appl[ies] them to Foucault in a completely different way."[68] Hjelmslev's double articulation generates, in Deleuze's *Foucault*, an analysis of two distinctive Foucauldian formations: the visible and the articulable. In his 1985 course Deleuze explains that the former is the regime of seeing of the general hospital in *History of Madness* or the prison in *Discipline and Punish*, while the latter is the regime of utterance in medicine (discourse about unreason) and penal law (discourse about delinquency). While one seems to flow from the other, the two regimes of the visible and the articulable—hospital and medical discourse, prison and penal discourse—are not isomorphic. Rather, one doubles the other in a crisscrossing encounter.

This crossing of nonequivalences exposed by the double articulation of the visible and the articulable Deleuze finds in Foucault helps us to see how the seeming stasis of chiastic representation generates the mobile mirroring of chiastic becoming. As we will see, that transformation has ontological significance. Returning to the new sentence on page 86—"There is a becoming of forces not to be confused with the history of forms, because it operates in another dimension"—chiasmus reemerges as sameness made different. What looked like a hole in the ground of a self-replicating shield becomes the generativity of ever-new relations in a "middle" of differences without ground. Retrospectively, the appearance of the new sentence on page 86 exposes the heterogeneity that was covered over by the assumption of rhetorical equality in the static figure of chiasmus.

Thus chiasmus becomes diagram in the Deleuzian sense: diagram as an effect of *doubling*. That doubling is a repetition not in the sense of *extended* quantity or isomorphic multiplications of a thing. Rather, doubling here marks an "*intensive* change in a quality."[69] In other words, as a rhizomatic book, *Foucault* doubles or repeats its own sentences as instances of intensive or exponential change. The archive "doubled" of the starting sentence is not the multiplication of archives (archives X 2) but archive to the power of two (archive2).[70] This exponential change in archive generates the Foucauldian archive as a diagram. In so doing, this "doubling" of archive also produces an ontological shift. Here in *Foucault* doubling is not repetition in quantitative terms according to principles of identity, with the same dimension but different quantities, where a diagram would equal two archives. Rather, repetition here generates an intensive change in a quality: diagram emerges as exponent of archive, archive2, in a different dimension. This sense of doubling as exponential (intensive change, to the power of) aligns with Deleuze's ontology of becoming.[71]

The new sentence makes all of this clear: "There is a becoming of forces not to be confused with the history of forms, *because it operates in another dimension*."[72] In the doublings generated from my starting sentence, "a becoming of forces" opens "the history of forms" to its exponential doubling. The effect of doubling as exponential ("to the power of") is an extroverting intensive change that puts outside as exponent (*ex-ponere*, to put outside) the interiorizing movement of mirroring self-reflection. Doubling "to the power of" is quite literally a thought of the exponent, a thought of the outside. This doubling generates the change in a quality Deleuze calls intensity. It literally generates "a becoming of forces" that "operates in another dimension."[73]

This thought of the exponent as thought of the outside in *Foucault* is explicitly aligned with a conception of the outside Foucault takes up in his 1966 essay on Blanchot, "The Thought of the Outside." The whale line in *Foucault* repeatedly circles back to that essay. In "The Thought of the Outside," Foucault described what he called the thought of thought, or "reflective discourse" (i.e., philosophy) in relation to "literary discourse" or the speech of speech.[74] He described the former, reflective thought, as a discourse which, in repeating itself (thought thinking itself), *confines the outside* by bringing the outside into the interiority of the mind. This conception of thought would correspond to Gide's lacunary shields and the rigid separation of ontological levels we find in the static mirror. By contrast, Foucault describes the latter, literary speech, as a discourse which, in repeating itself (speech speaking itself), "leads us . . . to the outside in which the speaking subject disappears."[75]

In *Foucault*, Deleuze takes up the ontological implications of that essay. Returning to the disjunction or "non-relation [that] is still a relation"[76] of the two elements in the double articulation—the regime of the visible and the regime of the articulable—Deleuze links the "outside" with the gap of that disjunctive relation. "Seeing is thinking, and speaking is thinking, but thinking occurs in the interstice, or the disjunction between seeing and speaking."[77] This "contact with Blanchot" is "the appeal to the outside" as "an 'abstract storm'" that refuses to "reunite the visible and the articulable."[78] Rather than reuniting the interval that separates the two elements of the double articulation, the outside "eats into the interval and forces or dismembers the internal."[79] This dismemberment of "the internal" as the "beautiful interiority" of thinking—the familiar understanding of thinking as the bringing of concepts into the interiority of the mind—produces a "liberation of forces which come from the outside and exist only in a mixed-up state of agitation, modification, and mutation. In truth, they are dice-throws, for thinking involves throwing the dice."[80]

Retrospectively, we can hear Foucault's implicit question in his 1966 essay on Blanchot as a question about the mirroring language of mise en abyme. How does the self-referential discourse of philosophy—thought that thinks itself—be taken to what Deleuze calls "another dimension"? How can thought thinking itself be an experience of thinking's transformation rather than the confinement of thinking? Again, in "Language to Infinity," Foucault offers a clue: "From the depths of the mirror," Foucault writes, "another language can be heard."[81] That other language opens a poetic space of rhizomatic difference, of speech speaking itself: as in the Klein bottle, the thought of the outside as thought of the exponent generates a relation of non-relation, a juxtaposition without edges. This intensive thought is a mobile mapping of the very middle between them: the eternal return as "a world the very ground of which is difference, in which everything rests on disparities, upon differences of differences which reverberate to infinity (the world of intensity)."[82]

Mutual Capture

Do the ontological shifts I've traced in this ad hoc encounter with a rhizomatic sentence in *Foucault* offer, in Deleuzian words, a "faithful" rendering of Foucault's thought? There's no question that Deleuze's Foucault is twisted. But perhaps those twists speak to the recoiling movement of fidelity defined not as the degree to which a representation matches an original. Such a conception would obviously be out of sync with both Deleuze's ontology and Foucault's genealogical approach to difference. If we rethink fidelity as trust, as *tâtonnement*, perhaps we can imagine that hesitating touch intensifying in the disjunctive embrace—a relation of non-relation—in the middle of the rhizomatic book. Such a thinking together makes possible, agonistically, in the gap that separates them, something like what Deleuze calls in his Foucault course a "mutual capture" (*capture mutuelle*), an embrace of fighters (*étreinte de lutteurs*): thinking as erotic struggle, as disjunctive embrace in the space Blanchot called the outside.

In the "mutual capture" that is *Foucault*, Foucault the "new archivist" becomes a poet whose raw material, the archive, should not be confused with the history of forms. Foucault's archive—"the severe poetry of what is said"[83]—is hardly the archive of traditional historians. Rather, the archive generates thought as diagram, thought "to the power of" ad infinitum. In *Foucault*, the archive of positivists is transformed into the generative movement of a relational intensity that opens thinking to the thought of the outside. Correspondingly, the historical a priori—the subject of much debate among Foucault scholars—is not a formal a priori endowed with history. Rather, as Deleuze puts it, "There is . . . a becoming of forces *not to be confused with the history of forms*."[84] Foucault's historical a priori operates, ontologically, "in another dimension."[85]

So too with both the "content" and "expression" of the archive. The content of the archive is not, Foucault tells us in *The Archeology of Knowledge*, the sum of texts and documents a culture has preserved. Nor is its expression the institutional apparatus that makes it possible to record, collect, and store what a culture wishes to remember. The archive is a *practice* that takes place in a gap "*between* the *language* [langue] that defines the system of constructing possible sentences, and the *corpus* that passively collects the words that are spoken."[86] The archive is like the operating system of a computer: the rules that allow some statements and events to "shine, as it were, like stars" while others grow pale and disappear.[87] This conception of the archive is, in effect, rhizomatic. Its purpose is not descriptive but diagnostic: it "deprives us of our continuities and dissipates [our] temporal identity; . . . it breaks the thread of transcendental teleologies; . . . it bursts open the other, the outside."[88]

Renvoi

Deleuze reflects on his friendship with Foucault in an interview:

> When someone you like and admire dies, you sometimes need to draw their picture. Not to glorify them, still less to defend them, not to remember, but rather to produce a final likeness you can find only in death, that makes you realize "that's who they were." A mask, or what he himself called a double, an overlay. . . . It's not a question of points I thought we had in common, or on which we differed. What we shared was bound to be rather indefinite, a sort of background that allowed me to talk with him.[89]

The Foucault-as-poet Alexa and I both loved generated a background that allowed us to think and talk together. The eternal return plunges me again into that background of talk, now doubled and undone by silence. The *renvoi* of death feels like a letter returned to its sender, unopened. Alexa is gone: there can be no more talk between us. The talk-space we once shared no longer holds us: her absence exposes the murmuring background as a groundless mise en abyme. Since Alexa's passing, I have experienced this mise en abyme made real by her death in the mode of the static mirror: a hollow, an abyss, a terrifying void.

But reading *Foucault* with Alexa in this chapter has opened up new possibilities. If Alexa's writing is what remains of my connection to her—of the Foucault-talk we shared—I can take up that writing as a "poem-life" in the archive, doubled as a diagram that opens internalizing lacunary thinking to the thought of the outside. And if, as Deleuze writes, "it is still from the outside that a force affects, or is affected by others,"[90] the force of that diagram is never exhausted. The singular poem-life-diagram that *is* Alexa will continue "to 'draw' new ones."[91]

Not long after her graduation from Emory, Alexa gave me a matryoshka doll as a reminder of the mise en abyme we had shared through years of thinking and writing together. Reading her again, as I have in this chapter, allows

Figure 8.4 Russian Matryoshka Doll "Alexa's Gift." *Source*: Author's own image.

me to reencounter her writing as a gift of nested dolls. That writing targets me, like Deleuze's arrows, in an exchange I now call *le plus beau*: the most beautiful thing in Alexa. Touching this gift, again and again, in my own faithful method of *tâtonnement*, the dolls speak "from the depths of the mirror" in a joyous reverberation where "nothing ends, since nothing has begun, but everything is transformed"[92] (figure 8.4).

NOTES

1. Cucopulos, Alexa. "Poiesis and Death: Foucault's Chiastic Undoing of Life in *The History of Sexuality Volume 1*." Honors Thesis. Philosophy Department, Emory University, 2016, 10.
2. Cucopulos, *Poiesis and Death*, 11.
3. Cucopulos, *Poiesis and Death*, 11.
4. Cucopulos, *Poiesis and Death*, 75.
5. Cucopulos, *Poiesis and Death*, 75.
6. Cucopulos, *Poiesis and Death*, 75.
7. Cucopulos, *Poiesis and Death*, 75.
8. Cucopulos, *Poiesis and Death*, 75.

9. Foucault, Michel. "Language to Infinity." Trans. Donald F. Bouchard and Sherry Simon. In *Essential Works of Foucault, 1954-1984*, ed. James D. Faubion. 3 vols. (New York: New Press, 1998), 2: 89–101.

10. Dickmann, Iddo. *The Little Crystalline Seed: The Ontological Significance of* Mise en Abyme *in Post-Heideggerian Thought* (Albany, NY: SUNY Press, 2019), 12.

11. Foucault, "Language to Infinity," 90.

12. Foucault, "Language to Infinity," 90.

13. Foucault, "Language to Infinity," 90.

14. Derrida, Jacques. *The Post Card: From Socrates to Freud and Beyond*. Trans. Alan Bass (Chicago: University of Chicago Press, 1987). See the translator's introduction, xxi, for a detailed etymology of the *envois* of Derrida's book.

15. Deleuze, course on Foucault, http://www2.univ-paris8.fr/deleuze/article.php3?id_article=403.

16. Deleuze, course on Foucault, http://www2.univ-paris8.fr/deleuze/article.php3?id_article=403.

17. Huffer, Lynne. *Foucault's Strange Eros* (New York: Columbia University Press, 2020), 1–2. Also see Eng, Michael. "Foucault, Blanchot, and Deleuze: Writing the Outside in the University," unpublished manuscript, *Foucault Circle*, April 7, 2018, 3.

18. Deleuze, Gilles. *Foucault*. Trans. Seán Hand (Minneapolis: University of Minnesota Press, 1988), 44.

19. Melville, Herman. Moby-Dick, or The Whale. Herfordshire, UK: Wordsworth Editions, 1993, 234.

20. Foucault, "Preface to Transgression," 75.

21. Cucopulos 11.

22. Dickmann, *The Little Crystalline Seed*, 1.

23. Dällenbach, Lucien. *The Mirror in the Text*. Trans. J. Whitely (Chicago: University of Chicago Press, 1989), 111, emphasis added.

24. Dällenbach, *The Mirror*, 111.

25. Huffer, Lynne. "Foucault and Sedgwick: The Repressive Hypothesis Revisited." *Foucault Studies* 14 (2012): 32.

26. Dickmann, *The Little Crystalline Seed*, 5.

27. Dickmann, *The Little Crystalline Seed*, 33.

28. Dickmann, *The Little Crystalline Seed*, 140.

29. Dickmann, *The Little Crystalline Seed*, 12.

30. Deleuze, course on Foucault, http://www2.univ-paris8.fr/deleuze/article.php3?id_article=403.

31. Deleuze, Gilles. *Difference and Repetition*. Trans. Paul Patton (New York: Columbia University Press, 1994), 55.

32. Hanley, Christopher. "Thinking with Deleuze and Guattari: An Exploration of Writing as Assemblage." *Educational Philosophy and Theory* 51, no. 4 (2019): 414.

33. See Deleuze, Gilles, and Félix Guattari. *A Thousand Plateaus: Capitalism and Schizophrenia*. Trans. Brian Massumi (Minneapolis: University of Minnesota Press, 1987), citing Lovecraft: "The cube and the sphere, of three dimensions, are thus cut

from corresponding forms of four dimensions, which men know only through guesses and dreams" (251). For an explanation of the 4th dimension see Carl Sagan, https://www.youtube.com/watch?v=N0WjV6MmCyM#action=share.

34. Dickmann, *The Little Crystalline Seed*, 206.
35. Deleuze and Guattari, *Thousand Plateaus*, 251.
36. Dickmann, *The Little Crystalline Seed*, 136.
37. Dickmann, *The Little Crystalline Seed*, 136.
38. Deleuze and Guatarri, *Thousand Plateaus*, 243.
39. Deleuze and Guatarri, *Thousand Plateaus*, 250.
40. Scott, Charles. *The Question of Ethics: Nietzsche, Foucault, Heidegger* (Bloomington: Indiana University Press, 1990), 1.
41. Deleuze, *Foucault*, 195.
42. Deleuze, 43, trans. Modified; in the French: "L'histoire des formes, archive, est doublée d'un devenir des forces, diagramme," 51.
43. Deleuze, *Foucault*, 44, emphasis in original.
44. Deleuze, *Foucault*, 43, emphasis added.
45. Deleuze, *Foucault*, 43, emphasis added.
46. Deleuze, *Foucault*, 34.
47. Dickmann, *The Little Crystalline Seed*, 195.
48. "Rien ne ferme réellement, chez Foucault," 51.
49. Foucault, *Discipline and Punish*, 301. The French original reads, "le carceau carcéral n'a pas de dehors" (*Surveiller et punir* 352).
50. Deleuze, *Foucault*, 43.
51. Dickmann, *The Little Crystalline Seed*, 216.
52. Dickmann, *The Little Crystalline Seed*, 217.
53. Dickmann, *The Little Crystalline Seed*, 89.
54. Dickmann, *The Little Crystalline Seed*, 89.
55. Deleuze, *Foucault*, 89.
56. Cucopulos, *Poeisis and Death*, 75.
57. Deleuze, *Foucault*, 89.
58. Deleuze, *Foucault*, 43.
59. Deleuze, Foucault, 85, trans. modified; in French: "*Il y a un devenir des forces qui double l'histoire*," 91, emphasis in original.
60. Cucopulos, *Poiesis and Death*, 43.
61. Cucopulos, *Poiesis and Death*, 43.
62. Deleuze, *Difference and Repetition*, 243.
63. Deleuze, *Difference and Repetition*, 56.
64. Deleuze, *Difference and Repetition*, 57.
65. Deleuze, *Difference and Repetition*, 57.
66. Deleuze, *Difference and Repetition*, 243.
67. Deleuze, *Foucault*, 86; in French: "Il y a . . . un devenir des forces qui ne se confond pas avec l'histoire des formes, puisqu'il opère dans une autre dimension," 92.
68. Deleuze, *Foucault*, 47.

69. Mader, Mary Beth. "Whence Intensity?: Deleuze and the Revival of a Concept." In *Deleuze and Metaphysics*, ed. Alain Beaulieu, Ed Kazarian, and Julia Sushytska (Lanham, MD: Rowman and Littlefield, 2014), 225, emphasis added.

70. Many thanks to Ingrid Diran for her helpful comments on an earlier draft of this chapter, where she pointed out the importance of the "thought of the exponent."

71. Mader, "Whence Intensity?" 225.

72. Deleuze, *Foucault*, 86, emphasis added.

73. Deleuze, *Foucault*, 86.

74. Foucault, *The Thought of Outside*, 149.

75. Foucault, *The Thought of Outside*, 149.

76. Deleuze, *Foucault*, 63.

77. Deleuze, *Foucault*, 87.

78. Deleuze, *Foucault*, 87.

79. Deleuze, *Foucault*, 87.

80. Deleuze, *Foucault*, 87.

81. Foucault, *Language to Infinity*, 90

82. Deleuze, *Difference and Repetition*, 241.

83. Deleuze, *Foucault*, 18.

84. Deleuze, *Foucault*, 86, emphasis added.

85. Deleuze, *Foucault*, 86.

86. Foucault, *The Archeology of Knowledge*, 130.

87. Foucault, *Archeology*, 129.

88. Foucault, *Archeology*, 131.

89. Deleuze, Gilles. *Negotiations, 1972-1990*. Trans. Martin Joughin. New York: Columbia University Press, 1995, 102.

90. Deleuze, *Foucault*, 89.

91. Deleuze, *Foucault*, 89.

92. Deleuze, *Foucault*, 89.

REFERENCES

Cucopulos, Alexa. "Poiesis and Death: Foucault's Chiastic Undoing of Life in *History of Sexuality Volume 1*." Honors Thesis. Philosophy Department, Emory University, 2016.

Dällenbach, Lucien. *The Mirror in the Text*. Trans. J. Whitely. Chicago: University of Chicago Press, 1989.

Deleuze, Gilles. Course on Foucault (1985-86). La voix de Gilles Deleuze en ligne, Université de Paris 8. http://www2.univ-paris8.fr/deleuze/article.php3?id_article=403, accessed July 31, 2020.

Deleuze, Gilles. *Difference and Repetition*. Trans. Paul Patton. New York: Columbia University Press, 1994.

Deleuze, Gilles. *Foucault*. Paris: Minuit, 1986.

Deleuze, Gilles. *Foucault.* Trans. Seán Hand. Minneapolis: University of Minnesota Press, 1988.

Deleuze, Gilles. *Negotiations, 1972-1990.* Trans. Martin Joughin. New York: Columbia University Press, 1995.

Deleuze, Gilles and Félix Guattari. *A Thousand Plateaus: Capitalism and Schizophrenia.* Trans. Brian Massumi. Minneapolis: University of Minnesota Press, 1987.

Derrida, Jacques. *The Post Card: From Socrates to Freud and Beyond.* Trans. Alan Bass. Chicago: University of Chicago Press, 1987.

Dickmann, Iddo. *The Little Crystalline Seed: The Ontological Significance of* Mise en Abyme *in Post-Heideggerian Thought.* Albany, NY: SUNY Press, 2019.

Eng, Michael. "Foucault, Blanchot, and Deleuze: Writing the Outside in the University," unpublished manuscript, Foucault Circle, April 7, 2018.

Foucault, Michel. *The Archeology of Knowledge and The Discourse on Language.* Trans. Alan Sheridan. New York: Pantheon, 1982.

Foucault, Michel. *Discipline and Punish: The Birth of the Prison.* Trans. Alan Sheridan. New York: Random House, 1977.

Foucault, Michel. "Language to Infinity." Trans. Donald F. Bouchard and Sherry Simon." In *Essential Works of Foucault, 1954-1984*, ed. James D. Faubion. 3 vols, 2: 89–101. New York: New Press, 1998.

Foucault, Michel. "A Preface to Transgression." Trans. Donald F. Bouchard and Sherry Simon. In *Essential Works of Foucault, 1954-1984*, ed. James D. Faubion. 3 vols., 2: 69–87. New York: New Press, 1998.

Foucault, Michel. *Surveiller et punir: Naissance de la prison.* Paris: Gallimard, 1975.

Foucault, Michel. "The Thought of the Outside." Trans. Brian Massumi. In *Essential Works of Foucault, 1954-1984*, ed. James D. Faubion. 3 vols., 2: 147–170 New York: New Press, 1998.

Gide, André. *The Journals of André Gide*, vol. 1. Trans. J. O'Brien. New York: Vintage Books, 1956.

Hanley, Christopher. "Thinking with Deleuze and Guattari: An Exploration of Writing as Assemblage." *Educational Philosophy and Theory* 51, no. 4 (2019): 413–423.

Huffer, Lynne. "Foucault and Sedgwick: The Repressive Hypothesis Revisited." *Foucault Studies* 14 (2012): 20–40.

Huffer, Lynne. *Foucault's Strange Eros.* New York: Columbia University Press, 2020.

Mader, Mary Beth. "Whence Intensity?: Deleuze and the Revival of a Concept." In *Deleuze and Metaphysics*, ed. Alain Beaulieu, Ed Kazarian, and Julia Sushytska, 225–248. Lanham, MD: Rowman and Littlefield, 2014.

Melville, Herman. *Moby-Dick, or The Whale.* Herfordshire, UK: Wordsworth Editions, 1993.

Scott, Charles. *The Question of Ethics: Nietzsche, Foucault, Heidegger.* Bloomington: Indiana University Press, 1990.

Section 2

OBEDIENCE, REVOLUTION, AND RESISTANCE

Chapter 9

You Can't Always Want What You Get

The Psychoanalytic Ambivalence of Michel Foucault

Julian Bourg

What is the status of Michel Foucault's and Gilles Deleuze's critiques of Sigmund Freud and psychoanalysis? The general contours of their different, yet resonate and at times overlapping, criticisms—from the genealogy of sexuality to the castigation of Oedipal "familialism"—can for our purposes be largely assumed. Their mutual offensive against psychoanalysis that crescendoed in the 1970s, a single moment in a longer series of engagements since the 1950s, is familiar. To ask about the status of their critique, therefore, points to a more basic question: What is the nature of Foucault's and Deleuze's relationship to Freud and psychoanalysis? What was it, and what is it to us?

A first option reflects the obvious outcome of an assault. It is the nature of critique to strike its target. Foucault and Deleuze were engaged in an anti-psychoanalytic campaign. At a certain limit, the assumptions, criteria, and conclusions of psychoanalysis are incompatible with aspects of the Foucauldian and Deleuzean orientations. As Peter Hallward puts it, "You can't have it both ways: Deleuze or Lacan."[1] Or as Connor MacLeod says in the film *Highlander* (1986), "There can be only one."[2] This either/or asymmetry is reinforced on the other side of the ledger by psychoanalytically minded theorists. Joel Whitebook can stand in for others with his charge that Foucault misapprehends the Freudian tradition. First, he references Foucault's disqualifying personal animus toward psychotherapy, and second and more powerfully, he plays the card of authoritative realism: "Although analysts are split subjects like their patients, they are more firmly planted in the world of consensual meaning."[3] More firmly planted, that is, than the rootless "the mad" and their supposed partisans. Anti-psychoanalytic dismissal meets its mirror reversal in the *reductio ad Freudum.* This standoff entrenches confrontational battle lines already evident during the 1970s when Foucault and Deleuze directly debated psychoanalysts.[4]

Another alternative is dialogue: possible mutual translation processes of two language games that face one another, from analogical, similarity-in-difference to a rather unlikely fusion of hermeneutic horizons. Yet there is not much evidence that Foucault, Deleuze, and psychoanalysis have been brought together in sustained communication and durable conceptual interpenetration, convergence, or generation. This volume itself testifies to open questions posed amid dialogues of the deaf and unsaid. After all, dialogics itself is a square on the psychoanalytic chessboard. On this occasion, exchange tends to tilt toward incommensurability. For example, in the end Dominick LaCapra's serious treatment of Foucault reads a paraphrased notion of the transgressive sublime through the grid of trauma.[5] Ultimately, critique cares more for its arrows than its targets.

These straw men positions are simplistic, reductive, unsatisfying, and yet in some sense verifiably accurate. Completing this dialectical foursquare is a last possibility. After mutual asymmetry ($a > b$, $b > a$) and blocked communication ($a \neq b$), one is left with another form of relation: the arrow is eventfully connected to its target. Here, again, a plausible psychoanalytic move, or rather one compatible with a certain psychoanalytic frame without perhaps being exclusive to it: critique as negation and attachment. The rebel respects the law enough to violate it. The arrow quivers in flight. Ambivalence ($=/\neq$) might be a Freudian concept elastic and capacious enough to capture aspects of Foucault's and Deleuze's relationships to Freud and psychoanalysis: ambivalence, ambiguity, oscillation, shuttling back and forth between contrary poles, not only between Foucault and Deleuze, on the one hand, and Freud and psychoanalysis, on the other hand, but also, for each of them, between renunciation and attachment, and also between Foucault and Deleuze themselves ("they" being less perhaps than the handsome couple "Deleuze and Guattari" but allies who nevertheless became estranged), and also between us and them.

Ambivalence, meaning quite literally strength and value on both sides, contradictorily mixes relation and distinction, and also enables us to approach Freud as a heuristic thinker of complexity alongside the reading of him as a paternalist who reduced everything to drive or signifier. Difference, then, would involve a certain division and thus resolution of ambivalent indecision; it might amount to being-in-difference, that is, becoming in-different. Foucault and Deleuze eventually came to this point: the harshest critic no longer speaks of her object at all. She changes the subject. She quivers her arrows and takes them elsewhere. Ambivalence was perhaps only resolved (a deceptive, seemingly dialectical term, which actually means to dissolve or disintegrate) when Foucault moved on to Christians, Romans, and Greeks, and Deleuze, with Guattari, answered the question, "What is philosophy?" Moving on, like Ida Bauer ("Dora") who completed her analysis by walking out of Freud's waiting room. Or did she? Until ways part, the ambivalent logic of *or/and*, with its infinite interpretations of difference and repetition, is at work.

In the supreme *reductio*, Freud's understanding of ambivalence may have ultimately originated in his unresolved relationship with his own mother.[6] Elements of the *theory* of ambivalence, however, were taking shape in the early 1900s—the "pairs of opposites" of sadism/masochism, looking/being looked at, masculinity/femininity, activity/passivity; Little Hans hitting and then kissing his father's hand; love driving hate into the unconscious where it "is able to persist and even to grow."[7] Freud only began systematically using the term "ambivalence" in two telling essays written in 1912. In "The Dynamics of Transference," he argued that positive and negative transferences were found in all "normal" people and to a heightened degree in "obsessional neurotics." The latter suffered from early splitting, and such "ambivalence"—"one of their constitutional preconditions"—bolstered their resistance to treatment. In contrast, paranoiacs drifted exclusively toward negative transference and were untreatable.[8]

The second, more substantial discussion of ambivalence appeared in one of four essays published together as *Totem and Taboo: Some Points of Agreement between the Mental Lives of Savages and Neurotics* (1913). Freud identified similarities between so-called primitive taboos (an equivocal notion meaning sacred as well as dangerous/forbidden and applicable to people, conditions [e.g., puberty], or things possessed by contagious "'demonic' power") and the behaviors of obsessional neurotics ("touching phobia" or "washing mania"). In both cases, prohibitions had unclear motives, were driven by fear, were contaminable/displaceable, and led to compulsive or ritualistic acts. It is here that Freud introduced the Foucauldian "repressive hypothesis" in order to explain, so to speak, what was really going on. "Touching phobia" originated in the repression of a child's masturbatory impulse as he or she internalized a prohibition, presumably a parent's admonition. Proscription remained conscious while the desire to touch one's genitals was banished to the unconscious where it nonetheless persisted. The result was "the subject's *ambivalent* attitude towards a single object, or rather towards one act in connection with that object." The original motives forgotten, compulsive behavior expressed a tense "impasse"—*don't do this/desire wants to do it*. Again thanks to Foucault, we know that Freud had inherited broader cultural anxieties about the figure of the masturbating child that had accumulated over the course of the nineteenth century.[9] The links among a "child's primitive psychical constitution," the infantilization of non-Europeans, and culturally framed abnormality are self-evident.[10]

Subsequent to these 1912 articles on transference and totemism, the term "ambivalence" entered Freud's vocabulary more regularly. It was used to describe issues such as bisexuality and sexual object choice, Oedipal attachment/revolt, ego/world, pleasure/unpleasure, and so forth. It played a key role in his metapsychological and socio-civilizational texts, and he added it to edited versions of earlier writings.[11] Freud was always forthright that he took the term "ambivalence" from Eugen Bleuler, head of the Zürich school at Burghölzli, who coined it together with the neologisms *autism* and *schizophrenia.* Alongside association and affectivity, ambivalence was one of the "simple functions" that became "altered" in schizophrenics. Its three forms—affective (pleasant/unpleasant feeling), volitional (to act/to not act), and intellectual (thought/counter-thought)—tended to be mixed along a continuum. A certain degree of ambivalence was part and parcel of everyday life, and schizophrenia involved differences of degree not of kind, intensifications rather than categorical, generic distinctiveness. "Even for the healthy," Bleuler wrote, "everything has its two sides. The rose has its thorns." People have mixed feelings, can be indecisive, or even act against their conscious intentions. He offered a timeless example: "Standing in a large store, I wish to get something at a particular counter; I carefully determine the one I do not want to go to, but then it is that very one to which I go." In dreams, "many ideas are almost always expressed by their opposites," and in conscious life, more generally, "synthesis may be omitted." Sorry, Hegel.

The schizophrenic expressed an amplification of this ordinary ambivalent capacity: he "loves the rose because of its beauty and hates it because of its thorns"; "usually appearing as merely two aspects of the same affect . . . hate and love are infinitely closer to each other than to indifference." Such positive and negative "indicators" of a "concept" could appear either "side by side" or they could alternate. Herein lay a major paradox in Bleuler's account: on the one hand, schizophrenics reflected a passional ambivalence, an incapacity to differentiate, the kind of heightened, roving, nomadic complexity later celebrated from surrealist aesthetics to Guattaro-Deleuzean schizoanalysis, and on the other hand, as he put it elsewhere in his book, they displayed

> an indifference to everything—to friends and relations, to vocation or enjoyment, to duties or rights, to good fortune or to bad . . . schizophrenic indifference is in contrast to the labile, irritable, anxious, or demanding nature of the neurotic.[12]

Ambivalence was caught in-between, overly invested, whereas indifference was elsewhere, disinvested.

In spite of interwar promoters such as Eugène Minkowski and Juliette Favez-Boutonier, Bleuler was not well-known in France for most of the twentieth century.[13] Although Henri Ey published an excerpt in 1969, *Dementia Praecox, or The Group of Schizophrenias* did not appear in French in its entirety until 1993.[14] Both Foucault and Deleuze were familiar with the Swiss psychiatrist, if they tended to mangle and misrepresent him. Foucault elided him in his famous 1954 introduction to Ludwig Binswanger's *Dream and Existence*, although the author had studied with Bleuler. Three years later he mistakenly ascribed to Bleuler a sharp distinction between "the schizoid type (tendency to fold in on oneself, to autism, to rupture of contact with reality) and the cycloid character (tendency toward expansion, to affective lability, to permanent contact with the exterior world)."[15] That opposition had actually been advanced by Ernst Kretschmer, although perhaps Foucault had meant Bleuler's contrast of the schizoid and the syntone (or cyclothymia).[16] Similarly, Deleuze and Guattari referred to the founding father of schizophrenia as having merely supplied one of

> three concepts that constitute its trinitary schema: dissociation (Kraepelin), autism (Bleuler), and space-time or being-in-the-world (Binswanger). . . . [Autism] is an ideational concept indicating the specific nature of the effect of the disorder: the delirium itself or the complete withdrawal from the outside world, "the detachment from reality, accompanied by a relative or an absolute predominance of [the schizophrenic's] inner life."

The unattributed citation was from *Dementia Praecox*.[17] While it is true that Bleuler had introduced autism as a possible characteristic of schizophrenia, reducing schizophrenia to autism betrays the vast complexity of his account, which discussed a myriad of other factors: catatonia, delusions, dementia, fugue states, hallucinations, mania, melancholy, negativism, paranoia, and so forth. The widespread tendency to equate Bleuler's understanding of schizophrenia with autism has obfuscated these other dimensions, including, for our purposes, ambivalence—a term that held no conceptual significance for either Foucault or Deleuze.[18]

For a time, the influences of Freud and Bleuler cut both ways, and during the first decades of the twentieth century, psychoanalysis and psychiatry frequently overlapped.[19] "Without Freud," Bleuler said, "there would be no psychopathology."[20] He linked autism, for instance, to Freud's concept of "autoeroticism," thus once again reintroducing the specter of the masturbating child.[21] Yet differences were real. For Freud, dreams symptomatized neurosis, whereas Bleuler considered the possibility that schizophrenia bore a fundamental "relation" to dream life. "One of our patients spontaneously verbalized the fact"; he observed, "The human dream-life is identical with the sphere of the voices of the insane."[22] Indeed, as we have seen, Freud reserved ambivalence as a meaningful category for understanding neurotics not paranoiacs, and the crosscurrents between "primitive" taboo and obsessive neurosis revealed through the hermeneutics of depth and *aletheia* the unresolved tensions of repressed instincts that returned. For Bleuler, almost by definition, ambivalence possessed a wide semantic range: non-synthetic emotions, acts, and thoughts; the continuum between "normals" and schizophrenics; the opposition ambivalence/indifference. The issue to raise at this point is, "Which Freudian ambivalence to emphasize? Was ambivalence something to *resolve*—for which psychoanalysis and the psychoanalyst were mediating, neutralizing, and normalizing third terms—or something *to live with*—an inevitable feature of psychic and social life?" The question performs the very vacillation to which it refers—turtles all the way down. It also evokes the Janus-faced image of the *two Freuds*: on the one hand, the pioneering advocate of desire's essential value who cautioned against costly repression, on the other hand, the champion of normality and normalization encouraging "realistic" adaptation to social conventions. Ambivalence becomes a concept by which to approach Freud and psychoanalysis altogether. Doing so has implications for anti-psychoanalytic critique, since it turns its object into a moving, oscillating target. As we have just seen earlier in Foucault's and Deleuze's rendezvous manqué with Bleuler, reduction is an equally opportunity trap. Who is the Freud being criticized? Is critique a form of determinate negation and thus an expression of attachment, however ambivalent? What of indifference? For reasons of space, I must limit the analysis to Foucault. Intellectual history is a forensic science—*une science medico-légale*.

Foucault's relationship to Freud obviously began in the 1950s: the previously cited 1954 introduction to Binswanger and 1957 survey of psychology, where he reproached psychoanalysis's "naturalist origins and metaphysical and moral prejudices."[23] There are undoubtedly many rich veins to explore from this early era—for instance, the "sovereign violence of a *return*" initiated by Freud and Pierre Janet mentioned in *Folie et déraison* (1961)—but we will focus on the period between the 1964 Royaumont conference on Friedrich Nietzsche and the 1976 publication of *La volonté de savoir*. At Royaumont, Foucault offered an appreciation of Freud who, together with Karl Marx and Nietzsche, made interpretation as an "infinite task."[24] As he wrote five years later, the "author function" replacing the author, Freud was an "initiator of discursivity" who "made possible a certain number of differences with respect to his texts, concepts, [and] hypotheses"; in other words, psychoanalytic discourse itself was generative, capacious, and ambiguous enough to open outward toward interpretive plurality.[25] Although Foucault certainly did not put it like this, psychoanalysis, like Marxism, was a living tradition. The grid Marx-Nietzsche-Freud functioned in *Les mots et les choses* (1966) as an apex of and thus crisis point for the modern human sciences. Yet "more than any other," Freud's exegetical and philological method foregrounded "an analysis in terms of norm, rules, and systems." In the celebrated final pages, Foucault presented psychoanalysis and ethnology as mirroring "counter-sciences" of the unconscious that exposed the boundaries and thus the conditions of possibility for knowledge of the human subject. With Freudianism, representation faltered before the limit of "finitude"—death, desire, and the law—toward which it nonetheless "advances indefinitely (in interminability)." In other words, the incapacity of psychoanalysis to grasp its epistemological object exposed the fault lines of positive human science in general. Both psychoanalysis and ethnology expressed such disquiet and "perpetual oscillation," their "double articulation" having appeared in that founding text of psychoanalytic ambivalence, Freud's *Totem and Taboo*.[26]

The breakup of the holy family of Marx, Nietzsche, and Freud continued in *L'Archéologie du savoir* (1969). All three had decentered subjectivity, although Marx and Nietzsche faced contemporaneous recuperation by, respectively, humanism and transcendental philosophy. In contrast, "archeology touches on a question that is being posed today by psychoanalysis," namely, how to define enunciations without a subject. Repeating the claim of *Les mots et les choses*—that "man himself . . . could not account for his sexuality and his unconscious"—Foucault also remarkably set forth the programmatic agenda for what he initially called "the archeological description of 'sexuality,'" a nineteenth-century discourse culminating in "the rupture brought about by Freud," centered not merely on scientific epistemology but on "a system of prohibitions and values . . . what we might call the ethical."[27] The genealogy of power, of course, would provide the relay between episteme and ethics. The topos of decentered subjectivity was developed further in Foucault's famous review of *Difference and Repetition* (1968) and *Logic of Sense* (1969), where he highlighted Deleuze's use of Freud to address the question of what it means to think: "Let us read Freud who tells us how *thought* can think." The attack on the Cartesian subject and the turn toward impersonal forms were welcome. Indeed, Foucault furthermore wondered if Deleuze's approach was itself "rigorously Freudian" since he undertook sideways readings of the "interruptions, lacunae, and not really important, small things left behind by philosophical discourse." Also in this review Foucault expressed his exasperation with the growing trend of Freudo-Marxism ("Freud with Marx, Marx with Freud, and both, if you please, with us"), a complaint that would become a cri de coeur by the mid-1970s.[28] As that decade opened, it seemed that Foucault was thinking *with* Freud as much as *against the grain* of Freudianism. Thus in his December 1970 inaugural Collège de France lecture, "L'ordre du discours," he mused that "one day, too, we must take a look at Freud's role in psychoanalytic knowledge."[29] Promises, promises.

The need to differentiate his historicization of the subject from other methods and projects sharpened the critique of Freud and psychoanalysis. No, he said in the résumé to his first course at the Collège (1970–1971), a psychoanalytic approach to history was not viable.[30] In 1972, forever disavowing structuralism, he nevertheless noted widespread contemporary attention to "unconscious structures." The idea that such structures could be reduced to "the unconscious in the Freudian sense" was mistaken and naive. Still, implicitly evoking Jacques Lacan, he found promising the view that the Freudian unconscious itself was "a place where this system of formal relations acts," just as such relations operate in "language, formal thought, and can also be found in certain social structures." In short, perhaps the Freudian unconscious was "'traversed' by this structural unconscious." One might have thought he would have referred to the *Les mots et les* chose to make his point, but he did not. Asked by his interlocutor, Giulio Preti, if this move involved a retreat to Carl Jung's notion of the collective unconscious, Foucault instantly replied, one imagines with a chuckling, broad grin, "Of course not."[31] As these examples indicate, between 1964 and 1972, Freud figured variously as a seemingly laudable initiator of infinite interpretation and discursive pluralization, as a decentered nonauthor whose texts helped approach the depersonalized *how* of thought and as the fountainhead of frustrating dead ends (unpromising politics, hollow psycho-historiography, naive inversion of the useful notion of a structural unconscious). All of these views made sense for a chair in "the history of systems of thought" at the Collège de France. Yet they also reflected a messy form of ambivalence: the hodgepodge.

Anti-Oedipus decisively focused Foucault's views on Freud and psychoanalysis. In a 1975 interview, he put things plainly (if slighting Guattari, as everyone does): "Deleuze's book is the most radical critique of psychoanalysis that has ever been made. . . . Deleuze did it in the name of something new. And with enough vigor that it provoked physical and political disgust with psychoanalysis." An entire Parisian intellectual culture was disrupted, one in which the "two absolutely fundamental activities" were writing a book and "babbling at your psychoanalyst's office."[32] Foucault gave this interview in Brazil during one of his five visits to the country (1965, once a year 1973–1976). Anecdotally, one might note that he always seemed more unsparing in his criticisms of psychoanalysis when abroad or speaking with foreigners, although he would also complain that the ambience in São Paulo was characterized by "Freud and Marx to infinity."[33] Two years earlier in 1973 lectures also delivered in Brazil, he had presented his first public appraisal of *Anti-Oedipus*, summarizing Deleuze and Guattari's arguments as an on-ramp to his own treatment of the seemingly "outdated" story of Oedipus. They had shown that Oedipus was "not the secret content of our unconscious, but the form of constraint that the psychoanalytic cure tries to impose on our desire and unconscious. Oedipus is an instrument of power," with respect to the analyst-analysand relation and to the channeling containment of desire within the family.

Foucault's own topic (he had given this lecture several times before) was the role of Sophocles's Oedipus in establishing a "relation between power and knowledge . . . from which our civilization has not yet liberated itself." To a discussion question on whether *Anti-Oedipus* would lead to the disappearance of psychoanalysis, Foucault averred, commenting that Deleuze and Guattari were still writing and working things out. To his mind, the issue of "minimal and maximal" notions of Oedipus—did it refer just to psychoanalysis or to all power relations of pathologization and medicalization?—was unsettled, and their "notion of schizophrenia [was] not clear."[34] Foucault's distance from Deleuze and Guattari was also apparent in a passing comment in the introduction to his opening lecture where he acknowledged some value in the Freudian enterprise. "Psychoanalysis," he said,

> has surely been the practice and the theory that has re-evaluted at the most fundamental level the somewhat sacred priority conferred on the subject, which has been established in Western thought since Descartes. . . . Psychoanalysis has insistently questioned this absolute position of the subject.[35]

The central poles of Foucault's ascending view of psychoanalysis—critical exposure of its normalizing relationship to power, recognition of its historical role in rethinking the subject—were henceforth in place. These May 1973 lectures were followed by his November 1973 to February 1974 Collège lectures on psychiatric power. Foucault made much more of Freud in the course summary than he did in the actual lectures: psychoanalysis was one of two forms of depsychiatrization; deinstitutionalization was accompanied by a reconstitution of medical power as a producer of truth; transference and monetization ensured that the production of the truth did not become a counterpower. Anti-psychiatry was opposed to such depsychiatrization.[36] To an extent, mixed judgments about *Anti-Oedipus*—the authors had furthered the critique of psychoanalysis as a knowledge-power regime, yet unanswered questions and imprecisions remained—provided an opening, however limited, for a reassessment and reappreciation of the historical positivity of Freudianism. The critique of anti-Oedipalism would sharpen.

In another interview published in Brazil in 1974, he noted that the value of psychoanalysis lay in the fact that it "enabled a series of critiques of psychiatry." While not involving a "total and radical rupture" with the nineteenth-century psychiatry that helped give rise to it, the psychoanalytic frame did lead to forms of deinstitutionalization and demedicalization.[37] Quite simply, as he declared in one his lectures in Rio de Janeiro that year, "we can affirm that psychoanalysis was the first form of anti-psychiatry."[38] One might see in this view another point of contact with debates energized by *Anti-Oedipus*, although, here too, Foucault seemed ambivalent since he had made the opposite claim in the Collège lectures on psychiatric power: deinstitutionalization was an anti-psychiatric ambition, but psychoanalysis also reconfigured and reinforced knowledge-power, thus extending the psychiatric project. Indeed, in the interview just cited, Foucault underscored the present-day "coexistence" and "mutual support" of psychoanalysis and psychiatry, a relationship that required further historicization. He made the key admission that he "would like in the future to study the extent to which psychoanalysis prolonged or broke with psychiatric power." It is of no small consequences that the promise of a full-scale, direct engagement with psychoanalysis would remain mortally unfulfilled. Here, he could only suggest that the "vulgarized" idea of interiorized repression be replaced by the analysis of "social control" and the ways that power operated through individualization.[39]

Yet the value of psychoanalysis was not confined to its disruption of nineteenth-century psychiatry. With explicit reference to Brazil, Eastern Europe, and the Soviet Union, he noted in 1975 that psychoanalysis could play "a positive political role by denouncing the complicity between psychiatrists and power." He was less sanguine about such prospects in France, where psychoanalysis tended toward "control and normalization."[40] The aporetic disjunction among these positions—psychoanalysis as liberating vis-à-vis psychiatry, psychoanalysis as normalizing control, and the admission that "No, in truth, I have not yet closely studied the functioning of psychoanalysis"—culminated in the full-throated rejection of Freudo-Marxism.[41] The "struggle" against this adversary, he said in 1975, "has already been going on for ten years."[42] Even then he continued to refer to *Anti-Oedipus* as a pivotal reference. Yet implicit in the rejection of Freudo-Marxist liberation were signs of an incipient rejection of the philosophy of desire with which Deleuze and Guattari had associated themselves. "The 'familialization' of psychoanalysis," he said, "is an operation that Deleuze has shown with great force, a critique that as a theoretician of desire he makes from inside, and that I as a historian of power am only capable of making from the outside."[43] And yet, as he remarked a year later, "we are always inside. The margin is a myth. Speech from the outside is a ceaselessly renewed dream."[44] Not liberation, but power; not desire, but unconscious discursive structures; the historical forces of knowledge-power—what one *got*—irrespective of whatever one *wanted*. Altogether, such reversals marked Foucault's quivering equivocality. He praised *Anti-Oedipus* for having opened a new front in the assault on psychoanalysis, while at the same time expressing reservations about its imprecisions and directing its arguments toward his own concerns with power, knowledge, and discourse. Even though psychoanalysis had and continued to function in tandem with psychiatry, it could be appreciated both for its deinstitutionalizing effects on nineteenth-century psychiatry and as a critical apparatus with which to respond to present-day authoritarianism. Freudo-Marxism could be categorically rejected; however, Freud and psychoanalysis themselves were for the most part approached only indirectly. The stage was set for the first volume of the *The History of Sexuality: La volonté de savoir*, where the critique of liberation in the guise of Freudo-Marxism and the philosophy of desire lay in ambivalent tension with his own version of repressive desublimation.[45]

The four extant volumes of *The History of Sexuality* can, of course, be read as "an archeology of psychoanalysis."[46] The fact that Freud and his method are scarcely mentioned in them tends to throw us off the trail, although one does not need to overread presence through the aperture of absence. In the introductory *La volonté du savoir* (1976), Foucault presents Freud as both epitomizing the "repressive hypothesis" and pioneering the critique of repression that would culminate in sexual revolution and Freudo-Marxism. The previous positions we have seen are succinctly restated. New is the explicit extension of suspicions about Freudo-Marxism to the Guattaro-Deleuzean philosophy of desire, the critique of repression doubling over into a critique of liberation. For the sexual frankness through which "desire" becomes the locus of a supposed emancipation turns out to be, through Foucault's reconstruction of the development and "deployment" of sexuality in the nineteenth and twentieth centuries, another tightening of the screw in a paradigm in which we suffer the obligation to make sexuality the center of subjectivity. The remarkable thing is not that sexuality is repressed or that desire longs to be free, but that we are talking about sex at all.

The familiar arguments of *La volonté de savoir* are worth recalling. Freud figures immediately in part one as one of the four basic elements and protagonists, alongside repression, "other Victorians" (prostitutes and pimps, etc.) and anti-Freudian sexual revolutionaries ("we 'other Victorians'"). From one perspective, he had helped remediate sexual repression. From another point of view, however, psychoanalysis resulted in "another round of whispering in bed," albeit to "the most famous ears of our time."[47] Freudianism both inherited and disrupted the evasive silences of nineteenth-century science, whose mantle it claimed. Paradoxically, the sexual frankness Freud introduced eventually became the means to reject him for being still too repressive. Foucault has in mind Freudo-Marxism, the sexual revolution, transgression, and the philosophy of desire, those who preach the "great sexual sermon" according to which overcoming repression leads to a radiant emancipated future.[48] He immediately throws cold water on this progressivism by raising the possibility that the "state of oppression and the sermon are mutually reinforcing."[49] In a way, Foucault brushes up against the Freudian insight that rebellion and attachment come hand in ambivalent hand, the id and the superego functioning economically. The explicit point, however, is that nineteenth-century sciences of sex, psychoanalysis, and both neo- and anti-Freudian sexual revolutionaries share a common framework or grid of intelligibility: power-knowledge-pleasure.

Precisely midway through the first volume of *The History of Sexuality*, Foucault admits that he has not yet discussed the theme of desire and the implicitly Lacanian argument against the simplistic impulse/repression opposition and in favor of the mutual constitutiveness of desire and law (the rupture of imaginary unity comes together with the instauration of the law/name/no of the father). Foucault shares with Lacan the rejection of the Freudian theory of naturalistic drives: "Where there is desire, the power relation is already present."[50] Perhaps, too, Deleuze's vitalism is implicitly cast aside for the sake of the structuring structures of power; there is no desire *before* power but only *through* power. In truth, as with the Freudian proximity mentioned earlier, Foucault is closer to Lacan than he admits. He agrees that there is no "sex" prior to its discursive manifestation qua composition. We do not learn anything of this possible adjacency because he immediately changes the subject, turning sharply toward another point: the critique of sovereign power and law on which both the liberationists of desire and the unmentioned Lacan ("You are always-already trapped") depend.[51] The fact that Foucault wants to explore his novel notion of biopolitical power as distinct from sovereign power poses no problem.[52] Still, it is not clear that arguing over the form of power frees him from a possibly deeper conjunction with an implicitly Lacanian view that, like the unconscious, the figure of desire is constituted by an interactive field of relations. The contrast with the anti-Oedipal presentation of productive desiring machines cannot be stronger. When Foucault writes that "power is tolerable only on condition that it masks a substantial part of itself," could the same formula not also apply to the unconscious?[53] Is his critical approach to psychoanalysis in some sense a narcissism of minor differences?

The argument vacillates once again when he later revives Deleuze and Guattari's assault on familialism in order to point out how psychoanalysis, in spite of the apparent dangers it posed by provisionally removing sexuality from the family, ultimately reinforced "the law of alliance, the involved workings of marriage and kinship." Psychoanalysis obeys the law, propping up the rickety family system and "the rules of alliance by saturating them with desire."[54] As in *Anti-Oedipus*, capitalism plays a role in his analysis. Freudian familialism reinforced the nineteenth-century reproduction of productive labor. This line of agreement with Deleuze and Guattari is immediately undercut in a "second phase" of the deployment of sexuality: *Spätkapitalismus* no longer requires concealing sexuality or consigning it to the reproduction of the family; "it relies instead on a multiple channeling into the controlled circuits of the economy—on what has been called a hyper-repressive desublimation." Enter Marcuse: desiring revolutionaries are Freud's children, and liberation from repression reflects another modulation of power through the "production" of sexuality.[55] The subtle shift between the two phases of the deployment of sexuality, indexed to changing conditions of capitalism, is actually a devastating rebuke to Deleuze and Guattari: their desiring machines *are also* factories of late capital.

The pushback against *Anti-Oedipus* smoothed the way for Foucault to reaffirm his somewhat sympathetic assessment of Freudian psychoanalysis. As a mutation within the psychiatric model, it had disrupted the reigning "perversion-heredity-degeneration" model. His main comment should be cited at length:

> It is very well to look back from our vantage point and remark up on the normalizing impulse in Freud; one can go on to denounce the role played for many years by the psychoanalytic institutions; but the fact remains that in the great family of technologies of sex, which goes so far back into the history of the Christian West, of all those institutions that set out in the nineteenth century to medicalize sex, it was the one that, up to the decade of the 1940s, rigorously opposed the political and institutional effects of the perversion-heredity-degenerescence system.[56]

Switching positions yet again, however, Foucault returns to the question of psychoanalysis and class society and how Freud ratified another aspect of the nineteenth-century production of sexuality/sexuality of production: "social differentiation." The middle classes went to therapy to recount the truth of their terrible desires whereas lower classes, who could not help but violate bourgeois "taboos," could still be medicalized as the great unwashed of perversion-heredity-degeneration. It is here, Foucault says, that the concept of repression emerged: the incest taboo was considered a universal law, except that, for those who could afford it, therapy "allowed individuals to express their incestuous desire in discourse." Psychoanalysis relieved repressed desires while new legal and state management regimes punished incest behaviors among the popular classes.[57] Deleuze and Guattari could likely endorse this conclusion.

The preceding analyses, oscillating between propinquity to and critique of Freud, Lacan, and Deleuze/Guattari, culminated in Foucault's clearest summary statement of the complex ambiguities of psychoanalysis: all at once, it normalized familialism; it freed sexual instinct from heredity, eugenics, and racism; and it enabled the bourgeoisie to differentiate themselves by relieving their desires according to the very law of repression that policed others.[58] It was a short step from the framework of bourgeois sexual repression to its censure. In the interwar era, Wilhelm Reich (another avatar of anti-Oedipalism) connected sexual repression to "general mechanisms of domination and exploitation." Sixties revolutionaries preaching the "great sexual sermon" followed suit. In toto, the unconscious structure Foucault proposed to reveal, and for which Freud proved to have been the pivot, involved the replacement of the nineteenth-century injunction—*that which should not be mentioned (shhh! sex)*—by the twentieth-century obligation *to speak of sexuality*, to place it at the center our identities, social anxieties, and hopes for the future. The liberation of desire was another face of normalization via sexuality:

> This whole sexual "revolution," this whole "antirepressive" struggle, represented nothing more, but nothing less—and its importance is undeniable—than a tactical shift and reversal in the great deployment of sexuality. But it is also apparent why one could not expect this critique to be the grid for a history of that very deployment. Nor the basis for a movement to dismantle it.[59]

Dismantlement, it seems, would involve ceasing to speak of sexuality, changing the channel, what he called elsewhere "desexualization."[60]

Even as he rejected the notion of an emancipated future established by the liberation of desire and sexuality, Foucault was not opposed to thinking of times to come. In the well-known concluding pages to *La volonté de savoir* he took on the perspective of an ideal spectator. "In the future people will be amused" as they look back at both those shocked by Freud's alleged salaciousness and those who mocked such outrage as "residual prudishness." Freud did not invent sexuality. He stood at a weigh station on a long road. Historically accruing processes of knowledge and power had already "marked out" the zone where his "genius" intervened. Perhaps someday, the forward-looking Foucault famously suggested, the "austere monarchy of sex" whose sovereign law commands that one tell the truth about sexuality would be replaced by "a different economy of bodies and pleasures" that had nothing to do with "'liberation.'"[61] Against the compulsion—obligation, urge—to transparency, a little discretion and opacity; to talk a little less about this thing called sex; silence, or better yet, to speak of other things: the ultimate critiques of Freud and psychoanalysis.

Foucault's views on Freud were never one-sided. Neither bromides about complexity nor the dull observation that he repeatedly changed his mind get us far. One can identify multiple series of oscillating ambivalences over

Freud and psychoanalysis: the exegesis of open discursivity versus finite limit, and thus subject versus structure and science versus counter-science; psycho-ethnology and ethno-psychoanalysis of the masturbating child's *Urambivalenz*; a field to be studied closely on a someday that never came or dismissed for its hollow vulgarities and contribution to sermonic dreams; endorsing *Anti-Oedipus* while taking distance from it; a force for the deinstitutionalization, demedicalization, and deracialization of psychiatry, and an ally in psychiatric normalization; psychoanalysis =/≠ anti-psychiatry; somatic pleasure, yes, desire, no; Freud as critic of Freud, shaped by and shaper of history; a means to overthrow the tyranny of the Cartesian subject and/or reinscribe its domain; Freud mapping ahead of time the silent routes though which one would try to escape the discipline of his sovereign gaze, or/and performing the very open-ended irresolution apparent in both Foucault's ceaseless questioning and our own ongoing interrogation.

There is more to say, for instance, on the masked philosopher's tempestuous debates with the Freudians and his ambiguous relationship to Lacan or on the reconstructive hermeneutics of the subject and genealogical alternatives to sexualization.[62] It is also fair to object, with Deleuze and Guattari, that ambivalence might upon reflection tilt toward mastery. "Theories of arbitrariness, necessity, term-by-term or global correspondence, and *ambivalence*," they wrote, "serve the same cause: the reduction of expression to the signifier."[63] Or maybe ambivalence enacts an overlapping knotting of their own connective, disjunctive, and conjunctive syntheses.[64] In truth, this sense of being caught and not—of dispensing with Freud and thus proving him, approving him while seeking dispensation, and walking away without leaving—recalls another haunting thinker altogether.[65] From the *or/and* to the *yes . . . and* (the food is terrible, and in such small portions), to what extent can one *speak of* Freud without *being spoken for* by him? As Foucault said, "I do not think that we must fall into the old trap, set by Freud himself, that consists of saying that from the moment our discourse enters the psychoanalytic field, it falls under the domination of the analytic interpretation."[66] And yet, by not explicitly making more of Freudian theoretical ambivalence, did Foucault perhaps act it out? For the distance between living with problems for which there is no cure and stylizing an aesthetics of existence for a life in which everything is dangerous may not be so great. After all, we still have the discontented Freud archaeologizing the mind as if it were Rome and conceiving history in "spatial terms," positing the all-seeing superego that surveils the self "like a garrison in a conquered city," evincing "primordial ambivalence" on battlefields marked by always-suspicious knowledges, often-concealed powers, and irreconcilable conflicts.[67] Except in all the ways that he was not, Freud was Foucauldian, too.

NOTES

1. Peter Hallward, "You Can't Have It Both Ways: Deleuze or Lacan," in *Deleuze and Psychoanalysis: Philosophical Essays on Deleuze's Debate with Psychoanalysis*, ed. Leen De Bolle (Leuven: Leuven University Press, 2010), 33–50. Cf. Wendy Grace, "Foucault and the Freudians," in *A Companion to Foucault*, ed. Christopher Falzon et al. (Malden, MA: Wiley-Blackwell, 2013), 227.

2. Russell Mulcahy, dir., *Highlander* (1986; Thorn EMI Screen Entertainment, 116 min.).

3. Joel Whitebook, "Against Interiority: Foucault's Struggle with Psychoanalysis," in *The Cambridge Companion to Foucault*, ed. Gary Gutting, 2nd ed. (Cambridge: Cambridge University Press, 2003), 314–317, 329.

4. "Le jeu de Michel Foucault" (1977), in Foucault, *Dits et écrits: 1954–1988*, ed. Daniel Defert and François Ewald, 2 vols. (Paris: Éditions Gallimard, 2001 [1994]), 2:298–329. Hereafter *DE*. "Deleuze and Guattari Fight Back . . ." (1972), in Gilles Deleuze, *Desert Islands and Others Texts*, ed. David Lapoujade (Los Angeles: Semiotext(e), 2004), 221–229.

5. Dominick LaCapra, *History and Reading: Tocqueville, Foucault, French Studies* (Toronto: University of Toronto Press, 2000), ch. 3. Dominick LaCapra, *History and Its Limits: Human, Animal, Violence* (Ithaca, NY: Cornell University Press, 2009), ch. 4.

6. Joel Whitebook, *Freud: An Intellectual Biography* (Cambridge: Cambridge University Press, 2017).

7. Sigmund Freud, "Three Essays on the Theory of Sexuality" (1905), in *The Standard Edition of the Complete Psychological Works of Sigmund Freud*, ed. James Strachey et al., 24 vols. (London: Hogarth, 1955), 7:160. Hereafter *SE*. Freud, "Analysis of a Phobia in a Five-year-old Boy" (1909), *SE*, 10:42n1. Freud, "Notes Upon a Case of Obsessional Neurosis" (1909), *SE*, 10:239.

8. Freud, "The Dynamics of Transference" (1912), *SE*, 12:106–107.

9. Stuart Elden, *Foucault's Last Decade* (Cambridge: Polity, 2016), 20–24, teases out this figure in Foucault's Collège de France lectures on psychiatric power (1973–1974) and the abnormal (1974–1975).

10. Freud, "Taboo and Emotional Ambivalence" (1912), *SE*, 13:18, 24, 27–30.

11. For instance, Freud, "Instincts and Their Vicissitudes" (1915), *SE*, 14:131–133, and "Mourning and Melancholia" (1915; 1918), *SE*, 14:251–257. The section on ambivalence in "Three Essays on the Theory of Sexuality" (1905) was added in 1915 (*SE*, 7:199) and a similar footnote in "Notes Upon a Case of Obsessional Neurosis" (1909) in 1923 (*SE*, 10:239). The "ancient ambivalence" between the Goddess of Love and the Goddess of Death (1913) showed up later as "the inborn conflict arising from ambivalence, of the eternal struggle between the trends of love and death" (1930). Freud, "The Theme of the Three Caskets" (1913), *SE*, 12:299; *Civilization and Its Discontents* (1930), *SE*, 21:133.

12. Eugen Bleuler, *Dementia Praecox, or The Group of Schizophrenias* (1911), foreword Nolan D. C. Lewis, tr. Joseph Zinkin (New York: International Universities Press, 1950), 40, 53–55, 322, 374–376.

13. Eugène Minkowski's *La schizophrénie: psychopathologie des schizoïdes et des schizophrènes* (Paris: Payot, 1927) and Juliette Favez-Boutonier's *La notion d'ambivalence, étude critique, valeur séméiologique* (Paris: Legrand, 1938) appeared in multiple editions. On the interwar French reception of Bleuler, see Carolyn Dean, *The Self and Its Pleasures: Bataille, Lacan, and the History of the Decentered Subject* (Ithaca, NY: Cornell University Press, 1992), 100–109.

14. Eugen Bleuler, *Dementia Praecox ou Groupe des schizophrénies* (Paris: Théraplix, 1969). Eugen Bleuler, *Dementia Praecox ou Groupe des schizophrénies*, tr. Alain Viallard (Paris: EPEL, 1993). See also Eugen Bleuler, "La schizophrénie," *Congrès des médecins aliénistes et neurologistes de France et des pays de langue française, 30è session, Genève-Lausanne, 2–7 août 1926* (Paris: Masson, 1926), 93–101; Eugen Bleuler and Henri Claude, *La schizophrénie en débat* (Paris: L'Harmattan, 2001).

15. Foucault, "La psychologie de 1850 à 1950" (1957), DE, 1:161. Foucault gives no citation. Eugen Bleuler, "Die Probleme der Schizoidie und der Syntonie," *Zeitschrift für die gesamte Neurologie und Psychiatrie* 78 (1922): 373–399.

16. Ernst Kretschmer, *Körperbau und Charakter: Untersuchungen zum Konstitutionsproblem und zur Lehre von den Temperamenten* (Berlin: Springer, 1921). For the conflation of Kretschmer and Bleuler, see Henri Claude, Adrien Borel, and Gilbert Robin, "La constitution schizoïde (étude clinique et diagnostic différentiel)," *L'Éncéphale: journal du neurologie et de psychiatrie* 4 (April 1924): 209.

17. Gilles Deleuze and Félix Guattari, *Anti-Oedipus: Capitalism and Schizophrenia* (1972) (Minneapolis: Minnesota University Press, 1983), 22–23. Bleuler, *Dementia Praecox, or The Group of Schizophrenias*, 63.

18. Élizabeth Roudinesco, *Freud in His Time and Ours* (2014), tr. Catherine Porter (Cambridge, MA: Harvard University Press, 2016), 126, repeats the view.

19. Ernst Falzeder, "The Story of an Ambivalent Relationship: Sigmund Freud and Eugen Bleuler," *Journal of Analytical Psychology* 52 (2007): 343–368.

20. Bleuler cited by Abraham Brill, "Discussion of Papers by Drs. Riggs and Terhune, Mayer, and Williams," *American Journal of Psychiatry* 4, no. 3 (January 1925): 443.

21. Bleuler, *Dementia Praecox*, 63n19.

22. Bleuler, *Dementia Praecox*, 439–441.

23. Foucault, "La psychologie de 1850 à 1950," 155.

24. Foucault, *History of Madness* (1961), ed. Jean Khalfa, tr. Jonathan Murphy and Jean Khalfa (London: Routledge, 2006), 339. Foucault, "Nietzsche, Freud, Marx" (1964; pub. 1967), *DE*, 1:597.

25. Foucault, "Qu'est ce qu'un auteur?" (1969), *DE*, 1:833–834.

26. Foucault, *Les mots et les choses: une archéologie des sciences humaines* (Paris: Gallimard, 1966), 311, 371–372, 386–392.

27. Foucault, *The Archeology of Knowledge and the Discourse on Language* (1969, 1970), tr. A. M. Sheridan Smith (New York: Pantheon, 1972), 12–13, 192–193, 207.

28. Foucault, "*Theatrum Philosophicum*" (1970), *DE*, 1: 948–949, 954–955.

29. Foucault, *The Archeology of Knowledge and the Discourse on Language*, 233.

30. Foucault, "La volonté de savoir" (1971), *DE*, 1:1110.

31. Foucault, "Les problèmes de la culture: un débat Foucault-Preti" (1972), *DE*, 1:1242.

32. Foucault, "Asiles, Sexualité, Prisons" (1975), *DE*, 1:1645.

33. Daniel Defert, "Chronologie," *DE*, 1:65.

34. Foucault, "La vérité et les formes juridiques" (1973, pub. 1974), *DE*, 1:1421–1422, 1491–1492.

35. Foucault, "La vérité et les formes juridiques," 1408.

36. Foucault, "Le pouvoir psychiatrique" (1974), *DE*, 1:1551.

37. Foucault, "Folie, une question du pouvoir" (1974), *DE*, 1:1529.

38. Foucault, "Crise de la médecine ou crise de l'antimédecine?" (1974, pub. 1976), *DE*, 2:52.

39. Foucault, "Folie, une question du pouvoir" (1974), *DE*, 1:1530.

40. Foucault, "Pouvoir et corps" (1975), *DE*, 1:1626–1627.

41. "Michel Foucault: les réponses du philosophe" (1975), *DE*, 1:1681.

42. Foucault, "Asiles, Sexualité, Prisons," 1647–1648. Cf. Foucault, "Sur la sellette" (1975), *DE*, 1:1592.

43. "Michel Foucault: les réponses du philosophe" (1975), *DE*, 1:1683, cf. 1681–1682.

44. Foucault, "L'extension sociale de la norme" (1976), *DE*, 2:77, where he again rehearses the complex: psychoanalysis facilitated the critique of psychiatry, and also it forms with psychiatry part of a "network of medical 'control.'"

45. Herbert Marcuse, *One-Dimensional Man: Studies in the Ideology of Advanced Industrial Society* (1964), intro. Douglas Kellner (London: Routledge, 1991), 75–80.

46. Michel Foucault, *The History of Sexuality, Volume 1: An Introduction* (1976), tr. Robert Hurley (New York: Vintage, 1990), 130.

47. Foucault, *The History of Sexuality*, 5, 112.

48. Foucault, *The History of Sexuality*, 7.

49. Foucault, *The History of Sexuality*, 8

50. Foucault, *The History of Sexuality*, 81.

51. Foucault, *The History of Sexuality*, 83.

52. Foucault elsewhere suggests that, in its reliance on power as law and sovereignty, psychoanalysis was involved in a rearguard action, a "historical 'retroversion,'" because it did not grasp the biopolitical. Its notable resistance to degeneration, racism, and eventually fascism—in the person of the émigré Freud himself—was nevertheless based on a view of power as sovereignty/law that could not effectively respond to biopolitics. Liberalism, in other words, could not halt Nazism. Foucault concludes, "We must conceptualize the deployment of sexuality on the basis of the techniques of power that are contemporary with it." Foucault, *The History of Sexuality*, 150.

53. Foucault, *The History of Sexuality*, 86.

54. Foucault, *The History of Sexuality*, 113.

55. Foucault, *The History of Sexuality*, 114.

56. Foucault, *The History of Sexuality*, 119.

57. Foucault, *The History of Sexuality*, 128–130.

58. Foucault, *The History of Sexuality*, 130.
59. Foucault, *The History of Sexuality*, 131.
60. "Le jeu de Michel Foucault," 321.
61. Foucault, *The History of Sexuality*, 159.
62. "Le jeu de Michel Foucault." The strict opposition between Foucault and Lacan seems overdrawn. Nadia Bou Ali and Rohit Goel, ed., *Lacan Contra Foucault: Subjectivity, Sex, and Politics* (London: Bloomsbury, 2019).
63. Gilles Deleuze and Félix Guattari, *A Thousand Plateaus: Capitalism and Schizophrenia* (1980), tr. and foreword by Brian Massumi (Minneapolis: Minnesota University Press, 1987), 66 (emphasis added).
64. Deleuze and Guattari, *Anti-Oedipus*, 36–41, 110–111.
65. Jacques Derrida, "Beyond the Power Principle" (1986), tr. Elizabeth Rottenberg, *The Undecidable Unconscious: A Journal of Deconstruction and Psychoanalysis* 2 (2015): 7–17. Derrida, *Resistances of Psychoanalysis*, tr. Peggy Kamuf et al. (Stanford: Stanford University Press, 1998), ch. 3.
66. "Michel Foucault: les réponses du philosophe," 1683.
67. Freud, *Civilization and Its Discontents*, 69–71, 96, 124, 132.

REFERENCES

Bou Ali, Nadia, and Rohit Goel, ed., *Lacan Contra Foucault: Subjectivity, Sex, and Politics*. London: Bloomsbury, 2019.

Bleuler, Eugen, *Dementia Praecox, or The Group of Schizophrenias* [1911], foreword Nolan D.C. Lewis, tr. Joseph Zinkin. New York: International Universities Press, 1950.

Bleuler, Eugen, *Dementia Praecox ou Groupe des schizophrénies*. Paris: Théraplix, 1969.

Bleuler, Eugen, *Dementia Praecox ou Groupe des schizophrénies*, tr. Alain Viallard. Paris: EPEL, 1993.

Bleuler, Eugen, "Die Probleme der Schizoidie und der Syntonie," *Zeitschrift für die gesamte Neurologie und Psychiatrie* 78 (1922): 373–399.

Bleuler, Eugen, "La schizophrénie," *Congrès des médecins aliénistes et neurologistes de France et des pays de langue française, 30è session, Genève-Lausanne, 2–7 août 1926*, 93–101. Paris: Masson, 1926.

Bleuler, Eugen, and Henri Claude, *La schizophrénie en débat*. Paris: L'Harmattan, 2001.

Brill, Abraham, "Discussion of Papers by Drs. Riggs and Terhune, Mayer, and Williams," *American Journal of Psychiatry* 4, no. 3 (January 1925).

Claude, Henri, Adrien Borel, and Gilbert Robin, "La constitution schizoïde (étude clinique et diagnostic différentiel)," *L'Éncéphale: journal du neurologie et de psychiatrie* 4 (April 1924): 145–151.

Dean, Carolyn, *The Self and Its Pleasures: Bataille, Lacan, and the History of the Decentered Subject*. Ithaca, NY: Cornell University Press, 1992.

Defert, Daniel, "Chronologie," *DE*, 1.

Deleuze, Gilles, and Félix Guattari, *Anti-Oedipus: Capitalism and Schizophrenia* [1972]. Minneapolis: Minnesota University Press, 1983.
Deleuze, Gilles, and Felix Guatarri, "Deleuze and Guattari Fight Back..." [1972], in Gilles Deleuze, *Desert Islands and Others Texts*, ed. David Lapoujade. Los Angeles: Semiotext(e), 2004.
Deleuze, Gilles, and Félix Guattari, *A Thousand Plateaus: Capitalism and Schizophrenia* [1980], tr. and foreword by Brian Massumi. Minneapolis: Minnesota University Press, 1987.
Derrida, Jacques, "Beyond the Power Principle" [1986], tr. Elizabeth Rottenberg, *The Undecidable Unconscious: A Journal of Deconstruction and Psychoanalysis* 2 (2015): 7–17.
Derrida, Jacques, *Resistances of Psychoanalysis*, tr. Peggy Kamuf et al. Stanford: Stanford University Press, 1998.
Elden, Stuart, *Foucault's Last Decade*. Cambridge: Polity, 2016.
Falzeder, Ernst, "The Story of an Ambivalent Relationship: Sigmund Freud and Eugen Bleuler," *Journal of Analytical Psychology* 52 (2007): 343–368.
Favez-Boutonier, Juliette, *La notion d'ambivalence, étude critique, valeur séméiologique*. Paris: Legrand, 1938.
Foucault, Michel, *The Archeology of Knowledge and the Discourse on Language* [1969, 1970], tr. A. M. Sheridan Smith. New York: Pantheon, 1972.
Foucault, Michel, *Dits et écrits: 1954–1988*, ed. Daniel Defert and François Ewald, 2 vols. Paris: Éditions Gallimard, 2001 [1994].
Foucault, Michel, *History of Madness* [1961], ed. Jean Khalfa, tr. Jonathan Murphy and Jean Khalfa, 339. London: Routledge, 2006.
Foucault, Michel, *The History of Sexuality, Volume 1: An Introduction* [1976], tr. Robert Hurley. New York: Vintage, 1990.
Foucault, Michel, *Les mots et les choses: une archéologie des sciences humaines*. Paris: Gallimard, 1966.
Freud, Sigmund, *The Standard Edition of the Complete Psychological Works of Sigmund Freud*, ed. James Strachey et al., 24 vols. London: Hogarth, 1955.
Grace, Wendy, "Foucault and the Freudians," in *A Companion to Foucault*, ed. Christopher Falzon et al. Malden, MA: Wiley-Blackwell, 2013.
Hallward, Peter, "You Can't Have It Both Ways: Deleuze or Lacan," in *Deleuze and Psychoanalysis: Philosophical Essays on Deleuze's Debate with Psychoanalysis*, ed. Leen De Bolle. Leuven: Leuven University Press, 2010.
Kretschmer, Ernst, *Körperbau und Charakter: Untersuchungen zum Konstitutionsproblem und zur Lehre von den Temperamenten*. Berlin: Springer, 1921.
LaCapra, Dominick, *History and Its Limits: Human, Animal, Violence*. Ithaca, NY: Cornell University Press, 2009.
LaCapra, Dominick, *History and Reading: Tocqueville, Foucault, French Studies*. Toronto: University of Toronto Press, 2000.
Marcuse, Herbert, *One-Dimensional Man: Studies in the Ideology of Advanced Industrial Society* [1964], intro. Douglas Kellner. London: Routledge, 1991.
Minkowski, Eugène, *La schizophrénie: psychopathologie des schizoïdes et des schizophrènes*. Paris: Payot, 1927.

Mulcahy, Russell, dir., *Highlander*, 1986; Thorn EMI Screen Entertainment, 116 min.
Roudinesco, Élizabeth, *Freud in His Time and Ours* [2014], tr. Catherine Porter. Cambridge, Mass.: Harvard University Press, 2016.
Whitebook, Joel, "Against Interiority: Foucault's Struggle with Psychoanalysis," in *The Cambridge Companion to Foucault*, ed. Gary Gutting, 2nd ed. Cambridge: Cambridge University Press, 2003.
Whitebook, Joel, *Freud: An Intellectual Biography*. Cambridge: Cambridge University Press, 2017.

Chapter 10

On Foucault and Deleuze's Disagreement about Desire and Pleasure

Desire as an Object of Veridiction

Agustín Colombo

After the publication of *The History of Sexuality Volume 1*, Gilles Deleuze wrote a letter to Michel Foucault in which he pointed out the divergences between his and Foucault's account of desire.[1] At the core of such divergence there is a contrast regarding the political dimension of desire, which the letter particularly illustrates by drawing a distinction between two notions: "desire" and "pleasure." As Deleuze observes, in *The History of Sexuality Volume 1*, the notion of "pleasure" plays a key role in the problematization of "phenomena of resistance,"[2] and, therefore, it is conceived as a strategic instance which tends to undermine the mechanisms of power at work in the *dispositif* of sexuality. Desire, instead, constitutes in Foucault's view a synonym of "lack" or "repression"[3] or a concept inexorably associated with repression. For Deleuze such a perspective is hardly conceivable because, in his view, pleasure cannot have a positive value. This is because pleasure interrupts the immanent process of desire and therefore allows the constitution of organisms and strata of power.[4] How should such a contrast between these two thinkers, whose work is frequently seen in complementarity terms, be addressed? While other scholars have already investigated Foucault's and Deleuze's divergent perspective on desire by focusing on the influence that Marxism has in their work[5] and on suicide,[6] this chapter concentrates on the relation between desire and truth. My hypothesis is that Foucault's diagnosis of both the shaping and the way of working of the *dispositif* of sexuality relies on such a fundamental and constitutive link between desire and knowledge of individuals that results in the impossibility to grant desire any faculty or ability to challenge the dynamics of power in the modern disciplines of sexuality. More precisely, Foucault's perspective on the intimate connection between desire and truth is so radical that desire cannot be conceived otherwise than a crucial object of knowledge that ensures the way in which such disciplines work. Such a radical perspective makes desire unable to both initiate and display any form of resistance.

The idea that desire is a fundamental historical vector in the constitution of the modern medical approach to sexuality is at the core of *The History of Sexuality Volume 1*. Medical disciplines of sex were shaped through historical dynamics that have put individuals "under the sway of the logic of concupiscence and desire."[7] Accordingly, within these fields of knowledge, desire works "as a master key"[8] whenever it is a question of knowing and defining individuals' identity through sexuality. Desire constitutes, therefore, a central element or mechanism engaged in the "men's subjection"[9] at work in these disciplines. Consequently, after many years of the publication of *The History of Sexuality Volume1*, Foucault could still observe that desire should be conceived as "the historical transcendental on the basis of which we can and should think the history of sexuality."[10] Hence, desire, and not repression,[11] should be understood as the main and preeminent element of sexual activity which has made possible the formation of the modern disciplines of sexuality. From that perspective, it could be argued that there is a close connection between Foucault's and Deleuze's account of desire, given that, in Deleuze's view, desire works as a condition of possibility of the whole social production.[12] Desire is what allows the connection between the machines at work in the aforementioned production: "Desire causes the current to flow, itself flows in turn, and breaks the flow."[13] Consequently, schizoanalysis "sets out to explore a transcendental unconscious, rather than a metaphysical one; an unconscious that is material rather than ideological."[14] However, the historical approach of Foucault's transcendental role of desire supposes a critical difference with Deleuze. Crucial for Foucault is to understand when and how an intimate interplay between desire and knowledge emerged. In fact, such a line of analysis orients the genealogy of the *dispositif* of sexuality displayed by *The History of Sexuality Volume 1*, which gives confession a seminal importance. Through confession, Foucault is able to identify the Christian approach to flesh as a focal point of formation of the modern approach to sexuality. For this reason, Foucault's investigation of Christianity is so relevant to understand the extent of Foucault's view regarding the transcendental dimension of desire. While *The History of Sexuality Volume 1* focuses on Counter-Reformation, Foucault's late investigation on Christianity concentrates on Late Antiquity. This late part of Foucault's investigation of Christianity plays a pivotal role in the modifications introduced by *The History of Sexuality Volume 2: The Use of Pleasure* to the whole research project of *The History of Sexuality*.[15] In 2018, after almost 35 years of Foucault's death, *The History of Sexuality Volume 4: Les Aveux de la chair*, Foucault's major work on the Church Fathers, was finally published. The last section of this book is entirely dedicated to analyzing St. Augustine's account of desire. Through both this analysis and Foucault's early 1980s research on ancient philosophy, this chapter examines how, in Foucault's view, a fundamental event in the history of sexuality takes place within Christianity: desire becomes an object of knowledge able to define what individuals are. To put it in terms of the Foucaldian vocabulary, through Christianity, desire gets constituted as an "object of veridiction," namely an element susceptible to being defined in terms of true or false,[16] through which individuals' identity can be defined. Foucault's perspective on such capital milestone in the history of sexuality allows to better grasp the terms of Foucault's and Deleuze's divergence about the political role of desire.

UNDOING AN ENSEMBLE

If, as Foucault argues, desire constitutes the historical transcendental of the history of sexuality, that means that, prior to being conceived as an object of veridiction by Christianity, desire possessed a different status. Understanding what could be considered as a pre-Christian and non-epistemological account of desire in ancient thought requires brief reference to Foucault's investigation on aphrodisia, the term that Foucault employs to define the ancient Pagan account of sexual ethics.

While Foucault generally defines aphrodisia as "acts, gestures, and contacts that produce a certain form of pleasure,"[17] he particularly insists on the idea that what characterizes aphrodisia was their dynamics instead of their form. The status of desire in the Greek ethics of aphrodisia becomes clear when the terms of such dynamics are considered. Aphrodisia's dynamics is defined by the "movement that linked *aphrodisia* to the pleasure that was associated with them and to the desire to which they gave rise."[18] More precisely, "the attraction exerted by pleasure and the force of the desire that was directed toward it constituted, together with the action of the *aphrodisia* itself, a solid unity."[19] Even if from both a conceptual and analytical point of view, pleasure, desire, and aphrodisia could be considered as different elements, in the Pagan "experience of *aphrodisia*" they were "closely bound one another."[20] Accordingly, the object of the moral reflection of Greeks in matters of sexual conducts was the dynamics, in particular the "force" that joined all pleasure, desire, and the sexual acts (aphrodisia) "in a circular fashion."[21] Therefore, in such a perspective on sexual activity, desire could be conceived neither as an isolated element nor as a preeminent dimension of sexual ethics.

In Foucault's view, both the Christian sexual ethics elaborated through the concept of "flesh" and the modern medical account of sexuality are marked by the dissociation of these three elements which were closely connected in the Greek approach to aphrodisia. Interestingly, in order to briefly describe the different ways through which such dissociation takes place, Foucault draws on the terms that dominate his divergence with Deleuze, namely pleasure and desire. On the one hand, the dissociation of the elements that composed the ensemble of *aphrosidia* implied "a certain 'elision' of pleasure," which in Christianity took place through the "injunction given by the clergy (*pastorale chrétienne*) against the pursuit of sensual pleasure (*volupté*) as the goal of sexual activity," whereas in the medical account of sexuality entailed a "theoretical devaluation shown by the extreme difficulty of finding a place for pleasure in the conception of sexuality."[22] On the other hand, the undoing of the ensemble of aphrodisia was marked by "an increasingly problematization of desire," which in the Christian ethics of flesh was dominated by a reflection on "the primordial sign of the fallen nature," whereas in the medical modern account of sexuality it was conceived in terms of "the structure characteristic of the human condition."[23] Now, in spite of mobilizing both pleasure and desire to describe the main modifications involved in the dissociation of aphrodisia, it is through desire that Foucault examines the continuities between the Christian ethics of the flesh and the modern approach to sexuality. Desire, more precisely, the "principle of desiring man," is in fact the main element that in his view characterizes both the Christian experience of the flesh and the modern experience of sexuality.[24] Actually, Foucault's diagnosis regarding the continuity between Christianity and modernity relies on the role of desire as an object of veridiction. This is for, the "genealogy" of the desiring man, which is the cornerstone of the whole project of *The History of Sexuality*, focuses on the practices by which individuals were led to acknowledge themselves "as subjects of desire, bringing into play between themselves and themselves a certain relationship that allows them to discover in desire, the truth of their being."[25]

Before focusing on the novelty engaged by the Christian perspective on desire, it is worth considering Foucault's investigation on aphrodisia one last time in order to identify two milestones that show crucial displacements relating to the role of desire in Pagan sexual ethics, prior to development of the Christian ethics of the flesh: (1) Plato's conception of true love and (2) the status of desire that results from Stoic ethics of marriage. In doing so, Foucault's perspective on the historical turning point that Christianity represents vis-à-vis desire will be easier to grasp.

According to the last chapter of *The Use of Pleasure*, Plato's *Symposium* and *Phaedrus* introduced key modifications within Greek sexual ethics. One of these modifications consisted in the problematization of the being of love within the debate on the love of boys. According to Foucault, in the traditional account of aphrodisia, "love and the intense and forceful movement that takes holds of the lovers [were] presupposed."[26] Grounded on that preexisting perspective on love, the main ethical issue regarded the conduct that lovers should have, namely how the two partners, the adult male and the boy, ought to conduct themselves within their relationship. In contrast, Plato's *Symposium* and *Phaedrus* introduce a debate regarding the "very being" of lovers' love, "its nature and its origin."[27] Such a displacement leads to an ontological inquiry of love and provokes a change of the object of the ethical reflection. Henceforth, establishing the nature of lovers' love becomes a crucial ethical issue. Consequently, instead of dealing with "pleasure and its dynamics," the Platonic reflection on love built up in both the *Symposium* and the *Phaedrus* pivots on an inquiry that concerns "the desire that must be led to its true object (which is truth) by recognizing it for what it truly is."[28] In order to do so, the soul must be able to sustain a struggle against the violence of her appetites which involves a twofold relation to truth: "a relation to her own desire questioned in its being, and a relation to the object of her desire recognized as a true being."[29] In short, with Plato emerges the necessity of inquiring the truth of desire as a crucial feature of sexual ethics. Thus, Plato's *Symposium* and *Phaedrus* show "where ground is broken for a future inquiring into desiring man,"[30] which will be later developed by Christianity.

The Stoic ethics of marriage also introduced significant modifications with regard to the role played by desire in the Greek traditional account of aphrodisia. Through such modifications, desire is conceived as an isolated element of the male's ethical conduct and becomes a preeminent dimension of the self which has to be managed and controlled. This is what Foucault calls a process of "objectivation" because desire is problematized in terms of "the very root of the sexual activity that has to be constituted within oneself as the object of a control, of a permanent observation."[31] Foucault's analysis of the principle of symmetrical conjugality developed by Musonius Rufus illustrates well this new account of desire. According to that principle, "only marriage can constitute the naturally legitimate tie for sexual relations."[32] The role that male's desire plays in the justification of the symmetrical conjugality is clearly explained in Foucault's lectures at the Collège de France *Subjectivity and Truth*, much more than it is in *The Care of the Self*. In Musonius Rufus's view, Foucault highlights, the prohibition to commit adultery does not rely on the juridical equality between man and wife, which could be allowed by Stoic doctrine. Rather, it was grounded on a moral inequality between them. In the conjugal relationship, the husband has to play a pedagogical role: his real role is to be "the wife's guide, it is for him to show the right way, to show how to live, to give the living example of the way of living."[33] In order to be able to play such role, the husband must be master of himself. By committing adultery, he would show that "the desire for sexual relations is so intense and violent in him that he cannot control it, that he is not master of himself."[34]

Therefore, having control of his own desire was central to the ethical position that he has in the couple. Accordingly, desire (*epithumia*) is conceived as the element that

> I must check and master, that I must observe and take into account at its source in order to assure myself that I will be able to establish, maintain, and renew throughout my behavior the caesura necessary to the relation I have to my own sex.[35]

Desire is therefore "isolated as the element that will anchor the subjectivation of *aphrodisia*: it is in the form of desire that I will establish the permanent relationship I have to my own sex."[36] This approach to desire introduces significant discontinuities to the traditional account of aphrodisia, in particular regarding the attitude that male individuals need to have toward their own desire in order to master or govern themselves and exert the government over the others.[37] Yet, for the purpose of this chapter, it is worth focusing on the consequences that Foucault assigns to this new perspective on desire with regard to the unity that characterizes the traditional account of aphrodisia. In his view, the technologies of the self, developed through the Stoics' reflection on sexual ethics, "extract" "the element of desire from *aprhodisia*" and grant it a privileged role.[38] This results in a considerable reduction of the relevance of the act that characterized aphrodisia, in which "the movements of the body and the soul were independent, bound to each other in a sort of paroxysmal unity."[39] Within such a unity, desire was only one aspect of a manifestation of an organic mechanism, namely the accumulation of humors, and "was linked to a pleasure that was itself the side, the soul's side, of an activity a mechanism of spermatic expulsion."[40] Hence, the bloc of aphrodisia is "dismantled (*disloqué*)" and a "re-centering of the whole problem of *aphrodisia* around desire" takes place.[41] On the wake of this dislocation, Christianity will organize a new bloc which, according to Foucault, will pivot on the "analytic of the subject of concupiscence."[42]

THE TRUTH OF THE SELF THROUGH DESIRE

If one compares both Foucault's investigation on the ethics of aphrodisia and Christian flesh, Christianity seems to develop a twofold capital displacement regarding the role of desire: desire becomes (1) the characteristic trait of human condition and (2) an element susceptible to be analyzed through ascetical techniques involving confession. Foucault's diagnosis about the "the analytic of the subject of concupiscence" developed by Christianity relies on such displacements: Christianity would have elaborated techniques through which it is possible to decipher the secret truth of the subject by focusing on desire. Yet, Foucault's hypothesis on the Christian origin of the analytic of the subject of concupiscence constitutes one of the more problematic features of the project of *The History of Sexuality*. As I have already explained,[43] this hypothesis relies on the intimate interplay between two elements which Foucault was not fully able to account for: the perspective on the human condition involved in St. Augustine's account of libido and Cassian's hermeneutical techniques of thoughts. The difficulties of grasping the connections between these two elements make plain the extent to which Foucault's death prematurely curtailed the project of *The History of Sexuality*. Nonetheless, despite these difficulties, Foucault's reflection on the Christian formation of the analytic of the subject of concupiscence is crucial to understand the genealogical dimension that he assigns to Christianity in the shaping of the modern account of sexuality. For the purpose of this chapter, I will draw on *The History of Sexuality Volume 4: Confessions of the Flesh* to show how Foucault tries to find in Christianity a seminal moment for the history of Western societies in which desire gets problematized as an object of veridiction, that is, an element susceptible to be defined in terms of true and false, through which the truth of the self can be revealed. In order to do so, I will analyze the aforementioned two elements implied in the syntagma "the analytic of the subject of concupiscence" separately.

The account of the human condition involved in St. Augustine's theory of libido is clearly exposed in the point 1 of the part II of the last section of *Confessions of the Flesh*, "The Libidinization of Sex." As Foucault explains, in St. Augustine's view the Fall was the consequence of a "movement" of the human soul through which it "turns away from God" and "takes pleasure in itself (*s'attache à elle même et s'y complaît*)."[44] This human action led to the formation of concupiscence or *libido*,[45] namely "the involuntary form of the urge" that characterizes sexual intercourse,[46] particularly illustrated by the image of erection.[47] In Paradise, prior to the Fall, all the elements which took part in the sexual act were under the absolute and complete control of the human will. Human disobedience to God provoked an alteration of human will. As a consequence of eating the forbidden fruit, God punished Adam and Eve by reproducing in them the attitude of disobedience that they have previously had toward him. In doing so, God's punishment was not located either between the body and the soul or between the matter and the spirit. Rather, it affected the whole subject. As Foucault explains, the change provoked by the Fall affects "the materiality of the body through the structure of the subject in terms of the relation of the will with itself (*la matérialité du corps à travers la structure du sujet comme volonté de soi sur soi*)":[48] the human will is internally split, and turned against its own self.

Such alteration of human will implied a modification of human nature, which, however, was not able to modify God's human creation. This is because the modification of human nature results in the "degradation of the being" that humans hold from God and not in the alteration of what God created:

> By turning away from God, and refusing to obey him, man thought he was becoming the master of himself: he believed he was emancipating his being. [Instead], he is only falling away from a being that only sustains itself through the will of God.[49]

The anthropological shift caused by St. Augustine's account of libido is considerable. Albercht Dihle affirms that St. Augustine introduces an anthropological account of will which displayed a strong contrast with Roman's legal approach to will.[50] However, what seems to have provoked a real turning point was the conception of human condition engaged by St. Augustine's theory of libido. As Peter Brown explains, "Augustine's handling of the history of the creation of Adam and Eve, and of their fall, made plain the extent to which he was prepared to shift the center of gravity of Christian thought on the human person."[51] Unlike other contemporary Christian writers like Ambrose, Gregory of Nyssa, and Jerome, who would agree in affirming that marriage and the creation of the family were a "result of a sad decline, by which Adam and Eve had lapsed from an 'angelic' state into physicality, and so into death,"[52] what remains a dark enigma to the bishop of Hippo "was the distortion of the will of those who now made up society": for him "the twisted human will [. . .] was what was new in the human condition after Adam's Fall."[53]

As far as Foucault's research on *The History of Sexuality* is concerned, the discontinuity introduced by St. Augustine's account of libido is substantial. If for the Stoics desire was a privileged element of the subject on which male's sexual activity had to pivot, with St. Augustine desire becomes a specific trait of human nature. Henceforth, desire is conceived not as an isolated element of the subject that has to be controlled but rather as what characterizes and defines human condition.

As Foucault explains, Augustine's perspective on desire had capital consequences for marriage sexual ethics because it opened the possibility to develop a juridical approach to sexual activity. Through notions such as *consensus* and *usus*, the bishop of Hippo defined the conditions under which marriage intercourse must take place in order to be permitted, and therefore not result in a sinful activity.[54] In doing so, he elaborated the "theoretical matrix" of a "very precise codification" of sexual relations, which will be later developed by Medieval Christianity since thirteenth century.[55]

However, this was neither the only nor the immediate consequence provoked by the account of desire built up by Augustine. At the time Augustine lived, his conception of concupiscence as "evil" lead to the possibility to "combine (*joindre*), through the theme of spiritual combat, the exercise of virginity to the practice of marriage."[56] Such an interplay was possible because, in Foucault's view, both kinds of practices relied on the same account of concupiscence. However, these two practices involve two different modes of relationship of the subjects to their own selves, namely two different dynamics of subjectivation.[57] In the case of marriage, subjects' relationship to their own selves was anchored in both the consent and use of their own concupiscence, whereas in the case of virginity it involved the use of ascetic techniques elaborated by monasticism. The objective of these techniques is to discover the deep truth of the "subject of desire."[58] The general dynamic of these techniques is well summarized in Foucault's analysis of *exagoreusis* based on John Cassian.

Monastic *exagoreusis* consists in an intimate interplay between the examination of thoughts (*cogitationes*, *logismoi*) and confession. The aim of *exagoreusis* is to obtain the conditions to make the flow or movements of individuals' thoughts as orderly and pure as possible. This is for the thoughts may be distressful and therefore able to perturb soul's quest of God's contemplation.[59] Accordingly, individuals need to identify the kind of thoughts that come to their mind and separate true thoughts from illusions. This is a crucial task because, since the Fall, Satan is able to penetrate the human body, weaken the human soul, and send it "suggestions, images, thoughts, whose origin is hard to determine."[60] Such a task could only be accomplished if combined with confession to the elder monk, because humans are incapable of determining the origins of their thoughts by their own means, given that Satan could always mislead them. The simple fact of expressing the soul's inner secrets to others through words gives confession its own "performative force (*force opératoire*)": confession has the ability to tell, show, expel, and free from sin.[61]

In Foucault's view, the combination of these two elements, that is, Augustine's sexual ethics of marriage and monastic techniques of examination of thoughts, through a univocal account of concupiscence resulted in the shaping of the "analytic of the subject of concupiscence." This provoked a sort of an earthquake in the moral reflection of Late Antiquity and led to a brand-new experience of sexual activity. The "paroxysmal bloc" through which the sexual act was conceived as a "unified convulsional event (*unité*) where the individual would lose themselves in the pleasure of their interaction with the other, to the point of mimicking death,"[62] was undone. Christianity dissociated and reshaped that "bloc." In doing so, the bloc was not grounded on of "pleasure and relationship" anymore but it pivoted on "desire and subject."[63]

This new unity was reshaped in such a way that its "diffraction remains and its analysis possible."[64]

Despite the problems involved,[65] Foucault's historical diagnosis seems to be quite clear: the dislocation of the bloc of aphrodisia by Christianity resulted in a reorganization of an ethical bloc in which knowing the truth of individuals' desire constitutes a central activity. In Foucault's own terms, Christianity introduced "a fundamental question in the relationship to the truth (. . .): what about the truth of my concupiscence? Or, as we will say in our terminology, what about the truth, what is truth of my desire?"[66] In doing so, a major displacement vis-à-vis the role of desire takes place. The fact of inquiring into the nature of lovers' desire is not the crucial ethical question, as it was in Plato. Rather, in the Christian experience of the flesh, the capital ethical issue consists in discovering the truth of subject's desire, as desire constitutes a characteristic feature of the subject. In other words, it is a matter of knowing the truth of the self through desire.

CONCLUSIONS

In an interview with G. Raulet in 1983, Foucault made plain his perspective on the different impact that Nietzsche had on both his work and Deleuze's. In his view, the effects of Deleuze's reading of Nietzsche are visible in Deleuze's "theory of desire," whereas, his appropriation of Nietzsche's philosophy was always related to "the question of truth, of telling the truth, the *Wahr-sagen*—what it is to tell the truth—and the relation between telling the truth and forms of reflexivity, of self upon self."[67] Nietzsche's account of *Wahrsagen* is exactly what inspires Foucault's approach to "veridiction."[68] In the light of the previous analysis, and even though Deleuze studied in depth Nietzsche's approach to truth,[69] Foucault's understanding of desire through the problem of veridiction seems to provide a key insight into Foucault's and Deleuze's divergence regarding the role of desire.

In Foucault's view, once desire is problematized as an object of veridiction capable of revealing subject's hidden truth, it becomes the cornerstone of the historical formation of the modern approach to sex. The dislocation of the bloc of aphrodisia and the organization of the experience of the Flesh constitutes a historical turning point which pushed pleasure into the background of the problematization of sexual activity and made desire a crucial object of self-analysis. Consequently, if, as Foucault argues, through his interpretation of the original sin Augustine conceptualizes the "metahistorical event" which reorganizes the sexual act in its original form,[70] it would be possible to affirm, evoking Nietzsche's influence on Foucault again, that the constitution of the analytic of the subject of concupiscence is the major genealogical event of

Foucault's diagnosis of the formation of the modern account of sexuality.[71] Yet, what seems to be crucial to understand Foucault's divergence with Deleuze is the radicality of Foucault's perspective on that event. In his view, once desire becomes the object of subject's self-veridiction it gets inevitably immobilized in that epistemological position, which constitutes the historical matrix of the modern disciplines of sexuality. In doing so, desire both works as the cornerstone of historical shaping of the aforementioned disciplines and guarantees the dynamics of power on which they rely and that they reproduce. Accordingly, the possibility of challenging these dynamics cannot rely upon desire. In other terms, desire cannot be the immanent element through which the analytic machine grounded on Oedipus could be internally reversed and, therefore, become an "indispensable part of a revolutionary machinery."[72] This is because, in Foucault's view, the epistemological status that desire acquires with Christianity makes impossible the exercise of freedom and autonomy. Resistance must therefore draw on an element which is not involved in *dispositif* of sexuality functioning. That is why pleasure could be able to challenge the dynamics of power organized by the aforementioned *dispositif.*

NOTES

1. Deleuze Gilles, "Desire and Pleasure" in Davidson Arnold, *Foucault and His Interlocutors* (Chicago: Chicago University Press, 1997), 183–192, translated by Daniel Smith.
2. Deleuze, "Desire and Pleasure," 188.
3. Deleuze, "Desire and Pleasure," 189.
4. Deleuze, "Desire and Pleasure," 189.
5. Grace Wendy, "Faux Amis: Foucault and Deleuze on Sexuality and Desire," *Critical Inquiry*, 36 (Autumn 2009): 52–55.
6. Harper Michela P., "Bewilderingly, *Forcefully*: Drawing the Line Outside," *Journal of Philosophy: A Cross-Disciplinary Inquiry*, 17 (Spring 2012), 60–69.
7. Foucault Michel, *History of Sexuality vol. 1: An Introduction* (New York: Pantheon Books, 1978), 78.
8. Foucault, *History of Sexuality Vol. 1: An Introduction*, 78.
9. Foucault, *History of Sexuality Vol. 1: An Introduction*, 60.
10. Foucault Michel, *Subjectivity and Truth. Lectures at the Collège de France 1980-1981* (London: Palgrave McMillan UK, 2017), 288.
11. The critique of the "repressive hypothesis" constitutes one of the main lines of analysis that structure Foucault's whole project of *The History of Sexuality*. Through this hypothesis, Foucault particularly criticizes psychoanalysis, especially the work of Wilhelm Reich.
12. Deleuze Gilles and Guattari Félix, *Anti-Oedipus* (Minneapolis: the University of Minnesota Press, 1983), 28.

13. Deleuze, Guattari, *Anti-Oedipus*, 5.

14. Deleuze, Guattari, *Anti-Oedipus*, 109.

15. Foucault Michel, *History of Sexuality Vol. 2: The Use of Pleasure* (New York: Vintage Books, 1985), 3–13.

16. In his late work, Foucault utilizes the term "veridiction" to define the historical perspective that he developed. A crucial aspect of the "history of veridiction" consists "of determining under what conditions something can become an object for a possible knowledge [*connaissance*], how it may have been problematized as an object to be known, to what selective procedures [*procédure de découpage*] it may have been subjected, the part of it that is regarded as pertinent." Foucault Michel, "Foucault" in Foucault Michel, *Essential Works 2: Aesthetics, Methods, an Epistemology* (New York: New Press, 1998), 460.

17. Foucault, *The Use of Pleasure*, 40.

18. Foucault, *The Use of Pleasure*, 42.

19. Foucault, *The Use of Pleasure*, 42.

20. Foucault, *The Use of Pleasure*, 42.

21. Foucault, *The Use of Pleasure*, 43.

22. Foucault, *The Use of Pleasure*, 42. Foucault Michel, *Histoire de la sexualité 2. L'Usage des plaisirs* (Paris: Gallimard, TEL, 1997), 58.

23. Foucault, *The Use of Pleasure*, 42.

24. Foucault, *The Use of Pleasure*, 5.

25. Foucault, *The Use of Pleasure*, 5.

26. Foucault, *The Use of Pleasure*, 236.

27. Foucault, *The Use of Pleasure*, 236.

28. Foucault, *The Use of Pleasure*, 244.

29. Foucault, *The Use of Pleasure*, 244.

30. Foucault, *The Use of Pleasure*, 244.

31. Foucault, *Subjectivity and Truth*, 284–285.

32. Foucault Michel, *History of Sexuality 3: The Care of the Self* (New York: Pantheon Books, 1986), 172. Prior to the Stoic's conception of conjugal fidelity, adultery was mostly conceived in terms of taking someone's else wife. *The Care of the Self*, 171, *Subjectivity and Truth*, 264.

33. Foucault, *Subjectivity and Truth*, 264.

34. Foucault, *Subjectivity and Truth*, 264. *The Care of the Self*, 173.

35. Foucault, *Subjectivity and Truth*, 286.

36. Foucault, *Subjectivity and Truth*, 286.

37. Foucault, *Subjectivity and Truth*, 265–267.

38. Foucault, *Subjectivity and Truth*, 286.

39. Foucault, *Subjectivity and Truth*, 286.

40. Foucault, *Subjectivity and Truth*, 286.

41. Foucault, *Subjectivity and Truth*, 287. Foucault Michel, *Subjectivité et vérité. Cours au Collège de France 1980-1981* (Paris: Seuil/Gallimard, 2014), 291.

42. Foucault Michel, *History of Sexuality Vol. 4. Confessions of the Flesh* (New York: Pantheon, 2021), 285.

43. Colombo Agustín, "What Is a Desiring Man?," *Foucault Studies*, 29 (2021): 76–84.

44. Foucault, *Confessions of the Flesh*, 268. *Les Aveux de la chair* (Paris:Gallimard, 2018), 341.

45. Foucault, *Confessions of the Flesh*, 268. In the course of his debate with Julian of Eclanum, St. Augustine will admit the existence of human concupiscence before the Fall. He will also develop a conceptual difference between the *concupiscentia nuptiarum*, which could have existed in Paradise, and the *concupiscentia carnis*, which was absent from Paradise. Clark Elizabeth, "L'Augustin de Foucault au risque de l'œuvre augustinienne" in Büttgen et al. *Foucault, les Pères et le sexe. Autour des Aveux de la chair* (Paris: Éditions de la Sorbonne), in press. Cf. Foucault, *Confessions of the Flesh*, 262, note 18.

46. Foucault, *Confessions of the Flesh*, 262.

47. Foucault, *Confessions of the Flesh*, 265.

48. Foucault, *Les Aveux de la chair*, 333. Passage not included in the English translation.

49. Foucault, *Confessions of the Flesh*, 269.

50. Dilhe Albrecht, *The Theory of Will in Classical Antiquity* (Berkeley, Los Angeles: University of California Press, 1982), 143.

51. Brown Peter, *The Body and Society. Men, Women, and Sexual Renunciation in Early Christianity* (New York: Columbia University Press, 1988), 399.

52. Brown, *The Body and Society*, 399.

53. Brown, *The Body and Society*, 404.

54. Foucault, *Confessions of the Flesh*, 277–283. Individual's *consensus* is a "supplement," a human act through which the subject accepts and wants the concupiscent form of his/her own will (278). Through *usus*, individuals can make good use of their concupiscence depending on the objective of the sexual act, that is, procreation or avoid partner's fornication (281).

55. Foucault, *Confessions of the Flesh*, 283–284.

56. Foucault, *Confessions of the Flesh*, 284. *Les Aveux de la chair*, 360.

57. Foucault defines subjectivity "as the mode of relation of self to self." Foucault Michel, *On the Government of the Living. Lectures at the Collège de France 1979-1980* (London: Palgrave McMillan UK, 2014), 225.

58. Foucault, *Confessions of the Flesh*, 285.

59. Foucault, *Confessions of the Flesh*, 102.

60. Foucault, *Confessions of the Flesh*, 99.

61. Foucault, *Confessions of the Flesh*, 108. Foucault also admits that the elder monk plays an important role in the monastic practice of confession, *Confessions of the Flesh*, 100.

62. Foucault, *Confessions of the Flesh*, 285.

63. Foucault, *Les Aveux de la chair*, 361. Passage not included in the English translation.

64. Foucault, *Confessions of the Flesh*, 285.

65. See Colombo, "What Is a Desiring man?," *Foucault Studies*, 29 (2021), 84–86.

66. Foucault, *Subjectivity and Truth*, 158.

67. Foucault Michel, "Structuralism and Post-structuralism," in Foucault Michel, *Essential Works 2: Aesthetics, Methods, an Epistemology* (New York: New Press, 1998), 446.

68. Foucault Michel, *Wrong-doing, Truth-telling. The Function of Avowal in Justice*. Edited by F. Brion and B. Harcourt (Presses universitaires de Louvain/The University of Chicago Press, 2014), 20.

69. Deleuze Gilles, *Nietzsche et la philosophie* (Paris: Presses universitaires de France, 1962), 108–111.

70. Foucault, *Les Aveux de la chair*, 329.

71. Genealogy "must record the singularity of event outside any monotonous finality" which characterizes historical approaches based on "linear development[s]." Foucault Michel, "Nietzsche, genealogy, and history" in Foucault Michel, *Essential Works 2: Aesthetics, Methods, an Epistemology* (New York: New Press, 1998), 369. Through the analysis of events Foucault aims to break the evidences on which rely "our knowledge, our consent, our practices." Foucault Michel, "Table ronde du 20 mai 1978," in Foucault Michel, *Dits et écrits II* (Paris: Gallimard, 2001), 842.

72. Deleuze, Guattari, *Anti-Oedipus*, 82.

REFERENCES

Brown, Peter. *The Body and Society. Men, Women, and Sexual Renunciation in Early Christianity*. New York: Columbia University Press, 1988.

Büttgen, Philippe, Philippe Chevallier, Agustín Colombo, and Arianna Sforzini (ed.), *Foucault, les Pères et le sexe. Autour des Aveux de la chair*. Paris: Éditions de la Sorbonne, 2021.

Colombo Agustín, "What is a Desiring Man?" *Foucault Studies*, no. 29 (2021): 71–90.

Deleuze, Gilles. "Desire and Pleasure." In *Foucault and his interlocutors,* edited by Arnold I. Davidson, 183–192. Chicago: Chicago University Press, 1997.

Deleuze, Gilles. *Nietzsche et la philosophie*. Paris: Presses universitaires de France, 1962.

Deleuze, Gilles, and Félix Guattari. *Anti-Oedipus. Capitalism and schizophrenia*. Minneapolis: the University of Minnesota Press, 1983.

Dilhe, Albrecht. *The theory of will in classical antiquity*. Berkeley, Los Angeles: University of California Press, 1982.

Foucault, Michel, "Foucault," In Foucault, Michel. *Essential works 2: Aesthetics, methods, an epistemology,* edited by James D. Faubion. New York: New Press, 1998.

Foucault, Michel. *Histoire de la sexualité 2. L'Usage des plaisirs*. Paris: Gallimard, TEL, 1997.

Foucault, Michel. *Histoire de la sexualité 4. Les Aveux de la chair*. Paris: Gallimard, 2018.

Foucault, Michel. *History of Sexuality vol. 1: An Introduction*. New York: Pantheon Books, 1978.

Foucault, Michel. *History of Sexuality vol. 2: The Use of Pleasure*. New York: Vintage Books, 1985.

Foucault, Michel. *History of Sexuality vol. 3: The Care of the Self*. New York: Pantheon Books, 1986.

Foucault, Michel. *History of Sexuality vol. 4. Confessions of the Flesh*. New York: Pantheon, 2021.

Foucault, Michel, "Nietzsche, genealogy, and history" in Foucault, Michel. *Essential Works 2: Aesthetics, Methods, an Epistemology*, edited by James D. Faubion. New York: New Press, 1998.

Foucault, Michel. *On the Government of the Living. Lectures at the Collège de France 1979-1980*. London: Palgrave McMillan UK, 2014.

Foucault, Michel, "Structuralism and Post-structuralism" in Foucault, Michel. *Essential Works 2: Aesthetics, Methods, an Epistemology*, edited by James D. Faubion. New York: New Press, 1998.

Foucault, Michel. *Subjectivité et vérité. Cours au Collège de France 1980-1981*. Paris: Seuil/Gallimard, 2014.

Foucault, Michel. *Subjectivity and Truth. Lectures at the Collège de France 1980-1981*. London: Palgrave McMillan UK, 2017.

Foucault, Michel, "Table ronde du 20 mai 1978", in Foucault Michel, *Dits et écrits II* (Paris: Gallimard, 2001).

Foucault, Michel. *Wrong-doing, Truth-telling. The Function of Avowal in Justice*, edited by F. Brion and B. Harcourt. Presses universitaires de Louvain/The University of Chicago Press, 2014.

Grace, Wendy, "Faux Amis: Foucault and Deleuze on Sexuality and Desire," *Critical Inquiry*, 36 (Autumn 2009): 52–55.

Harper, Michela P., "Bewilderingly, *Forcefully*: Drawing the Line Outside," *Journal of Philosophy: A Cross-Disciplinary Inquiry*, 17 (Spring 2012): 60–69.

Chapter 11

Desire's Tyranny

Deleuze and Guattari on Desire, Capitalism, and Authoritarianism in the Contemporary Moment

Geoff Pfeifer

As Wendy Brown, Peter Gordon, and Max Pensky have recently argued, we need a new—or at least renewed—critical theory that can help provide theoretical resources in making sense of this moment in which we are watching a reemergence of authoritarian politics and authoritarian impulses around the globe.[1] These impulses have expressed themselves in a variety of ways from Trump's United States, in which long-standing—but sometimes submerged—racism, xenophobia, and general hostility toward difference (and the social whole as such) have been unleashed and allowed to flourish in the open in new ways, to Bolsonaro's Brazil, Orban's Hungary, and other places where we are watching similar trends take shape.

Though it is the case that Trump was defeated in the 2020 presidential election, the attempted right-wing putsch during the certification of the election results on January 6, 2021 at the U.S. capitol building and the ongoing campaign to "decertify" those election results by the right both inside and outside the mainstream of the republican party, along with a renewed interest in passing laws that restrict the voting rights of the working poor, and BIPOC voters (who tend not to vote with conservatives in large numbers) should tell us that this movement is far from over, that it is now firmly entrenched in U.S. politics as it is in many places around the world.[2] As further evidence for this in the United States, we only have to look at the 2020 election results themselves where almost half the record number of voters came out and voted for Trump's chaotic authoritarianism despite his severe mishandling of the pandemic and his administration's many failures over the three-and-a-half years leading up to the election.[3] And even now, support for the ex-president remains extremely high among the right in this country.[4] What accounts for this? How can we understand its emergence on the political scene now? I hope here to offer a small contribution to the larger and ongoing project of building a critical theory to help our understanding this authoritarian turn. I want to do this here by looking to Deleuze and Guattari's work on the role that desire plays in the production and reproduction of social relations and also the ways in which, as they argue, desire is produced and channeled by capitalist social relations. Specifically, this chapter will, after offering a more general accounting of Deleuze and Guattari's elaboration of desire's capture, look at the role that desire's production plays in this moment, in ushering in and sustaining the renovation of right-wing authoritarianism that we are currently living through.

DESIRE'S PRODUCTION, OR, DESIRE AS SOCIAL PRODUCT

> *There are no internal drives in desire, only assemblages. Desire is always assembled; it is what the assemblage determines it to be.*[5]

> *Desire works in the infrastructure, invests it, belongs to it. . . . Desire thereby organizes power: it organizes the system of repression.*[6]

It is nothing new to say that for Deleuze and Guattari desire is political. As they see it, our individual desires and their structures are first found outside of us, in the larger social world, and they are (re)produced and channeled in us, by that larger social whole that we are born into and exist as a part of such that the structure of desire in the individual comes to mirror that of the larger social whole. This also means that the structure of one's desire comes to serve the continuity and reproduction of a given set of social relations that exist at a given time and in a given place.

As Jason Read has shown us, Deleuze and Guattari's understanding of the origins of affects like desire and others is grounded in the thought of both Spinoza and Simondon.[7] From Spinoza, Deleuze and Guattari take the idea that our affective life, that is, our capacities to affect and be affected, are part and parcel of our social relations, the encounters we have with others, the structures we participate in and come to inhabit, and the collectives we are a part of. As Read writes here for Spinoza,

> Political collectives are defined more by common structures of feeling than common notions or ideas. . . . Affects are thus necessarily both anti-humanist,

defining all of existence in various ways, and transindividual, passing in and through relations with others.[8]

For Spinoza (and for Deleuze and Guattari), the social is, in this way, the condition upon which the individual and her affects are premised. From Simondon then, Deleuze and Guattari take and build on the idea that individuation and individual subjective awareness is, as Read also states, "a process, not a default state of being. This process moves from a milieu that is considered pre-individual, made up of tensions and relations, to a process of individuation that increasingly encompasses different levels and aspects, biological, psychic, an social."[9] This is what, in a condensed form, is expressed between the two quotations that make up the epigraph for this section of the chapter: that desire is "assembled" in particular ways as a part of—and by—a larger social assemblage and it is so also as a result of its being part of the Marxist "infrastructure" or "base" rather than, as it is often thought in Marxist discourse, as a part of the ideologically mystified superstructure. This is why, as we will see later, in order to properly make sense of Deleuze and Guattari's understanding of desire in this way, it is my contention that we must read it in light of their reading of Marx in addition to what they import from Spinoza and Simondon.

To briefly recall the classic Marxist theory of base and superstructure, the material base is comprised of both the "forces of production," described by Marx as the technologies, tools, land, and so on, and labor power that exist in a particular amalgamation at a given time and also the "relations of production," or those relationships individuals are required to enter into in order to produce and reproduce their means of existence—also at a given time—so relationships of wage labor in various forms are the primary example here, but also other relations that surround wage labor such a contractual relations and the like are also a part of the relations of production.[10] In the classical story told by Marxist thinkers, the material base gives rise to superstructural relations which serve to justify and bring stability to that base—the kinds of things that exist as a part of the superstructure are (again, classically) things like legal codes, familial structures—think here about the Fordist family structure during the heyday of that mode of production wherein the raced, gendered, and heteronormative division of labor was constructed in such a way as to allow one adult member of the household (mostly white men) to work outside the house and earn enough money for the other adult member (mostly white women) to stay home and do the work of childcare and other forms of domestic labor—educational institutions, religious institutions, political structures, and also beliefs about what is natural and necessary, and so forth.

This latter category, ideas about what is natural and necessary, is what is classically captured by the term "ideology"—it is in ideology that we exist, for instance, when we think that capitalism is a natural fit for humanity, as we believe that it mirrors some foundational competitive "human nature." For the classical Marxist, this ideology is mistaken in its identification of a competitive human nature as existing in the ways that we experience it prior to capitalist economies and in a way that is fundamental to humanity. Rather, Marxist critique shows that we come to view ourselves as (fundamentally) competitive in the ways that we do as a result of the material and social relations put into place and reinforced by capitalism. This ideology, however, has a purpose—it serves to prop up and justify capitalist social relations (and thus to help reproduce them). In this traditional model then, subjective desires are a part of the superstructure insofar as they are conditioned by activity in the base to be as they are such that they support and reproduce an existing set of forces and relations of production. Critical here is that, to the classical theory, ideology is a *mistaken* relation to the real conditions of our existence and can be set right with the proper form of critique. As many recent Marxist thinkers have argued, however, there is not such a neat separation between the base and superstructure as what I am calling here the classical or simplified theory would have it. Further, for many, the idea that ideology is a matter of a mistaken relation is an inaccurate way to think it—rather it just is the way our relation to the world is constructed by capital. So there is no mistaken relation here—we just are constructed in the ways that we are.[11]

Returning to the complex relations and lack of separation between base and superstructure with this in mind then, feminist theorists of the concept of social reproduction (also known as Social Reproduction Theory or SRT), for instance, have argued that this is the case for care work, which includes everything from education, to health care, to the housework and child-rearing found in traditional family life—all of which had been seen in the more traditional model as part of the superstructure and hence less part of the economic base and more relegated to the sphere of the noneconomic and nonmaterial superstructure.[12] This is a problematic view of care work for many reasons. One of which is, as Melinda Cooper has recently pointed out, that it "serves to obscure and sentimentalize the existence of women's unpaid labor in the home at precisely the moment when the boundaries between the labor market and the private family were being established."[13] Furthermore, care work, wherein there is often still a gendered and raced division of labor, is itself productive—and so always properly located in the base—insofar as socially reproductive work is sometimes waged and is itself a regime of labor that combines both labor power and the technologies of the forces of production in its activities. Care work also, moreover, participates in the relations of production in that such socially reproductive work is a relation that many individuals (again—often in gendered and raced ways) must participate in as it is sometimes the only labor relation available to them and it creates the conditions of the economic labor outside of the house for others, in the proverbial factories. So here in socially reproductive care work, we see the blurring of the lines between the base and the superstructure.

For Deleuze and Guattari, desire, much like socially reproductive care work for many Marxist feminists, also straddles this divide. It is produced by a given set of social relations as we saw earlier in their extension of Spinoza and Simondon, in a particular way, but it is also critically (re)productive of those relations such that it acts to reproduce and sustain that given set of social relations and forces of production that instantiate it in a given moment. The experience of desire under capitalism is also not, as with the theory of ideology, a mistaken experience—it is real, and it is what it is as a result of its entanglement in capitalist social relations. The process of this double move—the real production and subsequent reproduction of desire by capital—arises in relation to what Deleuze and Guattari term the "inscribing socius."[14] The socius—or the social machine—is the agglomeration of all of the various sets of practices—both economic and thus those that exist in the base, and also superstructural—that preexist (and exist external to) the life of individuals in the socius. These form the backdrop of a given society into which such individuals are inserted and through which desire is formed. To say more about this here, we can see that Deleuze and Guattari describe this as the process of the coding of the "flows of desire" and thus, they describe the work of the social machine in this way:

> The social machine is literally a machine, irrespective of any metaphor, inasmuch as it exhibits an immobile motor and undertakes a variety of interventions: flows are set apart, elements are detached from a chain, and portions of tasks to be performed are distributed. Coding the flows implies all of these operations. This is the social machine's supreme task inasmuch as the apportioning of production corresponds to the extractions from the chain resulting in a residual share for each member, in a global system of desire and destiny that organizes the production of productions.[15]

Following Daniel Smith, we should see the concept of "flow" as at the foundation of Deleuze and Guattari's political philosophy in a way that also helps us understand the production of desire in the infrastructure.[16] As Smith argues, the concept of "flow" is central for Deleuze and Guattari much like the concept of the "social contract" is the foundation of the political philosophy of Hobbes and other contract theorists, or the "hegemony" is for Gramsci, and so forth. It is the coding of all kinds of flows that is at the heart of social and political relations and at the center of the political philosophy offered in *Anti-Oedipus* and, as Smith shows us, is key for making sense of how Deleuze and Guattari understand the relation between the individual and the social machine. It is also key for understanding the processes by which social relations that exist as a part of a given social machine produce individual awareness and affect such that these fit with, and work to reproduce, those larger social relations.

In this way, the inscribing socius then, as described in the quote earlier, "codes" these various flows in particular ways so as to both make them legible to individuals as a part of their social milieu and channel and direct those flows toward particular ends that extend and reproduce the conditions of production that exist in a given social structure. So in making sense of, or offering an account of, a given set of social relations, Deleuze and Guattari look to the ways in which flows are coded by the socius. This tells us about how the social machine functions and the ways that it produces and reproduces itself (and in so doing, the ways it produces and reproduces individuals and individual awareness as a part of this). In making certain flows legible in certain ways, the inscribing socius sets the rules and boundaries for what counts as proper modes of production, distribution of social and commercial goods, practices, and traditions.[17] It is then, the coded flows that set the terms of the social within which individuals become subjects—my coming to understand myself in the myriad ways that I do; for instance, as gendered in particular ways, raced, classed, as having a particular religion (or not), as having the ability to enter into certain professions (or not), as wanting certain things, fearing others, in short, my own social positioning and subjective awareness along with all its attendant abilities and limitations both social and individual is a result of my entering into a social world with certain sets of flows coded in certain ways so as to both position me in particular ways in relation to a given set of social conditions, practices, and traditions, and to make that positioning legible to me (and to others) in ways that help me understand myself and my social world (and help others understand me also).

This also connects me with history and tradition. These codes are also akin to a larger social memory that help me make sense of my place within them and connects me to the larger social whole in ways that both allows its reproduction in and through me via the social position that I inhabit, and also the habits, traditions, and practices that come to shape who I am and how I understand myself. It also enables, as mentioned earlier, my seeing of myself as part of that social whole. And when societies transition from one set of codes to another, as in say, when there is a move from feudal society to capitalist society, this involves the decoding of certain sets of flows to make those available to capital and their recoding in different ways that reinforce and facilitate capitalist social relations at the level of political economy. As Deleuze and Guattari show us in their most Marxist moments when they talk of the ways in which labor is decoded under capitalism so as to become available for sale in ways it was not in feudal society and so forth.[18] This is the result of the process of the decoding of the ways flows of labor existed in the precapitalist world and their recoding in ways that enable capitalist labor relations.

Returning then to the discussion of desire, it too is coded, decoded, and recoded in various ways at various times as a part of this process such that it comes to mirror the larger social and machinic practices and traditions such that it reproduces those in the individual who, as a result, comes to desire in ways that are legible in a given social machine. This is Deleuze and Guattari's addition, then, to Marx's analysis: they help us see that, as they argue, the libidinal economy is the same as the political economy.[19] Smith puts this point nicely (and in reference to the first epigraph in this section of the chapter earlier):

> Put differently, "desire is part of the infrastructure" (104; cf. 63): our impulses and affects, and even our unconscious drives, what seems to be the most individual and personal part of ourselves (libidinal economy), are themselves immediately part of what Marx called the economic infrastructure, that is, the material base of every social formation (political economy). In other words, it is impossible to posit a mental or psychic reality to desire that is different from the material reality of social production.[20]

If there is no psychic reality without social production, and if social production is material and external to the individual in the ways described above, then psychic realty is nothing more than the internalization of the preexisting social—we are truly social products even in our psychic and affective life and this most intimate part of ourselves serves the reproduction of a given social machine.

This brings us then also to the second part of the second epigraph given earlier: Desire organizes power—the power of individuals, the power of the market, and the power of politics. And none of these are neatly separable. Desire is bound up with those other forces and relations of production such that it is produced, or "assembled"—to return again to the first epigraph—in the particular ways it is by those existing social relations in the base that individuals must enter into in order to live (the relations of production) and, at the same time, it is reproductive of those relations such that desire expresses them in individuals and their actions, in economies in their relations, in social practices and traditions, and in politics.

Now, if we take Deleuze and Guattari's picture of desire's central role in both organizing the power of individuals and the social, and its role as being organized by those things in the mode of the external-to-the-subject social machine or the inscribing socius, we can begin to build a critical theoretical accounting of the ways in which such desire is implicated in this new authoritarian politics and one that also helps us see the mechanisms through which authoritarian desire is produced in us and put in the service of the reproduction of authoritarian social relations. In order to do this, I want to think briefly first about what other kinds of social and political economic relations exist in the present such that desire is organized in the particular ways that it is.

NEOLIBERAL CAPITAL, NEOLIBERAL DESIRES

For decades now we have seen the emergence and deepening of what many call neoliberal capitalism. Neoliberalism's foundations are in the creation of what Quinn Slobodian (with reference to Hayek and Mesis) has recently described as a kind of dual governmentalism wherein the realm of the economy and capitalist markets are governed in ways that protect them from the "problems" of democratic rule—neoliberalism seeks to, as Slobodian says, "encase" the market in ways that free it from this mass democratic rule.[21] And so neoliberal governments work to take economic activity out of the hands of the demos by working (paradoxically) to "free" it from democratic governance—to privatize institutions such that they are not, or at least they are less, subject to democratic control. Under neoliberalism, modern, democratic states cannot be trusted with economic activity because they are subject to the whims of democracy and so the economy must be divorced from the democratically controlled aspects of the state.

William Davies has offered a nice periodization of neoliberalism that I think helps in understanding both its current manifestations and its roots in what neoliberal thinkers saw as the threat posed by the rise of socialism and socialist policy making.[22] Davies divides neoliberal thought and policy into three distinct periods. Two of which are positioned prior to the 2008 financial crisis and the third which exists in that crisis's wake. The first period, what Davies calls "combative neoliberalism," runs roughly between 1979 and 1989 and emerges out of, as just mentioned, the critique of socialist and Keynesian economic programs offered (beginning much earlier) by Ludwig von Mises. Davies points out here that Mises offered a thoroughgoing criticism of socialist rationality and Keynesian economics in large part by lumping these distinct traditions together and setting up "seemingly obvious binary choices between liberal market capitalism and everything else."[23]

Davies argues, with reference to Mirowski, that this binary choice—which lays at the heart of early and later neoliberal thinking—sets up a kind of Schmittian friend/enemy distinction and is primarily concerned with, as we also saw in Slobodian's description, insulating executive decision-making about the market and economies from the whims of the democratic populous.[24]

This leads to the belief that what is needed is a technocratic elite who can maintain the "rationalism" of the market and is insulated in these ways. This project required an ideological and political war on the many forms of democratic collectivism that neoliberals saw as impeding the project of safeguarding the autonomy and supposed rationality of liberal capitalist market relations. So in this period we see then not just neoliberal ideas and policy as moving in the direction of combating socialism as it existed in places like Russia and China but also, and more importantly for us, what it deemed as collectivist and socialist challenges to markets in the core capitalist democracies of Europe and the United States and the budding social democracies in other places around the world. So the war on trade unions and other forms of nonmarket, democratic, and rights-based collectivism become a mainstay of neoliberal programs in this period as they are seen as a part of this ideological project of the Schmittian enemy-making of all things that challenge or impede the market logic of liberal capitalism. As Wendy Brown notes here, for neoliberal thinkers of this period like Hayek, market rationalism and freedom prevail only "when there is no intentional human coercion" and such liberty must be enforced by rules, laws, and dictates against human intervention (Brown, 2016; Hayek 1960—constitution of liberty).[25] Hayek argues that the more markets can be "set free" from human intervention, the more we can discern their "truth."[26] It is this concern for and attempted prevention of human and democratic intervention—seen as the socialist enemy—in the independent "rationality" of markets, as Davies shows us here, that provided both the uniting force of various strands of neoliberal ideologies and also neoliberalism's "animating telos" in this period.

The second period identified by Davies is that which comes into existence at the end of the Cold War and runs roughly to the 2008 financial crash. He labels this the period of "normative neoliberalism." With the defeat of socialism at the end of Cold War, the animating telos of neoliberalism shifts toward the desire to push market rationalism into all corners of human existence. This is because market rationality is seen by the neoliberals as virtuous insofar as it

> provided a normative procedure through which value and knowledge could be ascertained. According to this logic, all spheres of human activity should therefore be reconstructed around the standards of competition so as to ensure that valuable products, services, artefacts, ideas, and people were discoverable.[27]

It is market rationality and market competition that provides a procedure of discovery for neoliberalism in which we become able to discern the good in all things and so such logics become a way of organizing the totality of society. Attempts to disrupt or regulate such market logics (both at the scale of the larger economy and at the scale of other types of social relations) are seen as suspect as such regulation interferes with the "scientific" process of discernment of the good. It is in this that the kind of entrepreneurial self of neoliberalism discussed by Foucault, and later Darot and Laval, becomes popularized and firmly entrenched in Western democracies.[28] As Davies points out here, under this form of neoliberal governance, the goal is to "ensure that 'winners' are clearly distinguishable from 'losers' and the contest is perceived as fair."[29]

The final phase of neoliberal governance that Davies outlines in his periodization is what he describes as "punitive neoliberalism." This is also sometimes referred to by others for good reason as "authoritarian neoliberalism."[30] This form of neoliberalism takes shape in the period after the financial crash of 2008 in which it becomes clear that debts (both individual and business/corporate) have been one of the defining features of the prior period and that what is needed is austerity to control this debt buildup. So this period is characterized by both the institution of austerity measures for individuals and public sector spending on what little social safety measures remains and the transfer of banking debt to governments so as to keep markets afloat. Here Davies notes that this period is accompanied by a general feeling that such debts are immoral and the fault of individuals and so the proper remedy is punishment (especially for those who have little political power in society):

> Under punitive neoliberalism, economic dependency and moral failure become entangled in the form of debt, producing a melancholic condition in which governments and societies unleash hatred and violence upon members of their own populations. . . . Studies of those living in poverty with problem debts found a prevalent psychology of melancholia, whereby debt exacerbates a sense of self re-crimination and the expectation of further punishment. Research on public attitudes to austerity confirms a similar internalization of financial morality, which produces the sense that we "deserve" to suffer for credit fueled financial growth.[31]

Davies is not the only one to recognize the growth of debt and financial moralization as a core feature of contemporary neoliberal governance and subjection. Maurizio Lazzarato has also made these connections in important ways.[32] Lazzarato, drawing on Foucault's analysis of neoliberal governmentality and biopolitical control and Deleuze's analysis of the former's transformation into control societies[33] partially via the expansion of debts, points out here that, in this subjective and social transformation, the debtor

> is not expected to reimburse in actual money but rather in conduct, attitudes, ways of behaving, plans, subjective commitments, the time devoted to finding a job, the time used for conforming oneself to the criteria dictated by the market

> and business, etc. Debt directly entails life discipline and a way of life that requires "work on the self," a permanent negotiation with oneself, as specific form of subjectivity: that of indebted man.[34]

To return to Davies—and to neoliberalism's Schmittian moment—here, we can see echoes of Lazzarato's claims about the need for self-recreation and discipline under punitive neoliberalism, but in the register of the social and political policy:

> The Schmittian worldview of the neoliberal pioneers, which pitted free-market capitalism against all varieties of non-capitalist system, has mutated into something equally paranoid and simplistic, but now apparently self-destructive. In contrast to the offensive against socialism, the "enemies" targeted now are largely disempowered and internal to the neoliberal system itself. In some instances, such as those crippled by poverty, debt, and collapsing social safety nets, they have already largely been destroyed as an autonomous political force. Yet somehow this increases the urge to punish them further.[35]

To add a further layer of analysis to help us understand the punitive or authoritarian shift in neoliberalism we should note also that others have pointed to the fact that this particular regime of neoliberal governance has also begun to make increased use of penal, policing, and criminal justice policy to enforce and extend its reach.[36] Here, Davies and others show us how, in this phase, neoliberalism produces the kinds of internal dynamics that we see animating our new authoritarian moment—the "socialist" enemy is within, and it is those who would continue to mistakenly desire a social safety net, who think that there exist structural injustices for which the government should enforce redress, and who generally think that governance is there to help make people's lives better rather than simply set the conditions for more and more competitive market relations in more and more corners of existence. In responding to these challenges, it resorts more and more to punitive means and, in doing so, as we can begin to see now, it reconstructs our affective life and desires to align with and reproduce this structure in ways that display the organizing force or particularities of the kinds of coding of flows that we see in the neoliberal inscribing socius and that include the coding of the flows of individual desire.

DESIRE'S AUTHORITARIAN TYRANNY

As we have seen, the three periods of neoliberal capital and their attendant ideological and policy commitments have included, among other things, a deepening suspicion of democratic and popular governance, first around economic activity as neoliberal policy and programs seek to wall off economies from democracy in ways that make such activity increasingly autonomous and controlled not by the democratic populous or moderated by unions and social safety nets but by technocrats and elites who work more and more to free markets from such controls and whose expertise is less and less questioned. Such policy, as it is extended in subsequent periods to areas beyond the economy, produces this distain for democratic and community-controlled processes in other corners of social life as well—think here about the war on public education and other social services—and in ways that privilege individualized competition (and continued, competitive self-improvement). This form of social organization sees the production of winners and losers as an inevitable and a natural cost of the "proper" social structure and any attempts to control for this as a nonnatural and problematic intervention. Further, as Davies notes, in its most recent iteration, punitive neoliberalism teaches that debt is incurred by individualized, poor decision-making at the same time that it extends more and more credit to individuals whose wages have not increased as the cost of living increases or who do not have the financial means to pay for increasingly expensive postsecondary educations at the same time that they are told that such education is the sole means to increasing class status.

Punitive neoliberalism also, as Davies argues, without an external enemy like socialism or communism, increasingly sees as the enemy an internal demos who is indebted and oppressed and seeking redress for these structural inequalities. This of course, in the context of continued neoliberal hollowing out of social safety nets, the existence of fewer and fewer stable well-paying jobs (even for those who are able to finance a university education), and the rise of part-time and contract work, sets the stage for an invigorated scapegoating of immigrants and others by those who have traditionally been in positions of relative power and security and who are now losing that as a part of the larger neoliberal economy. Jennifer Silva, speaking of this process in relation to her ethnographic studies of young working-class Americans, points out that all of this is the way in which individuals become "acquiescing neoliberal subjects, rejecting all kinds of government intervention, and affirmative action in particular, as antithetical, and thereby offensive, to their lived experiences."[37] As a result, she continues,

> In this way, potential communities of solidarity are broken apart by the strain of insecurity and risk, Men hold fast to the few remaining public sector jobs by vigilantly policing their boundaries against women and gay people. White people draw moral boundaries against blacks for taking government money and wasting their tax dollars . . . ultimately young working-class men and women

> believe that if they have to battle through life alone then everyone else should too.[38]

In the context of the present chapter, I should be clear to point out that the creation of such a neoliberalized subjectivity that Silva discusses here does not necessarily lead directly to support for the kinds of authoritarian politics we see emerging today. Nor do I mean to suggest that it is only young working-class folks that might support such a politics. In fact, as we know well, the amount of actual support for new authoritarian politicians like Trump among young voters is relatively small and that in 2016 he gained the majority of support from older more economically well off white voters (a majority of whom do, however, fall into the category of working class in the sociological literature insofar as they are noncollege educated).[39] But I do use this example to point out that neoliberal economic and political structures produce subjectivity and subjective affect and desires in particular ways such that what individuals desire comes to mirror the broader social and political structures and practices that are put in place by neoliberalism. And we can certainly see in Silva's example, the role this plays in provoking some right-wing authoritarian sentiments in some members of the working class and also further entrenching those same desires in others across the economic spectrum.

To return to the place we started, we can see clearly that in the aftermath of the 2020 presidential election and the sentiments that underlie the attack on the capital building in the United States, by more right-wing and authoritarian elements in this country, there is a deep suspicion of the electoral and democratic process: a desire to believe that the election was stolen and that it should be—or, in fact, for some, will, as some believe be—overturned at some later date and Trump will be reinstalled as president. Further, as mentioned earlier, we see an ongoing attempt, by members of the legislative branch, to wall off the process of selecting political officials from the larger democratic public that mirror the ways in which neoliberal politics seek to wall off the economy. All of these, along with the other moralizing sentiments Silva, Davies, and others describe around debt burdens and the need for government assistance by those who are structurally left out of economic and other forms of access to a flourishing life, as well as the growth in and support for punitive measures taken against those who seek redress for such structural inequities are perfectly in keeping with what we have seen in thinking through the ways neoliberalism props up and further entrenches capitalist social relations. And it does this not just by enacting social and economic policy but by worming into our very desires and subjectivity: producing along the way, antidemocratic sentiments across the body politic in ways that ground and reproduce such things at a structural level. While some analysts of authoritarian and punitive neoliberalism argue that, in the authoritarian turn, neoliberalism moves further away from seeking consent for its policies by the governed[40] and toward coercion, we should also recognize, as I have tried to lay out here, the ways in which such coercion itself produces affective consent by and through the coding of social flows in ways that also come to be mirrored in the very affective desires on individuals that are a part of the social machine itself.

Finally, there is an ongoing debate in the empirical political science and sociological literature about whether support for Trump's chaotic neoliberal authoritarianism is most caused by sentiments of economic anxiety in that the neoliberal economy has made it harder and harder to make ends meet or by sentiments attached to changing demographics in the United States, what this literature often refers to as "status threat"—that folks who have been on top in this country are increasingly faced with loss of place. [41] Both of these ways of understanding the authoritarian turn are on display in the quote from Silva's work above even though it predates and in many ways prefigures the rise of Trump and what we now call Trumpism in the United States. While I think, and have argued elsewhere, that it is not easily one of these or the other, but perhaps both of these things working in tandem, this analysis is not enough to explain it—we must see this as a result of the ways in which neoliberalism entrenches authoritarian sentiments at the level of our very desires.[42] Deleuze and Guattari can, as I hope I have begun to show here, help us with this. And it is this that can also help further build both a reckoning with the moment in which we find ourselves and avenues for working our way out of it even if the latter is still unclear.

NOTES

1. Wendy Brown, Max Pensky, and Peter Gordon, *Authoritarianism: Three Inquiries in Critical Theory* (Chicago: Trios, 2018), 4–5.

2. See Matt Vasilogambros, "Republican Wave of Voting Restriction Swells," *Pew Trusts*. March 25, 2021, https://www.pewtrusts.org/en/research-and-analysis/blogs/stateline/2021/03/25/republican-wave-of-voting-restrictions-swells ; Brennan Center for Justice, "Voting Laws Roundup: May 2021," May 28, 2021, https://www.brennancenter.org/our-work/research-reports/voting-laws-roundup-may-2021; and Anthony Salvanto, Fred Backus, and Jennifer De Pinto, "Republicans Weigh in on Liz Cheney and Direction of the GOP-CBS News Poll," *CBS News*, May 15, 2021, https://www.cbsnews.com/news/republicans-liz-cheney-opinion-poll/.

3. James Lindsay, "The 2020 Election by the Numbers," Council on Foreign Relations December 15, 2020, https://www.cfr.org/blog/2020-election-numbers.

4. Lisa Lerer, "Marooned at Mar-A-Lago, Trump Still Has Iron Grip on Republicans," *New York Times*. June 5, 2021, https://www.nytimes.com/2021/05/08/us/politics/trump-republicans-liz-cheney.html.

5. Gilles Deleuze and Félix Guattari, *Anti-Oedipus: Capitalism and Schizophrenia Vol. 1* (Minneapolis: University of Minnesota Press, 1983), 229.

6. Deleuze and Guattari, *Anti-Oedipus*, 104.

7. Jason Read, "The Age of Cynicism: Deleuze and Guattari on the Production of Subjectivity in Capitalism," in Ian Buchanan and Nicolas Thoburn (eds.), *Deleuze and Politics* (Edinburgh: Edinburgh University Press, 2008).

8. Read, "The Age of Cynicism," 105.

9. Read, "The Age of Cynicism," 106. See also Gilbert Simondon, *Individuation in Light of Notions of Form and Information (Volume 1)*. Translated by Taylor Adkins (Minneapolis: University of Minnesota Press, 2020).

10. See Karl Marx, "Contribution to the Critique of Political Economy" in David McLellen (ed.), *Karl Marx: Selected Writings, 2nd edition* (Oxford: Oxford UP, 2000), 424–450.

11. See, for instance, Louis Althusser, *For Marx*, translated by Ben Brewster (New York: Verso, 2005).

12. See, Katharyne Mitchell, Sally Marston, and Cindi Katz, C. "Introduction: Life's Work: An Introduction, Review, and Critique." *Antipode*, 35, no. 3 (2003): 415–442; Tithi Bhattacharya ed., *Social Reproduction Theory: Remapping Class, Recentering Oppression* (New York: Pluto Press, 2017); Susan Ferguson, *Women and Work: Feminism, Labor, and Social Reproduction* (New York: Pluto Press, 2019) and Melinda Cooper, *Family Values: Between Neoliberalism and the New Social Conservativism* (Cambridge and London: Zone Books, 2019).

13. Cooper, *Family Values*, 22–23.

14. Deleuze and Guattari, *Anti-Oedipus*, 139

15. Deleuze and Guattari, *Anti-Oedipus*, 139.

16. Dan Smith, "Flow, Code, and Stock: A Note on Deleuze's Political Philosophy," *Deleuze Studies* 5, supplement (2011): 36–55.

17. Read, "The Age of Cynicism," see also Geoff Pfeifer, "The Question of Capitalist Desire: Deleuze and Guattari with Marx," *Continental Thought and Theory: A Journal of Intellectual Freedom* 1, no. 4 (2017): 254–269.

18. Deleuze and Guattari, *Anti-Oedipus*, 222–240.

19. Deleuze and Guattari, *Anti-Oedipus*, 345, 381.

20. Smith, "Flow, Code, and Stock," 40.

21. Quinn Slobodian, *Globalists: The End of Empire and the Birth of Neoliberalism* (Cambridge: Harvard University Press, 2018), 5–7.

22. William Davies, "The New Neoliberalism," *New Left Review* 101 (2016): 121–134.

23. Davies, "The New Neoliberalism," 125.

24. Paul Mirowski and David Plehwe eds., *The Road from Mont Pelerin: The Making of the Neoliberal Thought Collective* (Cambridge, MA: Harvard University Press, 2009).

25. Brown "Authoritarianism" 15. See also F. A. Hayek, *The Constitution of Liberty* (Chicago: University of Chicago Press, 1978).

26. F. A. Hayek, "Competition as Discovery Procedure." Translated by Marcellus S. Snow. *The Quarterly Journal of Austrian Economics* 5, no. 3 (2002): 9–23.

27. Davies, "The New Neoliberalism," 127.

28. See Michel Foucault, *The Birth of Biopolitics*. Translated by Graham Burchell (New York: Picador, 2008) and Pierre Dardot and Christian Laval, *The New Way of the World: On Neoliberal Society*. Translated by Gregory Elliot (New York and London: Verso, 2013).

29. Davies, "The New Neoliberalism," 126.

30. Ian Bruff, "The Rise of Authoritarian Neoliberalism," *Rethinking Marxism* 26, no. 1 (2014): 113–129; Bruff, Ian and Cemel Burak Tansel, "Authoritarian Neoliberalism: Trajectories of Knowledge Production an Praxis," *Globalizations* 16, no. 3 (2019): 233–244; and Adam Fabry and Sune Sandbeck, "Introduction to Special Issue on 'Authoritarian Neoliberalism,'" *Competition and Change* 23, no. 2 (2019): 109–115.

31. Davies, "The New Neoliberalism," 130. See also William Davies et al., "Financial Melancholia: Mental Health and Indebtedness," Political Economy Research Centre, Goldsmiths, London 2015.

32. Maurizio Lazzarato, *The Making of the Indebted Man: An Essay on the Neoliberal Condition*. Translated by Joshua David Jordan (Los Angeles: Semiotext, 2011).

33. Gilles Deleuze, "Postscript on Societies of Control," 59 (1992): 3–7.

34. Lazzarato, *The Making of Indebted Man*, 104.

35. Davies, "The New Neoliberalism," 131.

36. See Luc Wacquant, *Punishing the Poor: The Neoliberal Government of Social Insecurity* (Durham, NC: Duke University Press, 2009); Joshua Page and Joe Soss, "Criminal Justice Predation and Neoliberal Governance," in *Rethinking Neoliberalism: Resisting the Disciplinary Regime*, edited by Sanford Schram and Marianna Pavlovskaya, 139–59 (New York: Routledge, 2018) and Geoff Pfeifer, "Balibar, Citizenship, and the Return of Right Populism," *Philosophy and Social Criticism* 46, no. 3 (2020): 323–341.

37. Jennifer Silva, *Coming Up Short: Working Class Adulthood in an Age of Uncertainty* (Oxford: Oxford University Press 2013), 109.

38. Silva, *Coming up Short*, 109.

39. See the Pew Center's report showing only 28 percent of voters aged 18–29 voted for Trump, "An Examination of the 2016 Electorate Based on Validated Voters," Pew Center, August 9, 2018, https://www.pewresearch.org/politics/2018/08/09/an-examination-of-the-2016-electorate-based-on-validated-voters/.

40. See Bruff, "The Rise of Authoritarian Neoliberalism," 116

41. See, for instance, Mutz, Diana Mutz, "Status Threat not Economic Hardship Explains the 2016 Presidential Vote."

PNAS 15, no. 19 (2017): E4330–E4339, and Stephen L. Morgan, "Status Threat, Material Interests, and the 2016 Presidential Vote," *Socius* 4 (2018): 1–17.

42. Pfeifer, "Balibar, Citizenship, and the Return of Right Populism."

BIBLIOGRAPHY

Althusser, Louis. *For Marx*. Translated by Ben Brewster. New York: Verso, 2005.

Bhattacharya, Tithi ed. 2017. *Social Reproduction Theory: Remapping Class, Recentering Oppression.* New York: Pluto Press, 2017.

Brennan Center for Justice, "Voting Laws Roundup: May 2021" May 28, 2021, https://www.brennancenter.org/our-work/research-reports/voting-laws-roundup-may-2021

Brown, Wendy, Peter Gordon, and Max Pensky. *Authoritarianism: Three Inquiries in Critical Theory*. Chicago: University of Chicago Press, 2018.

Bruff, Ian. "The Rise of Authoritarian Neoliberalism" *Rethinking Marxism* 26, no. 1 (2014): 113–129.

Bruff, Ian and Cemel Burak Tansel. "Authoritarian Neoliberalism: Trajectories of Knowledge Production an Praxis" *Globalizations* 16, no. 3 (2019): 233–244.

Cooper, Melinda. *Family Values: Between Neoliberalism and the New Social Conservativism.* Cambridge and London: Zone Books, 2017.

Dardot, Pierre and Christian Laval. *The New Way of the World: On Neoliberal Society*. Translated by Gregory Elliot. New York and London: Verso, 2013.

Davies, William. "The New Neoliberalism" *New Left Review* 101 (2016): 121–134.

Davies, William, Johnna Montgomerie, and Sara Wallin. "Financial Melancholia: Mental Health and Indebtedness," Political Economy Research Centre, Goldsmiths, London, 2015.

Deleuze, Gilles. "Postscript on Societies of Control" 59 (1992): 3–7.

Deleuze, Gilles and Félix Guattari. *Anti-Oedipus: Capitalism and Schizophrenia.* Minneapolis: University of Minnesota Press, 1983.

Fabry, Adam and Sune Sandbeck. "Introduction to Special Issue on 'authoritarian neoliberalism'" *Competition and Change* 23, no. 2 (2019): 109–115.

Ferguson, Susan. *Women and Work: Feminism, Labor, and Social Reproduction.* New York: Pluto Press, 2019.

Foucault, Michel. *The Birth of Biopolitics.* Translated by Graham Burchell. New York: Picador, 2008.

Hayek, F. A. "Competition as Discovery Procedure" Translated by Marcellus S. Snow. *The Quarterly Journal of Austrian Economics* 5, no. 3 (2002): 9–23.

———. *The Constitution of Liberty*. Chicago: University of Chicago Press, 1978.

———. *The Road to Serfdom.* Edited by Bruce Caldwell. Chicago: University of Chicago Press, 2017.

Lazzarato, Maurizio. *The Making of the Indebted Man: An Essay on the Neoliberal Condition.* Translated by Joshua David Jordan. Los Angeles: Semiotext, 2011.

Lindsay, James. "The 2020 Election by the Numbers," Council on Foreign Relations December 15, 2020, https://www.cfr.org/blog/2020-election-numbers

Lerer, Lisa. "Marooned at Mar-A-Lago, Trump Still has Iron Grip on Republicans," *New York Times,* June 5, 2021, https://www.nytimes.com/2021/05/08/us/politics/trump-republicans-liz-cheney.html

Marx, Karl. "Contribution to the Critique of Political Economy," in *Karl Marx: Selected Writings 2nd Edition*, edited by David McLellen, 424–450. Oxford: Oxford UP, 2000.

Mirowski, Paul and David Plehwe, eds. *The Road from Mont Pelerin: The Making of the Neoliberal Thought Collective*. Cambridge, MA: Harvard University Press, 2009.

Mitchell, Katharyne, Sally Marston, and Cindi Katz. "Introduction: Life's Work: An Introduction, Review, and Critique." *Antipode*, 35, no. 3 (2003): 415–442.

Morgan, Stephen L. "Status Threat, Material Interests, and the 2016 Presidential Vote," *Socius* 4 (2018): 1–17.

Mutz, Diana. "Status Threat not Economic Hardship Explains the 2016 Presidential Vote." *PNAS* 15, no. 19 (2017): E4330–E4339.

Page, Joshua, and Joe Soss. "Criminal Justice Predation and Neoliberal Governance." In *Rethinking Neoliberalism: Resisting the Disciplinary Regime*, edited by Sanford Schram and Marianna Pavlovskaya, 139–159. New York: Routledge, 2018.

Pew Center. "An Examination of the 2016 Electorate Based on Validated Voters," August 9, 2018, https://www.pewresearch.org/politics/2018/08/09/an-examination-of-the-2016-electorate-based-on-validated-voters/

Pfeifer, Geoff. "Balibar, Citizenship, and the Return of Right- Populism," *Philosophy and Social Criticism* 46, no. 3 (2020): 323–341.

———. "The Question of Capitalist Desire: Deleuze and Guattari with Marx," *Continental Thought and Theory: A Journal of Intellectual Freedom* 1, no. 4 (2017): 254–269.

Read, Jason. "The Age of Cynicism: Deleuze and Guattari on the Production of Subjectivity in Capitalism," in *Deleuze and Politics,* edited by Ian Buchanan and Nicolas Thoburn. Edinburgh: Edinburgh University Press, 2008.

Salvanto, Anthony, Fred Backus, and Jennifer De Pinto. "Republicans weigh in on Liz Cheney and Direction of the GOP-CBS News Poll," *CBS News*, May 15, 2021, https://www.cbsnews.com/news/republicans-liz-cheney-opinion-poll/

Silva, Jennifer. *Coming Up Short: Working Class Adulthood in an Age of Uncertainty*. Oxford: Oxford University Press, 2013.

Simondon, Gilbert. *Individuation in Light of Notions of Form and Information (Volume 1)*. Translated by Taylor Adkins. Minneapolis: University of Minnesota Press, 2020.

Slobodian, Quinn. *Globalists: The End of Empire and the Birth of Neoliberalism*. Cambridge: Harvard University Press, 2018.

Smith, Dan. "Flow, Code, and Stock: A Note on Deleuze's Political Philosophy," *Deleuze Studies* 5, supplement (2011): 36–55.

Vasilogambros, Matt. "Republican Wave of Voting Restriction Swells," *Pew Trusts*. March 25, 2021, https://www.pewtrusts.org/en/research-and-analysis/blogs/stateline/2021/03/25/republican-wave-of-voting-restrictions-swells

Wacquant, L. *Punishing the Poor: The Neoliberal Government of Social Insecurity*. Durham, NC: Duke University Press, 2009.

Chapter 12

Foucault's Troublesome Hypothesis

Notes on a New History

John Rajchman

The question posed by this volume goes back to a vital moment of contestation and debate in Paris no longer our own. Foucault, Deleuze, Psychoanalysis, the Politics of Desire—all this now appears to us as an entangled knot, with multiple strands, a legacy at once complex and unresolved. It is not clear we still have the same view today not only of desire and sexuality but also of politics and therefore the kinds of movements in which they might figure. We have long sought to rethink the larger legacy of May 68 itself. Already at the time, Deleuze and Guattari were pointedly asking why "May 68 didn't take place"; more recently, Jean-Luc Nancy has proposed to see 68 in terms of a disruptive truth in democratic politics rather than in terms of revolution or reform.[1] How then can we draw—or cross—the line that separates us from this earlier moment of contestation and struggle? What then would a politics of desire look like for us today? Where and for whom? How, in short, can we retrospectively see and take up this multiple legacy now, confronted with new forces and questions in a geopolitical setting no longer centered in Paris alone? Such is the larger cluster of questions I'd like to introduce into the discussion. What follow are notes for a new history in which to formulate and develop them. I take as a starting point a troublesome hypothesis Foucault introduced in 1976 and the new unresolved question it posed at the time—that of a politics of truth.

Foucault and Deleuze's relations with psychoanalysis of course go back much earlier. But we can now see this question of 1976 as initiating or exploring a disaccord, opening up divergent paths, later crossing with one another, and leading up to our situation today. Foucault came to imagine political movements or struggles as being at once singular and multiple, brought together in zones of contestation and questioning at a given moment, in particular, following 68 with the new feminist, sexual, anti-racist, movements of the day, and the role knowledge and power played in them. Such movement is always what comes first, opening up, in any given moment a new "we" not yet given. Looking back at the sexual liberation movements that had grown up after 68 in this way, he tried to introduce a new question. What it would it mean to see them not in terms of repressed desire or the law that structures it but in terms of the practice of confession or avowal (*l'aveu*) regarded as a kind of *Wahrsagen* in a new political history of truth?[2] Such was the new game he wanted to play, the new sort of history of sexuality he had hoped to open up. One can't say it was wildly popular—Baudrillard even said we should "forget Foucault"—and the hypothesis would prove troublesome in another way: for the development of Foucault's own thought. In his *The History of Sexuality*, he would move away from the original focus on "modern" sexuality in Europe; at the same, his new political history of truth would be elaborated along new lines and the game played in new ways. In 1976, in an interview on the function of the intellectual, he had declared, "The political question, to sum up . . . is truth itself."[3] In 1978, in a series of writings about Kant that would accompany him until the end, he added a new problem, captured in the phrase "We don't want to be governed like this anymore."[4] Such was the battle cry in the very idea of Critique that Kant had introduced and its relation to an ever changing "present." In this turn we can now see a new focus on disobedience, dissidence, and "counter-conduct" in the politics of truth, which Foucault would take up in his last courses on parrhesia in ancient Greece. As François Ewald suggests in a late interview,[5] it is not clear where this leaves the troublesome hypothesis he had introduced back in 1976 in his sketch of a modern *dispositif* of sexuality, centered in the normal and the pathological, inseparable from a rise in state biologizing racism and the idea of degeneracy, as well as in the new questions of truth and psychiatric power, posed by the hysterics in Charcot's clinic.

The great *Nachlass* of Foucault's writings that has appeared piecemeal since that time has shaped and sharpened all these questions, and in particular, the role of the "politics of truth" in them. As Daniel Defert puts it in his presentation of Foucault's inaugural Course at the Collège de France in 1970, we can now see "that the work of Michel Foucault only ever had one object: the truth."[6] The posthumous publication of Foucault's courses, unfinished projects, "sayings and writings," spread out over many years, has given us in effect a new Foucault, in many ways our contemporary. In 2004, 20 years later, Jacques Rancière was already talking about Foucault's "difficult legacy"—that of a style of thought that challenges us and mobilizes us without telling us what to do or think, which poses questions *to* politics rather than simply posing "political questions," often sounding themselves like the administrative matters Foucault had associated with "police science."[7] Sexual politics was one aspect of this difficult legacy: Rancière drawing in particular a contrast with David Halperin with respect to Foucault's relations with gay politics. Over the last 15 years, we have come to see this problematizing role of truth and truth-saying not only in the difficult legacy of Foucault's work but in our own unsettled and unsettling times today, in the renewed debate about truth and truth-saying and our politics and the populisms we now confront.

What then was Foucault's hypothesis back in 1976 in *La volonté de savoir*? Why was it so troublesome, upsetting relations and friendships given the new role psychoanalysis was acquiring in politics? This book, which Foucault had initially wanted to call "Sex and Truth," was rather different in kind from *Surveiller et punir*, published just a year before. It tried to introduce a "game of truth," with new stakes and uncertain outcomes, combining the politics of truth with a new way of thinking the "history of sexuality." It announced a monumental project in five volumes, which Foucault would abandon, taking up and rethinking his ideas in the courses and lectures that followed. Central to this new game was a political history of *L'aveu* in the history of sexuality. But we now know this was not the first or the last time that Foucault would take up the question. The trouble the book would cause, the "disaccord" to which it would lead, was due to its focus on psychoanalysis in the new sexual liberation movements of the time. To interconnect at once "sex without the law and power without the king"—such Foucault declared was the stakes of his new history of sexuality and the new game of truth he was trying to introduce into it.[8]

As Daniel Defert has shown, the question of a political history of *l'aveu* had been raised much earlier, already in his inaugural lecture at the Collège de France, in connection with his new questions about the "will to truth" in Nietzsche. In particular it was developed in a lecture Foucault had given in the United States called "The Knowledge of Oedipus," in which he proposed to read *Oedipus Rex* in terms of various "juridical forms" of *l'aveu*—a project he would later take up later in Rio and much later in Louvain.[9] But in these lectures the focus was never on psychoanalysis or Charcot, or hysteria. In Louvain the focus was instead on the strange game and "speech act" of "admitting to one's problems" in psychiatry, and an expanded history of "testimony" in law. For Foucault had started to move away from his focus on "modern sexuality" in Europe, looking back to its role in Christianity, its "pastoral power," its monastic institutions, its focus on the problem of "the flesh," so different from the ancient Greek problem of moderating the excesses of "aphrodisia," or the modern European questions of normality and sexual identity.

In 1976, Foucault's focus had been not only on psychoanalysis but on Lacan's way of refocusing it on truth and its new role in the women's movement. As he would later say, Lacan was the first since Freud to recenter psychoanalysis around the question of truth[10]—a truth betrayed in our symptoms but never fully said, calling for a new discourse outside the university, or psychiatry, indeed outside any "discourse of the Master," in which women would play a singular role. Lacan himself started to talk of a "femininity" irreducible to the logic of any constituted gender difference. In 1974 in his course on *Psychiatric Power*[11] Foucault had tried to trace politics of women in truth-saying back to the theatrical "battle of truth" waged by working-class women in Charcot's clinic. Today all this has now become well-known: the "invention" of hysteria, the new category of trauma and memory, and the role of women and psychoanalysis in it.

How then can we see the legacy of this formation today? Why did Foucault himself abandon it, taking his project of the politics of truth in new directions? What separates us from this earlier moment of protest and contestation? It seems we now no longer have at our disposal the larger field of "anti-" or "alternative" psychiatric practice on which Foucault could rely at the time, and in which he had already started to intervene with his *History of Madness* in the early 1960s. We no longer have the same attitudes toward sexuality and "mental health" and its workers. Anti-psychiatry today has now itself become for us a multiple and enigmatic legacy, found in one way with the role of Félix Guattari at La Borde and in another with Franz Fanon's work with François Tosquelles on the psychopathology of colonialism. Can the question of woman and truth now be rescued from its Lacanian setting, extending it to other areas, as with Antoinette Fouque's turn in the 1990s to the new issues surrounding women raised by the Islamic formation that was taking shape in Algeria?[12] With these questions about women in Islam, we find a complication of Foucault's tendency to focus on Christianity in his history of *l'aveu*. For that we need to look back instead at Foucault's interventions in Iran; in a striking new book about them, Behrooz Ghamari-Tabrizi, himself an activist at the time, has looked back at the actual role of women in the uprising there and the ways it was misunderstood by European and American feminists at the time.[13] Women and their singular ways of "truth-saying" have come to play a key role in the rise of new "leaderless" movements today, as, for example, with a writer like Chimamanda Ngozi Adichie in Nigeria, or in the current Harik uprising in Algeria, or indeed with the resistance of the 'Women's March' and then the Black Lives Matter movement.

The way sex and desire figure in the "politics of truth" thus goes beyond Foucault's new political history of *l'aveu* and the way it had figured in the psychoanalytically inflected movements that took shape in Paris following 68. But that was not the only kind of "truth-saying," the only kind of "veridiction" that mattered. When we look back at Foucault's last two courses, we see another line of investigation, mobilizing the sort of questions posed *to* politics that Rancière would see in Foucault's difficult legacy—a politics of refusal or disobedience in the ways we govern ourselves and one another, giving rise to new processes of subjectivization. Setting aside the story he told in the last two volumes of his *The History of Sexuality*, hastily put together as he was dying, Foucault would turn to these political questions in his last courses and related materials. He had already formulated this new problem in his various attempts, in 1978, to rethink the very idea of Critique in Kant and Kant's relations with Enlightenment and Revolution captured in the phrase "We don't want to be governed like this anymore." This sort of "voluntary insubordination" involved a politics of truth, to be found in movements of "dissidence" and "disobedience" across the borders of the Cold War divisions then still in force. "Critique," he declared,

> is the movement by which the subject gives himself the right to question truth on its effects on power and question power on its discourse of truth. Well then, critique will be the art of voluntary insubordination . . . a desubjugation of the subject in what, in a word, we could call a politics of truth.[14]

It was to such questions that Foucault would return in his extended analysis of truth-saying in fifth-century Athens, focused on the role of cynical parrhesia—on free or fearless speech, on public space and citizenship. In a recent essay,[15] Étienne Balibar has looked back at the implications of this analysis for current discussions of "free public expression," associated with a picture of democratic politics not based in any one political regime, mobilized instead by uprisings and related movements that interrupt the political institutions at a given moment, opening up new questions or potentials in them—what he proposes to call "contra-diction." In Foucault's own work he suggests this idea is already to be found in the "intolerance-investigations" carried on by the Group for Information on Prisons (GIP), then later in the "counter-conducts" in Christian "spirituality," as well as in later movements in Europe. It is this theme that Foucault then took up in the pre-Christian context of ancient Athens in his analysis of cynical "free speech," now regarded as a kind of truth-saying or *dire-vrai*.

This turn in Foucault's work retrospectively sheds light on yet another side of the debate about desire in 1976 and the role of psychoanalysis in it: his dramatic disaccord with Gilles Deleuze. The impact of May 68 on the politics of psychoanalysis marks a turning point in Deleuze's work. It was the start at once in style and thought of his new experiment in "multiple authorship" with Félix Guattari, which at first at least was an attempt to push Lacan in a new direction, no longer dependent on a constitutive law refracted in the family, but tied up instead with the emergence of "transversal groups," and in particular with the new questions of "intolerance" Foucault was raising at the time in GIP. Foucault's disagreement with Deleuze would come later, in 1976, following precisely his troublesome hypothesis about the politics of truth. Foucault had grown allergic to the very idea of desire, skeptical that there was anything "revolutionary" about it as such, wondering whether this idea might itself just be a by-product of the modern European *dispositif* of sexuality. Later he would simply declare that Deleuze's topic is desire, while mine is truth.[16] For his part, we now know, Deleuze sent Foucault, via François Ewald, a concerned letter in which he says he doesn't see how truth can be a matter of "resistance" and not simply of "power," as Foucault was using those terms.[17] The two would stop talking, coming back together only as Foucault was dying.

But we can now see how this division was complicated by the paths each would take afterward. Deleuze and Guattari would go on to introduce new questions of "territory" and "deterritorialization" into the notion of desire, seeing sexual politics in terms of "minority" and 'becoming', and Deleuze, for his part, would raise the question of truth in new ways, remarkable to read today. In his essay on Herman Melville's "Bartleby,"[18] seen in terms of the Revolutions in America and Russia, and the new kinds of solidarity they would introduce, he takes up the great pragmatist theme of "truth and trust" and the new question it raises: What happens when "trust" is lost? What are the politics of "distrust," when all belief in government is lost? In Melville, he already finds an answer: the rise of "confidence men," working in a world of manipulation where all is false. Along with what Nietzsche had called "the last men," this problem called for a new response, what Deleuze called a "belief in the world" that he would go on to elaborate in his study of film.[19] All along, Foucault and Deleuze had been allied in another way: on the question of "sex without the Law, power without the King," in opposition to Georges Bataille and "transgression," as well as to the sort of mysticism of the law, in a democracy or an insurrection to come, found in different ways in Jacques Derrida and Giorgio Agamben. Truth is a matter of this world, of other possibilities in this world, and of a sort of trust or belief in them, prior to any such mystical law or judgment.

How then did sexual politics figure in this attempt to reinsert the practice of cynical parrhesia into our picture of the slave owning, patriarchal, colonizing democracy of fifth-century Athens, with its tragic theater, its philosophical Academy, its agonistic debate in the *agora*, over sophistry, rhetoric, and the nature of philosophical truth? Let's take the case of Hipparchia, the first woman philosopher, the first "feminist" philosopher, who introduced a whole new kind of "gender trouble" in public and private, involving dress codes and scandalous acts, and a new role for women in public philosophical debate. Can we see something of this practice more generally in the role of "performance" in the theater of political movements and the new role that women and sexuality play have come to play in them? In what sense was such cynical counter-practice already at the time said to be "cosmopolitical"? In what ways was Hipparchia a "citizen of the world" rather than of any already constituted polis, her truth-saying opening up within it a new "outside"? In what ways was this outside a matter not of a True Life found in a Higher Realm of ideas and our access to them but rather of other possibilities of living, other ways of governing ourselves and one and another in *this* world? As with what Deleuze would call belief in the world the problem of cynical parrhesia was not only about scandalous counter-conduct in dress, marriage, and thinking but also about truth itself.

What then more generally might Foucault's troublesome hypothesis tell us today, not simply about desire and psychoanalysis but about our own current debates surrounding "big lies" and the ways they have come to figure in our new populisms and new media, and the role sex and gender now plays in them? The project Foucault left unfinished retains for us today a number of original features: as never before, Foucault introduced into our understanding of truth the question of the present, of *l'actuel*, and the role played in it by the kind of disobedient contestation that opens up the possibility of invention of a new people, a new "We" not already given. That is why no fixed or monolithic narrative can precede or contain it, why it must constantly be reinvented, and why its task is endless. Truth is thus a thing of this world and involves a realism about the regimes and operations of truth in it. In Paris in 1976 that meant a whole cluster of questions surrounding desire, psychoanalysis, psychiatric knowledge, and power. Perhaps our renewed debate about truth and democracy today can also be seen as a singular disruption without a single prior model, either in the Weimar Republic, or in Soviet propaganda and George Orwell's view of it, or even in the United States with the legacies of Jim Crow racism, drawing instead on many sources at once, and calling for new kinds of invention and resistance. We then find a second principle in the politics of truth in Foucault: that there are many truths, and many ways of saying it, rather as when Nietzsche's Zarathustra says, "I came to my truth by many ways, in many ways . . . for THE WAY does not exist." The politics of truth is thus always multiple and involves many new intersections, relations, and solidarities and new ways of working and thinking together. How then might the politics of desire figure in the global geographies of today and the new transnational spaces of interaction and intersection they call for? In a note for his last lecture that he was never able to finally say, Foucault wrote,

> What I would like to stress in the end is this: there is no establishment of truth without an essential position of otherness. Truth is never the same; there can only be truth in the form of another world, another life.[20]

Perhaps these last words now help us to see what makes Foucault our contemporary and to suggest how his troublesome hypothesis might serve as a source for new invention and new thinking for us today.

NOTES

1. Gilles Deleuze, "May '68 Did Not Take Place" in *Two Regimes of Madness: Texts and Interviews 1975-1995*, ed. David Lapoujade (Cambridge: Semiotext(e),

2007), 233–236; Jean-Luc Nancy, *The Truth of Democracy* (New York: Fordham University Press, 2010).

2. By drawing upon Nietzsche, Foucault calls *Wahrsagen* "the *act* of truth-telling" (Emphasis in original) in Michel Foucault, *Wrong-Doing, Truth-Telling: The Function of Avowal in Justice*, ed. Fabienne Brion and Bernard E. Harcourt, trans. Stephen W. Sawyer (Chicago: The University of Chicago Press, 2014), 20.

3. Michel Foucault, "Truth and Power" in *Power/Knowledge: Selected Interviews & Other Writings 1972-1977*, ed. Colin Gordon, trans. Colin Gordon, Leo Marshall, John Mepham, and Kate Soper (New York: Pantheon Books, 1980), 133.

4. Michel Foucault, "What Is Critique?" in *The Politics of Truth*, ed. Sylvère Lotringer, trans. Lysa Hochroth and Catherine Porter (Cambridge: Semiotext(e), 2007), 44.

5. Michel Foucault, "The Concern for Truth" in *Foucault Live*, ed Sylvère Lotringer, trans. Lysa Hochroth and John Johnston (New York: Semiotext(e),1996), 455–464.

6. Daniel Defert, "Course Context" in Michel Foucault, *Lectures on the Will to Know (Lectures at the Collège de France 1970-1971) and Oedipal Knowledge*, ed. Daniel Defert, trans. Graham Burchell (London: Palgrave Macmillan, 2013), 262–281. For a remarkable elaboration of this view see "Seminar with Daniel Defert: 'Reflections on Foucault's Will to Know,'" filmed May 2013 at the University of Chicago Political Science Department and The France Chicago Center, Chicago, IL, video, 1:52:04, https://www.youtube.com/watch?v=60R7hFuRnlg&list=PL4pJgpthYlJevfqlh_vH8asDnm5xKMWlg.

7. Jacques Rancière, "The Difficult Legacy of Michel Foucault, June 2004" in *Chronicles of Consensual Times*, trans. Steven Corcoran (London: Continuum, 2010), 124–128.

8. Michel Foucault, *The History of Sexuality Volume I: An Introduction*, trans. Robert Hurley (New York: Pantheon Books, 1978), 91.

9. Michel Foucault, "Oedipal Knowledge" in *Lectures on the Will to Know (Lectures at the Collège de France 1970-1971) and Oedipal Knowledge*, ed. Daniel Defert (London: Palgrave Macmillan, 2013), 229–257; Michel Foucault, "Truth and Juridical Forms" in *Power*, ed. James D. Faubion (New York: The New Press, 2000), 1–89; Michel Foucault, *Wrong-Doing, Truth-Telling: The Function of Avowal in Justice*, ed. Fabienne Brion and Bernard Harcourt (Chicago: The University of Chicago Press, 2014).

10. Michel Foucault, "6 January 1982: First Hour" in *The Hermeneutics of the Subject (Lectures at the Collège de France, 1981-82)*, ed. Frédéric Gros (New York: Palgrave Macmillan, 2005), 1–24. See "Lacan, le 'libérateur' de la psychanalyse" in Michel Foucault, *Dits et Écrits 1954-1988 IV*, ed. Daniel Defert and François Ewald (Paris: Éditions Gallimard, 1994), 204–205. Among Lacanian analysts, Jean Allouch would engage with the questions in Foucault's last phase.

11. Michel Foucault, "6 February 1974" in *Psychiatric Power (Lectures at the Collège de France 1973-1974)*, 297–323. Georges Didi-Huberman recalls Foucault's support of his own later research of the Charcot archives in 1981, noting an indifference to the issue of psychoanalysis ("all that doesn't matter") in "Knowing When

to Cut' in *Foucault Against Himself*, ed. François Caillat (Vancouver: Arsensal Pulp Press, 2015), 77–110.

12. Antoinette Fouque, *There Are Two Sexes* (New York: Columbia University Press, 2016).

13. Behrooz Ghamari-Tabrizi, *Foucault in Iran: Islamic Revolution after the Enlightenment* (Minneapolis: University of Minnesota Press, 2016).

14. Michel Foucault, "What Is Critique?" in *The Politics of Truth*, ed. Sylvère Lotringer, trans. Lysa Hochroth and Catherine Porter (Cambridge: Semiotext(e), 2007), 47.

15. Étienne Balibar, "Dire, contredire: sur les formes de *parrhesia* selon Foucault' in *Libre parole* (Paris : Éditions Galilée, 2008), 81.

16. Gérard Raulet, "Structuralism and Post-Structuralism: An Interview with Michel Foucault" in *Telos* XVL, no. 55 (Spring 1983): 195.

17. Gilles Deleuze, "Desire and Pleasure" in *Foucault and His Interlocutors*, ed. Arnold I. Davidson (Chicago: The University of Chicago Press, 1997) 183–192.

18. Gilles Deleuze, "Bartleby; or, The Formula" in *Essays Critical and Clinical*, trans. Daniel W. Smith and Michael A. Greco (New York: Verso, 1998), 68–90.

19. Deleuze returns to the question in an interview with Toni Negri in Gilles Deleuze, "Control and Becoming" in *Negotiations, 1972-1990*, trans. Martin Joughin (New York: Columbia University Press), 169–176, declaring, "To believe in the world is what we need most."

20. Frédéric Gros, "Course Context" in Michel Foucault, *The Courage of the Truth (The Government of Self and Others II) Lectures at the Collège de France 1983-1984*, ed. Frédéric Gros (London: Palgrave Macmillan, 2011), 356.

REFERENCES

Balibar, Étienne, "Dire, contredire: sur les formes de *parrhesia* selon Foucault' in *Libre parole*. Paris : Éditions Galilée, 2008.

Behrooz, Ghamari-Tabrizi, *Foucault in Iran: Islamic Revolution after the Enlightenment*. Minneapolis: University of Minnesota Press, 2016.

Defert, Daniel, "Course Context" in Michel Foucault, *Lectures on the Will to Know (Lectures at the Collège de France 1970-1971) and Oedipal Knowledge*, edited by Daniel Defert. Translated by Graham Burchell. London: Palgrave Macmillan, 2013.

Deleuze, Gilles, "Bartleby; or, The Formula" in *Essays Critical and Clinical*. Translated by Daniel W. Smith and Michael A. Greco. New York: Verso, 1998.

Deleuze, Gilles, "Control and Becoming" in *Negotiations, 1972-1990*. Translated by Martin Joughin. New York: Columbia University Press, 1997.

Deleuze, Gilles, "Desire and Pleasure" in *Foucault and His Interlocutors*, edited by Arnold I. Davidson. Chicago: The University of Chicago Press, 1997.

Deleuze, Gilles, "May '68 Did Not Take Place" in *Two Regimes of Madness: Texts and Interviews 1975-1995*, edited by David Lapoujade. Cambridge: Semiotext(e), 2007.

Didi-Huberman, Georges, "Knowing When to Cut' in *Foucault Against Himself*, edited by François Caillat. Vancouver: Arsensal Pulp Press, 2015.

Foucault, Michel, "Lacan, le « libérateur » de la psychanalyse" in Michel Foucault, *Dits et Écrits 1954-1988 IV,* edited by Daniel Defert and François Ewald. Paris: Éditions Gallimard, 1994.

Foucault, Michel, "Oedipal Knowledge" in *Lectures on the Will to Know (Lectures at the Collège de France 1970-1971) and Oedipal Knowledge,* edited by Daniel Defert. Translated by Graham Burchell. London: Palgrave Macmillan, 2013.

Foucault, Michel. *Psychiatric Power (Lectures at the Collège de France 1973-1974).* Edited by Jacques Lagrange. Translated by Graham Burchell. London: Palgrave Macmillan, 2006.

Foucault, Michel, "The Concern for Truth" in *Foucault Live*, edited by Sylvère Lotringer. Translated by Lysa Hochroth and John Johnston. New York: Semiotext(e),1996.

Foucault, Michel. *The Hermeneutics of the Subject (Lectures at the Collège de France, 1981-82).* Edited by Frédéric Gros. Translated by Graham Burchell. New York: Palgrave Macmillan, 2005.

Foucault, Michel. *The History of Sexuality Volume I: An Introduction.* Translated by Robert Hurley. New York: Pantheon Books, 1978.

Foucault, Michel, "Truth and Juridical Forms" in *Power,* edited by James D. Faubion. New York: The New Press, 2000.

Foucault, Michel, "Truth and Power" in *Power/Knowledge: Selected Interviews & Other Writings 1972-1977*, edited by Colin Gordon. Translated by Colin Gordon, Leo Marshall, John Mepham, and Kate Soper. New York: Pantheon Books, 1980.

Foucault, Michel, "What is Critique?" in *The Politics of Truth,* edited by Sylvère Lotringer. Translated by Lysa Hochroth and Catherine Porter. Cambridge: Semiotext(e), 2007.

Foucault, Michel. *Wrong-Doing, Truth-Telling: The Function of Avowal in Justice.* Edited by Fabienne Brion and Bernard E. Harcourt. Translated by Stephen W. Sawyer. Chicago: The University of Chicago Press, 2014.

Fouque, Antoinette. *There Are Two Sexes.* New York: Columbia University Press, 2016.

Gros, Frédéric, "Course Context" in Foucault Michel, *The Courage of the Truth (The Government of Self and Others II) Lectures at the Collège de France 1983-1984*, edited by Frédéric Gros. London: Palgrave Macmillan, 2011.

Nancy, Jean-Luc. *The Truth of Democracy.* New York: Fordham University Press, 2010.

Rancière, Jacques, "The Difficult Legacy of Michel Foucault, June 2004" in *Chronicles of Consensual Times.* Translated by Steven Corcoran. London: Continuum, 2010.

Raulet, Gérard, "Structuralism and Post-Structuralism: An Interview with Michel Foucault" in *Telos,* XVL, no. 55 (Spring 1983).

"Seminar with Daniel Defert: 'Reflections on Foucault's Will to Know'," filmed May 2013 at the University of Chicago Political Science Department and The France Chicago Center, Chicago, IL, video, 1:52:04, https://www.youtube.com/watch?v =60R7hFuRnlg&list=PL4pJgpthYlJevfqlh_vH8asDnm5xKMWlg.

Index

Note: Page numbers followed by 'n' refer to notes

Abnormal, 47, 50
Aeschylus, 9
Agamben, Giorgio, 184
ambivalence, 124–26, 128, 137
Anthropology from a Pragmatic Point of View, 27, 28
Antigone, 15
anti-Oedipalism, 131
Anti-Oedipus, 2, 6, 12, 34, 42, 130–32, 134, 135, 137, 165; in question, 48–50
"anti-psy," 42
anti-psychiatry, 131
aphrodisia, 147, 148, 150
apolitism, 45
The Archeology of Knowledge, 78, 113
Augustine, 58, 65, 66
authoritarianism, 161–76
authoritarian neoliberalism, 170, 173–74
autism, 126, 127

autoeroticism, 127
Baldwin, James, 5
Balibar, Étienne, 183
baptism, 59
Basil of Ancyra, 63
Bataille, Georges, 184
Benjamin, Walter, 7–13
Bergson, 79
Bibliothèque nationale, 58
Billings, Joshua, 20n40
Binswanger, Ludwig, 73, 81, 127, 128
biomechanics, 18n10
biopolitical power, 134
bishop of Hippo, 152
Black Lives Matter movement, 182
Blanchot, Maurice, 105
Bleuler, Eugen, 126–28
Braunstein, Nestor, 96
Brecht, Bertolt, 18n10
Brown, Peter, 152
Brown, Wendy, 161, 169
Burchell, Graham, 54n19

capitalism, 161–76
The Care of the Self, 149
care work, 164
Cassian, John, 61, 63, 153
Castel, Robert, 41–55
Charcot, Jean-Martin, 25–27
Chomsky, Noam, 94, 95
Christian ethics, 148
Christianity, 51, 57–67, 146, 147, 150, 153, 155, 181
Chrysostom, John, 58
The City of God, 64

Civilization and Its Discontents, 69
Cixous, Hélène, 26, 33
Clement of Alexandria, 59
concupiscence, 153, 154
Confessions of the Flesh, 58, 60, 62, 151
"Connaissance de l'homme et réflexion transcendentale," 27
constructivism, 18n10
contemporary moment, 161–76
Cooper, Melinda, 164
Copjec, Joan, 93, 96–98
Corriere della sera, 60
Creon, 11
crime fiction, 14
Cucopulos, Alexa, 101–15
culture of confession, 50–51

Davies, William, 168–73
da Vinci, Leonardo, 72
De Baptismo, 59
debt, 171
Defert, Daniel, 180, 181
Deleuze, Gilles, 1, 2, 6, 7, 13–18, 26, 32, 33, 36, 41–55, 70, 74, 75, 77, 78, 102, 103, 106–10, 112–14, 123, 124, 127, 132, 135, 145, 161–76, 179, 183
Dementia Praecox, 127
depsychiatrization, 131
Derrida, Jacques, 184
desexualization, 136
desires, 89, 94–96, 98; authoritarian tyranny, 171–74; disagreement on, 145–58; as object of veridiction, 145–58; production, 162–68; as social product, 162–68; truth of self, 150–54; tyranny, 161–76; *See also individual entries*
Dickmann, Iddo, 102, 104, 105, 108
Didi-Huberman, Georges, 25, 27
Difference and Repetition, 13, 14, 35, 79, 105, 129
Dihle, Albercht, 152
Discipline and Punish, 108, 111
discursive intersubjectivity, 72
Donzelot, Jacques, 54n27
dream, 70–71, 76–80
Dream and Existence, 73, 127
dual governmentalism, 168
Duhamel, Marcel, 6, 7, 13, 14

École Freudienne de Paris, 35
economic anxiety, 174
empiricism, 13
Empiricism and Subjectivity, 73
Encore, 92
ensemble, undoing, 147–50
envoi (for Alexa), 101–15; *Foucault*, 106–13; mise en abyme, 102–6; mutual capture, 113–14; renvoi, 114–15
eschatology, 30
essences, 73
ethnography, 30
Euripides, 9
Ewald, François, 180
exagoreusis, 153
exponential doubling, 112

family issue, 46–48
fascism, 34
Federation of Groups for Institutional Study and Research, 35
finitude, 129
Focuault, Michel: psychoanalytic ambivalence, 123–41
Folie et déraison, 128
Foucauldian genealogy, 42
Foucault, 102, 105–14
Foucault, Michel, 1, 2, 6–13, 24, 26–29, 32–34, 41–55, 58, 60, 63, 70, 74, 75, 77–79, 90, 92–96, 102, 130, 134, 137, 140n52, 145, 148, 151, 152, 155, 156n16, 181, 183; troublesome hypothesis, 179–85
Foucault-Deleuze crossing, 109
Foucault's Strange Eros, 103
fragmentary morphology, 19n15
freedom, 15
French Communist Party, 34

Freud, Sigmund, 1, 6, 8, 58, 62, 66, 69–71, 74, 75, 81, 82n12, 89, 98, 123, 125–28, 133, 136, 137
Freudian orthodoxy, 6
Freudo-Marxism, 133
Fromanger, Gerard, 78

The Gay Science, 75
genital pleasure, metaphorization, 63–64
Ghamari-Tabrizi, Behrooz, 182
Gide, André, 7, 8, 103, 104
Gordon, Peter, 161
governmentality, 62
Gregory of Nanzianze, 60
Gregory of Nyssa, 62
Guattari, Félix, 1, 26, 32, 33, 35, 41–55, 127, 132, 135, 161–76, 179, 183
Guattaro-Deleuzean schizoanalysis, 126
guilt, 11, 96

Hallward, Peter, 123
Halperin, David, 180
Hamlet in Tails, 8
Hayek, F. A., 169
Hellenism, 59
Henri Ey, 127
Highlander, 123
Hipparchia, 184
Hippocrates, 59
Hippocratic school, 25
History of Madness, 58, 73, 108, 111, 182
The History of Sexuality, 5, 6, 28, 32, 42, 58, 63, 78, 96, 133, 134, 145, 146, 151, 152, 180, 182
Hjelmslev, Louis, 110
Hobbes, 14, 165
Hölderlin, Friedrich, 7, 12, 14–17
hyper-repressive desublimation, 135
Hyppolite, Jean, 28
hysteria, 23, 25, 26, 36, 182
hysterical women, 25

ideology, 163–64
imaginal, concept, 82n3
imagination, 31, 69, 70, 73, 74, 77, 80
immortality, 15
Iser, Wolfgang, 105
Izcovich, Luis, 99n3

Janet, Pierre, 128
Jim Crow racism, 185
jouissance, 63, 65, 89, 98
Jung, Carl, 130

Kant, I., 13–18, 27, 28, 74, 183
"Kant: Anthropology, Introduction, Translation, Notes," 28
Keynesian economics, 168
Klein, Melanie, 72
Klossowski, Pierre, 75, 76, 79
knowledge, 7–13, 30; of beautiful souls, 24–27; and unconscious, 27–33
"The Knowledge of Oedipus," 181
Kretschmer, Ernst, 127

Lacan, Jacques, 35, 60, 66, 71–72, 75, 90–92, 95–98, 130, 134, 181; theory of discourse, 92
Laplanche, Jean, 70
L'Archéologie du savoir, 129
La voie communiste, 35
La volonté du savoir, 133
Lazzarato, Maurizio, 170
Lectures on the Will to Know, 6, 54n19
Leonard, Miriam, 11
Le Psychanalysme: L'ordre psychanalytique et le pouvoir, 42
Les mots et les choses, 129
Levine, Steven, 72
liberalism, 140n52
"The Libidinization of Sex," 151
Logic of Sense, 35, 129
L'Ordre psychiatrique: L'âge d'or de l'aliénisme, 42
Louis XIV, 24

MacLeod, Connor, 123
Madness and Civilization, 27, 42
Magritte, René, 77

"Many Thousands Gone," 5
market competition, 169
market rationality, 169
Marx, Karl, 128
Marxism, 34, 145
matryoshka doll, 114–15
Melville, Herman, 107, 184
mental illness, 41
Mental Illness and Personality, 52n3
Merleau-Ponty, Maurice, 72–77
Meyerhold, V. E., 18n10
Mirowski, Paul, 168
mise en abyme, 102–6
Moby Dick, 107
modern sexuality, 181
Mooney, Timothy, 76
multiple authorship, 183
multiple beginnings, 71–76
My tâtonnement, ad hoc encounter, 107

Nachlass, 180
Nancy, Jean-Luc, 179
neoclassicism, 8
neoliberal capital, 168–71
neoliberal desires, 168–71
neoliberal economy, 172
neologism, 59
Nietzsche, Friedrich, 75, 76, 154
normative neoliberalism, 169

obsessional neurotics, 125
obsessive neurosis, 128
Oedipal complex, 6
Oedipal "familialism," 123
Oedipal Knowledge, 6, 11, 12
Oedipal "triangle," 48
Oedipus, 8, 10, 14–17, 47, 131, 155; the detective, 13–18; modern disguises, 7–13
Oedipus, 6, 13; rethinking, 5–20
"Oedipus, or Rational Myth," 7
Oedipus Rex, 5, 9, 15, 17
ontology of discourse, 90
The Order of Things, 28, 29, 73, 74, 77
Orwell, George, 185

Parisian intellectual culture, 130
paroxysmal bloc, 153
pastoral governmentality, 62
pathological life, 25
Pensky, Max, 161
"perversion-heredity-degeneration" model, 135
Phaedrus, 149
phantasms, 31, 69–85
Phenomenology of Perception, 72
pleasure: disagreement on, 145–58
political engagement, 2
Pontalis, J. B., 76
positivism, 30
post-psychoanalysis, 51
power, 2, 7–13, 62, 94
power-knowledge complex, 12
Preti, Giulio, 130
primitive taboos, 125, 128
proscription, 125
psychiatric knowledge, 24
psychiatric power, 6
Psychiatric Power, 43, 182
psychiatry, 24–27, 43–46
psychic ontology, 98
psychic pressures, 82n12
psychoanalysis, 1, 2, 30, 31, 41, 43–46, 128, 129, 131–37, 179, 181, 185; alienation mechanism, 42; 'familialization' of, 132; Marxism and, 34; in question, 41–55; repressive hypothesis of, 96–97; social unconscious of, 44; *See also individual entries*
psychological culture, 50–51
psychotherapies, 81
psy-function, 42, 43, 46–48, 50
punitive neoliberalism, 170, 172, 173
The Punitive Society, 43

quasi-hieroglyphic form, 70

racism, 5, 25, 136, 161, 180, 185
Rancière, Jacques, 180
rationalism, 169

Raulet, G., 154
Read, Jason, 162, 163
Reich, Wilhelm, 136
renvoi, 114–15
repressive hypothesis, 5, 125, 133
reproductive jouissance, 63
residual prudishness, 136
Roussel, Raymond, 77
Rufus, Musonius, 149

Salpêtrière, 23–25, 27, 33, 36
same-sex rights, 95
Saussure, Ferdinand de, 73
schizoanalysis, 34–36, 49
schizophrenia, 49, 126, 127
schizophrenics, 126
Schreber, 35
Schuster, Aaron, 15, 16
scientific consciousness, 27
Scott, Charles, 106
self-consciousness, 17
selfhood, 6
self-knowledge, 6
sexual ethics of marriage, 153
sexuality, 6; Christian invention of, 57–67; deployment of, 41, 135, 140n52; as state of exception, 89–100
sexual liberation movements, 180
Shapiro, Gary, 76
Silva, Jennifer, 172–74
Simondon, Gilbert, 162, 163, 165
skepticism, 1, 74
Slobodian, Quinn, 168
Smith, Daniel, 165, 167
social differentiation, 135
socially reproductive care, 165
Social Reproduction Theory (SRT), 164
Sophocles, 6–9, 16
Soussloff, Catherine, 77
Spinoza, 162, 163, 165
St. Augustine, 64, 147, 151, 152
Stoic ethics of marriage, 149
subjectivation of desire, 66
Subjectivity and Truth, 149
sublimation, 72
sublime laws, 11
symbolic destiny, 72
symbolic function, 81
Symposium, 149

Tertullian, 59
This Is Not a Pipe, 77
A Thousand Plateaus, 79
Tosquelles, François, 182
Totem and Taboo: Some Points of Agreement between the Mental Lives of Savages and Neurotics, 125
touching phobia, 125
"transcendental-empirical" doublet, 76–80
transgression, 184
tribute, 101–18
truths, 93, 185

unconscious: of human knowledge, 29; and knowledge, 27–33; producing, 33–36

Vernant, Jean-Pierre, 6, 8, 11
vicissitudes, 69–85
The Virgin and Christ with Saint Anne, 72

Wahrsagen, 154, 180
What Is Philosophy, 32
Whitebook, Joel, 123
The Will to Knowledge, 32, 41, 43, 46, 50
Women's March, 182

xenophon, 59

Zupančič, Alenka, 28, 31, 32, 98

About the Author

Julian Bourg is associate professor of History at Boston College. He is author of *From Revolution to Ethics: May 1968 and Contemporary French Thought* (2007; 2nd ed. 2017), which won the 2008 Morris D. Forkosch book prize from the *Journal of the History of Ideas*. He is currently writing a book on the conceptual history of terrorism since the eighteenth century.

Agustín Colombo is a postdoctoral researcher of the Fonds de la recherche scientifique FRS-FNRS at the Institut supérieur de philosophie of the Université catholique de Louvain, Belgium. Through Michel Foucault's and Michel Henry's investigation on Christianity, his research develops the critique of subjectivity built up by contemporary French philosophy. His recent publications include "L'expérience des Pères: *Les Aveux de la chair* de Michel Foucault et la formation de l'expérience de la chair" (*Revue théologique de Louvain*, 52, 2021, p. 43–64) and "What Is a Desiring Man?" (*Foucault Studies*, Issue 29, p. 71–90). He is the editor of several books on the thought of Michel Foucault, most recently *Pensar con Foucault hoy* (2019) and *Foucault, Les Pères, le sexe. Autour des Aveux de la chair* (2021).

Frédéric Gros is PhD in philosophy and holds a HDR (*habilitation à diriger des recherches*). Former student of the l'Ecole Normale Supérieure de la rue d'Ulm, he is also "agregé" in philosophy. He is Professeur des Universités at Sciences-Po (Institut d'études politiques de Paris), where he teaches humanités politiques (*political humanities*). His research focuses on French contemporary philosophy, in particular Michel Foucault. He is the editor of Foucault's lectures at the College de France: *Subjectivity and Truth*, *The Hermeneutics of the Subject*, *The Government of the Self and Others*, and *The Courage of Truth*. He also edited Foucault's *Oeuvres* published in the collection "Bibliothèque de la Pléaide" by Gallimard. His main research topics are the foundations of the right to punish, the problems of war and security, and the ethics of the political subject (especially through the problem of obedience/disobedience). His current research focuses on shame as political affect. He is most recently author of *Désobéir* (Albin Michel, 2017) published in English in 2020 (*Disobey! A Philosophy of Resistance*).

Laura Hengehold is professor of philosophy at Case Western Reserve University in Cleveland, Ohio, where she teaches and researches political philosophy and theory of sexuality with continental European and African sources. Her previous book includes *The Body Problematic: Kant and Foucault on Political Imagination and Simone de Beauvoir's Philosophy of Individuation.* She is also editor (with Nancy Bauer) of the Blackwell Companion to Simone de Beauvoir and editor and translator of Jean-Godefroy Bidima's Law and the Public Sphere in Africa, as well as Seloua Luste Boulbina's Kafka's Monkey and Other Phantoms of Africa.

Lynne Huffer is Samuel Candler Dobbs Professor of Women's, Gender, and Sexuality Studies at Emory University. She is the author of a trilogy on Foucault's ethics of eros: *Foucault's Strange Eros* (2020), *Are the Lips a Grave?: A Queer Feminist on the Ethics of Sex* (2013), and *Mad for Foucault: Rethinking the Foundations of Queer Theory* (2010). She is also the author of *Maternal Pasts, Feminist Futures: Nostalgia, Ethics, and the Question of Difference* (1998) and *Another Colette: The Question of Gendered Writing* (1992). She has published academic articles on feminist theory, queer theory, Foucault, ethics, and the Anthropocene, as well as personal essays, creative nonfiction, and opinion pieces in mass media venues. She is also the author, with Jennifer Yorke, of *Wading Pool*, a collaborative artist's book (http://www.vampandtramp.com/finepress/h/Lynne-Huffer-Jennifer-Yorke.html). Her current book project is *Respite: 99 Anthropocene Fragments.*

Corey McCall taught philosophy for a number of years at Elmira College and now teaches for the Cornell Prison Education Program. His work focuses on ethical and aesthetic questions across Continental, American, and Africana philosophical traditions. His most recent book is the coedited collection *Decolonizing American Philosophy* (SUNY, 2021).

Edward McGushin is professor of philosophy at Stonehill College. He is author of Foucault's Askésis: *An Introduction to the Philosophical Life* (Northwestern University Press, 2007) and many articles and chapters on contemporary continental philosophy. He is the Coordinator of the Foucault Circle and an Affiliate Scholar at the Boston Psychoanalytic Society and Institute.

Geoff Pfeifer is associate professor of Philosophy and International and Global Studies at Worcester Polytechnic Institute in Massachusetts. In addition to a number of book chapters, his work can be found in *Philosophy and Social Criticism*, *Globalizations*, *Human Studies*, *The European Legacy*, *Crisis and Critique*, *Continental Thought and Theory*, *Contemporary Perspectives in Social Theory*, and *The Journal of Global Ethics*. He is also the coeditor (with West Gurley) of *Phenomenology and the Political* (2016) and author of *The New Materialism: Althusser, Badiou, and Žižek* (2015).

John Rajchman is a philosopher and a professor of Art History at Columbia University, where he has taught since 1999. He has written widely on art, architecture and technology, and the new role philosophy plays in them. His books and essays have been translated into many languages. During the course of his graduate work in philosophy at Columbia, he became a founding editor of *Semiotext(e)* and later joined the editorial board of *October* and then of *ANY* (a decade-long global symposium on architecture and urbanism in the 1990s). In the last 10 years, he has become increasingly involved in transnational exchanges notably with Asia and Latin America.

All along he has been engaged with the work and legacy of Foucault, Deleuze, and psychoanalysis. His *Truth and Eros* (1991) is an early study of the question of truth in the work of Lacan, Foucault, and their relations with one another. He has also written two books and many essays about the work of Deleuze and its implications for us today. With Étienne Balibar, he edited and introduced the anthology *French Philosophy since 1945: Problems, Concepts, Inventions.* Forthcoming is a new anthology, *Foucault in Asia*, introduced and coedited with Daniel Defert and Lydia Liu.

Serene Richards is a lecturer in law at New York University in London and an affiliated researcher at the École Pratique des Hautes Études. Her articles have appeared in several journals, including *Journal for Cultural Research*, *Crisis & Critique*, *Birkbeck Law Review*, and *Continental Thought and Theory*. She is currently completing a book detailing a genealogy of conduct in Western philosophical, theological, and juridical thought, focusing in particular on the concepts of dominium and *vitam instituere*, and the late medieval form-of-life, the Court of Miracles.

Philippe Sabot is full professor of philosophy at the University of Lille (France). He belongs to a research center called "Savoirs, textes, langage" (UMR 8163, Univ. Lille-CNRS). He has been president of the Michel Foucault Center since 2017. His research focuses on Michel Foucault's thought and his legacy in contemporary philosophy.

He has published two books on *The Order of Things* : *Lire Les Mots et les choses* (Paris: PUF, 2006; second edition 2014), *Le Même et l'Ordre. Michel Foucault et le savoir à l'âge classique* (Lyon: ENS-éditions, 2015). After contributing to the edition of the works of Michel Foucault in the Bibliothèque de la Pléiade (Paris: Gallimard, 2015), he edited a manuscript by Foucault devoted to *Phénoménologie et psychologie* (Paris: Le Seuil-Gallimard, 2021). He has also translated Judith Butler, *Sujets du désir. Réflexions hégéliennes au XXe siècle* (Paris: PUF, 2011) and Judith Butler, Ernesto Laclau, Slavoj Zizek. *Après l'émancipation. Trois voix pour penser la gauche* (Paris: Le Seuil, 2017). He is currently finishing a book entitled *Relations. Pouvoirs, normes, vulnérabilités* (Paris: Vrin, 2022).

Cindy Zeiher is a lecturer in human services at the University of Canterbury, New Zealand. She writes in the fields of Lacanian psychoanalysis and social theory and is currently in training as a Lacanian analyst.

www.ingramcontent.com/pod-product-compliance
Ingram Content Group UK Ltd.
Pitfield, Milton Keynes, MK11 3LW, UK
UKHW041637031026
15587UKWH00001B/342

9 781538 144244